CRIMINAL JUSTICE TECHNOLOGY IN THE 21st CENTURY

CRIMINAL JUSTICE TECHNOLOGY IN THE 21st CENTURY

Edited By

LAURA J. MORIARTY

Virginia Commonwealth University

and

DAVID L. CARTER

Michigan State University

CHARLES C THOMAS · PUBLISHER, LTD.
Springfield · Illinois · U.S.A.

Published and Distributed Throughout the World by

CHARLES C THOMAS • PUBLISHER, LTD.
2600 South First Street
Springfield, Illinois 62794-9265

© *1998 by* CHARLES C THOMAS • PUBLISHER, LTD.
ISBN 0-398-06902-6 (cloth)
ISBN 0-398-06903-4 (paper)

Library of Congress Catalog Card Number: 98-29807

Printed in the United States of America
CR-R-3

Library of Congress Cataloging in Publication Data

Criminal justice technology in the 21st century / edited by
Laura J. Moriarty and David L. Carter.
    p.   cm.
    Includes bibliographical references and index.
    ISBN 0-398-06902-6 (cloth). -- ISBN 0-398-06903-4 (pbk.)
    1. Criminal justice, Administration of--United States--Data
processing. 2. Criminal justice, Administration of--Study and
teaching (Higher)--United States--Data processing. I. Moriarty,
Laura J. II. Carter, David L.
HV9950.C74325 1998
364.973--dc21   98-29807
                                                      CIP

CONTRIBUTORS

David L. Carter (Ph.D., Sam Houston State University) is a Professor in the School of Criminal Justice at Michigan State University. He also serves as Director of the National Center for Community Policing and Director of the Criminal Justice Study Abroad Program. He has written numerous books and articles and served as a trainer and consultant to law enforcement agencies throughout the United States and several foreign countries.

Thomas J. Dover (MS, Virginia Commonwealth University) is a Criminal Intelligence Analyst with the Henrico County Police Department. He is an adjunct instructor in the Department of Criminal Justice at Virginia Commonwealth University. Mr. Dover previously has worked for the Criminal Justice Research Center as a Research Assistant for the Department of Criminal Justice Services, Richmond, Virginia.

Robert C. Haas (MA, Rutgers University) is the Chief of Police for the Westwood Police Department in Massachusetts and has served in this capacity for the last seven years. Prior to accepting his current position, he served fifteen years as a police officer in Morris Township Police Department in New Jersey where he rose to the rank of lieutenant. While serving as a police officer in New Jersey, he also taught extensively at the Morris County Police Academy as a certified police instructor in a variety of topical areas and served on the Board of Directors for the Jersey Battered Women's Services. He is presently attending the Law, Policy and Society Doctoral Program at Northeastern University. Chief Haas is a recipient of President Bush's "Points of Light" award in recognition of his work in the area of domestic violence within Morris County, New Jersey.

Keith N. Haley (MS, Michigan State University) is the Dean of the School of Criminal Justice at Tiffin University. He has also served in the following positions: Coordinator of the Criminal Justice Program at Collin County Community College in Texas; Executive Director of the Ohio Peace Officer Training Council, the state's law enforcement standards and training commission; Chairman of the Criminal Justice Department at the University of Cincinnati which offers B.S., M.S., and Ph.D. degrees in criminal justice; police officer in Dayton, Ohio; Community School Director in Springfield, Ohio; Director of the Criminal Justice Program at Redlands Community College in Oklahoma; electronics repairman and NCO in the U.S. Marines. Mr. Haley has written several books and book chapters, many articles and papers, and has served as a consultant to many public service, business, and industrial organizations.

Janet R. Hutchinson (Ph.D., University of Pittsburgh) is currently an Assistant Professor in the Department of Political Science and Public Administration, Virginia Commonwealth University in Richmond, Virginia where her principal teaching responsibility is Analytical Methods. She earned her Masters Degree in Public Administration from The American University and her doctoral degree in Public Policy Research and Analysis from the Graduate School of Public and International Affairs, University of Pittsburgh. Her research interests include applications of feminist theory to public administration teaching and practice, family policy, and applied constructivist methodologies.

Andra J. Katz is a doctoral canidate at Michigan State University. As a student, she worked in the National Center for Community Policing on related projects. Currently, she is an Assistant Professor in Criminal Justice at Wichita State University as well as a project director of a Regional Community Policing Institute funded by the C.O.P.S. office. As a co-instructor of the criminal justice overseas study program in England, she has had the opportunity to study the criminal justice system in the U.K. She was an invited speaker at a week long seminar on computer crime held in Pattaya, Thailand. Her research interests include: computer crime, community policing, and international organized crime issues.

James E. Mays (Ph.D., Virginia Tech) is an Assistant Professor of Statistics in the Department of Mathematical Sciences at Virginia Commonwealth University. His research interests include nonparametric and semiparametric regression techniques, with emphasis on smoothing considerations and the development of model-robust techniques. Dr. Mays is also involved in the development of introductory level (general education) statistics courses, including the implementation of interactive multimedia techniques in instruction.

Lorraine Green Mazerolle (Ph.D., Rutgers University) is the Director of the Center for Criminal Justice Research and an Assistant Professor in the Division of Criminal Justice at the University of Cincinnati. Professor Green Mazerolle is currently the Principal Investigator for several NIJ sponsored grants including an experimental evaluation of a civil remedy drug enforcement program in Oakland, California, a problem-solving project implemented across six public housing sites in New Jersey, and an evaluation of gunshot detection technology in Dallas, Texas and Redwood City, California. Professor Green Mazerolle is the author of a book entitled "Policing Places with Drug Problems" and numerous scholarly articles in the areas of policing, drug enforcement, displacement of crime, and crime prevention.

Peter J. Mercier (MA, Old Dominion University) is a Special Agent with the Naval Criminal Investigative Service, specializing in computer-related crimes. He has 16 years of law enforcement experience. An adjunct instructor at Old Dominion University and St. Leo College, Professor Mercier is working on research in domestic violence and computer deviance. He is co-editing a collection of research on domestic violence entitled "Battle Cries on the Home Front: Violence in the Military Family."

Jon'a Meyer (Ph.D., University of California at Irvine) is an Assistant Professor of Criminal Justice in the Department of Sociology at Rutgers University, Camden. She has published on many aspects of criminal justice, including sentencing, criminal courts, Native American legal systems, prison industry and reform, community oriented policing, and computer crime. She is the author of *Doing Justice in the People's Court: Sentencing by Municipal Court Judges* and *Inaccuracies in Children's Testimony: Memory Suggestibility or Obedience to Authority?*

Kevin I. Minor (Ph.D., Western Michigan University). is currently a Professor in the Department of Correctional and Juvenile Justice Studies at Eastern Kentucky University where he teaches courses in corrections, juvenile delinquency and justice, and theory. His books include *Prisons Around the World: Studies in International Penology* (with M. Carlie) and *Law-Related Education and Juvenile Justice* (with D. Williamson and J. Fox). Dr. Minor has published articles in *Crime & Delinquency, Journal of Criminal Justice, American Journal of Criminal Justice, Federal Probation,* and a variety of other professional journals.

Laura J. Moriarty (Ph.D., Sam Houston State University) is an Associate Professor in the Department of Criminal Justice and Assistant Dean, College of Humanities and Science at Virginia Commonwealth University. Her primary research interests include victimology, violent crime, and theory testing. She is the co-author (with Robert A. Jerin) of the textbook, *Victims of Crime* (1998, Nelson Hall). Her work has appeared in *Journal of Criminal Justice Education, Criminal Justice Policy Review, Criminal Justice Review, American Journal of Criminal Justice,* among others. In addition, she is the author of many book chapters and technical reports. Dr. Moriarty is currently co-editing (with Robert A. Jerin) a book entitled "Current Issues in Victimology Research" (Carolina Academic Press, in press).

Kenneth L. Mullen (Ph.D., State University of New York) is an Assistant Professor in the Political Science/Criminal Justice Department at Appalachian State University in North Carolina and has more than twelve years experience in law enforcement at the federal and city levels. He recently has had articles published by the "Community Policing Consortium" and by "The South African Journal of Criminology." Dr. Mullen's current research interests include career paths of police chiefs, computers in law enforcement, and academic cheating via the Internet.

Larry J. Myers is a doctoral candidate in educational human resource development at Texas A&M University. He received his masters degree in criminology from Florida State University. His research and teaching interests include policing, educational technology, computer crime investigation, and training and development. Recent publications include articles on visual interpretation of graphic material in *Journal of Visual Literacy* and criminal justice computer literacy in the *Journal of Criminal Justice Education.* He is currently completing his dissertation on training skills development of computer crime investigators.

Laura B. Myers (Ph.D., Florida State University) is an Associate Professor of Criminal Justice at Sam Houston State University. Her research and teaching interests include ethics, criminal justice education, cultural diversity, and criminal courts. Dr. Meyers' recent publications include an ethics chapter in the *Handbook of Criminal Justice Administration*, a public opinion and the courts chapter in *Americans View Crime and Justice*, and articles on criminal justice computer literacy in the *Journal of Criminal Justice Education*, the measurement of sentence disparity in the *Journal of Criminal Justice*, and gender-based differences in delinquency in *Justice Quarterly*.

Timothy O'Shea (Ph.D., University of Illinois at Chicago) is an Assistant Professor of Political Science and Criminal Justice at the University of South Alabama. Before joining the University of South Alabama he was a police officer with the Chicago Police Department, where he was employed for twenty years. His research interests are in the area of police officer and offender information processing operations. Dr. O'Shea is currently consulting with several rural police agencies in their efforts to reorganize according to a community policing model.

Stephan Sherman (MSW) is a program manager for the HATTS application for the Washington/Baltimore HIDTA program – a program funded by the Office of National Drug Control Policy. Mr. Sherman has worked with users in 12 jurisdictions to design, develop, and implement the application.

John Ortiz Smykla (Ph.D., Michigan State University) is Professor of Criminal Justice at the University of Alabama. He teaches corrections and research methods and uses technology to enhance his instructional performance and student learning. His current research is on measuring the "intensiveness" of ISP. With Frank Schmalleger, he is co-authoring a corrections textbook (*Corrections in the 21st Century*, Glencoe/McGraw-Hill) that will make full use of technology to enhance student learning and instructional performance and delivery. In 1997, Professor Smykla chaired the ACJS Program Committee at the invitation of then-ACJS President, Dr. Donna Hale. Technology was the conference theme. It was there that the idea for Moriarty and Carter's volume first originated.

Jeffrey T. Stone was born in Dayton, Ohio, on January 14, 1972, the son of Thomas and Ruth Stone. In 1990, Jeff entered The Ohio State University where he majored in Criminology and Criminal Justice and minored in Interpersonal and Organizational Communication. He graduated in 1995 with the Outstanding Undergraduate Criminology and Criminal Justice Award. In August of 1995, he entered the Graduate College at Arizona State University to pursue a Master's degree in Justice Studies. While at Arizona State, he received both Arizona Regent's In-State and Out-of-State Tuition Scholarships and served as a research assistant where he helped teach undergraduate Theories of Justice classes. He also worked as a Psychology Intern with the Maricopa County Sheriff's Office Psychological Services Unit, where he conducted research evaluating various components of a testing process used to select applicants applying for positions as Deputy Sheriffs and

Detention Officers. Currently, Mr. Stone is the Legal Liaison for the Maricopa County Sheriff's Office in Phoenix, Arizona.

Faye S. Taxman (Ph.D.) is an Associate Research Professor in the HIDTA Research Program and the Department of Criminology and Criminal Justice at the University of Maryland, College Park. Dr. Taxman's work is in corrections, sentencing, and program evaluation. She is currently the principal investigator evaluating the implementation of the 12 sites in the treatment and criminal justice component of the Washington/Baltimore HIDTA program and two evaluations of substance abuse treatment programs. Dr. Taxman has published in the areas of corrections, treatment, and evaluation.

Robert W. Taylor (Ph.D., Portland State University) is currently Professor and Chair of the Department of Criminal Justice at the University of North Texas in Denton, Texas. He has an extensive background in criminal justice, being an active consultant to various public, private, and international agencies and having served as a sworn police officer and major crime's detective (in Portland, Oregon) for over six years. He has authored or co-authored more than seventy-five articles, books, and manuscripts. Most of his research and publications have focused on police policy and administration including the evaluation of community policing in the United States, the investigation of computer fraud, and other techno-crimes, and the nexus between drugs, terrorism, and violence. Dr. Taylor is a co-author of the leading text, *Police Administration: Structures, Processes and Behavior*, currently in its fourth edition with Prentice-Hall. He is the recipient of numerous research and training grants with more than $1 million in funded projects.

James B. Wells (Ph.D., Georgia State University) is an Associate Professor of Correctional Services at Eastern Kentucky University. His main areas of interest are criminal/juvenile justice and education related evaluation research and the improvement of criminal justice training and university level teaching through the use of multimedia instruction. He has presented and published papers in both criminal justice and education related areas and has authored computer-assisted instruction software. Dr. Wells' recent articles have appeared in the *Journal of Criminal Justice Education, Federal Probation*, and the *Journal of Educational and Behavioral Statistics*.

To My Godchild and Her Twin Sister-
Lauren and Megan Gilbertson-
and to my Great Nieces-
Alyssa and Mariah Hetzel
May You All Know the Value of Education-LJM

FOREWORD

Next Wednesday is the last time I meet my two-way interactive graduate seminar on community corrections. Sixteen students on the campuses of the University of Alabama and the University of Alabama at Birmingham enrolled. Once a week for three hours we talked about the listserv discussion we had before coming to class, used the world wide web in class to investigate an issue, faxed student response papers between sites, and carried on lively debate without regard to the virtual reality of it all. My only regret? I didn't have Laura Moriarty and David Carter's volume four months ago. Thinking about how community corrections agencies use technology to inform the public, hire and train staff, collect and manage data, and sort and track offenders are natural issues for a course like this. The contributors, editors, and publisher are to be thanked for giving us this volume. I'm honored to join them in writing the introductory comment.

I'm not a techno-sapien. I'm a baby-boomer. I thought word-processing was the most important technological wonder over my Underwood manual typewriter and IBM Selectric that I would ever see. Boy was I wrong! Concern for ways to improve my instructional performance, provide computer-based learning opportunities at home for our son when he was in high school, and a need to understand what generational experiences my students were bringing to the classroom convinced me that learning about technology and incorporating it into my teaching was a must. Whether you're working in a criminal justice agency, teaching criminal justice, or learning about it as a student, this volume will inspire you.

What is *Criminal Justice Technology in the 21st Century?* It is a volume of 15 original chapters on the ways that technology is impacting criminal justice. It is the first academic volume of its kind. And because of that, it will serve as an important primer in the literature. Five of the papers were first presented at the 1997 annual meeting of the Academy of Criminal Justice Sciences. Professors Moriarty and Carter invited the others.

Criminal Justice Technology in the 21st Century represents the concerns of criminal justice teachers, practitioners, and students. The essays explore the level to which faculty are using computers in their teaching. We learn that having a positive attitude about computers as a teaching tool, possessing computer knowledge and skill, and receiving strong administrative support are core ingredients in successfully using computers to improve instructional performance. The essays also make us ask why "distance" learners hold more positive attitudes about distance learning than students on campus. The report card on distance learning is good.

Other chapters enlighten us on the ways criminal justice agencies are using the world wide web and automation to inform and interact with the public, hire and train staff, collect and manage better data, share data "seamlessly" solve field problems, and classify and track offenders.

The chapters also remind us that the digital age is producing new crime whose effects are beyond comprehension. The criminal's new weapons are keyboards and modems, not guns and knives. Might is no longer a criminal trait. Education is. Techno-crime means that criminal justice teachers, practitioners, and students cannot afford to get behind the learning curve. The internet and modem raised the bar of techno-crime and it's getting higher everyday.

These chapters challenge the crime control paradigms of the 20th century that many of us developed, taught, and practiced. It's understandable why we're slow to change and why many of us have fallen behind in the digital age. But techno-crime is not emerging slowly and techno-criminals hope we stay behind. Our goal must be to think and act differently in the classroom, in the agency, and in the field. The shift will not be easy. Fundamental change never is. But tomorrow there will be no part of criminal justice education or practice that doesn't use or feel the effects of technology. Imagine virtual classrooms and a virtual faculty. Imagine reporting crime to a "software agent" police officer at your local police department over the world wide web. Imagine corrections using the technology of electronically transmitted smells to monitor offender lifestyle. Imagine virtual courtrooms, digitally displayed evidence, and virtual tours of crime scenes. Don't imagine. They're already here.

Criminal Justice Technology in the 21st Century is reading for everyone in criminal justice. Whether your area of interest or work is police, courts, or corrections, the *essence* of each chapter can be thought about and discussed as an issue being faced elsewhere in the criminal justice system. In real time, the volume will shape the debate about one of the most virtual changes of our time.

JOHN ORTIZ SMYKLA

ACKNOWLEDGMENTS

This book is the result of many talented people who have graciously allowed us to publish their most recent research involving criminal justice technology. We thank all the authors for their thorough, conscientious, and innovative contributions. Without them, this book would never come to fruition.

In addition, we would like to recognize the support from our institutions–Virginia Commonwealth University and Michigan State University including our colleagues and students. We would also like to thank Charles C Thomas Publisher, especially our editor, Michael Thomas, who has been instrumental in seeing this project through to completion.

Lastly, we like to thank our families who have always supported us in this and all endeavors. Their love, patience, and understanding allows us to fulfill our academic pursuits.

CONTENTS

CRIMINAL JUSTICE TECHNOLOGY
IN THE 21st CENTURY

Chapter 1

TRADITION AND TECHNOLOGY: COMPUTERS IN CRIMINAL JUSTICE

Jon'a Meyer

The advent of new forms of technology over the past two decades has created a challenging new world for the criminal justice professional. Technology, from sophisticated information handling systems to robotic equipment to programs that control security and other routine systems, impacts our everyday lives in ways never imagined. Indeed, it is difficult to imagine a world without high-tech inventions that assist (and sometimes limit) us as we live. The technological innovation that has most impacted criminal justice is the computer.

COMPUTERS

Computers have revolutionized America's daily workings. It is difficult to imagine a facet of life that has not been affected by the now ubiquitous electronic devices. Nearly everything we do in society is now accomplished, regulated, or tracked through some computer system. Even this chapter is a product of the computer age; it was created, formatted, and spell-checked using WordPerfect software (a legal copy, of course).

The introduction of the desktop personal computer (PC) lead to an explosion in the number of computers in use in this country. In 1978, the total number of computers in the U.S. exceeded the 500,000 mark. By 1983, just five years later, the figure topped 10 million. Now, millions of personal computers are being produced and sold each year; in 1992 alone, more than twelve million PCs were shipped in the United

States (U.S. Census, 1994) and 40 percent of American households currently have at least one PC (CEMA, 1997, p. 55). Several factors have lead to this exponential growth, including computers' speed, reliability, storage capabilities, and availability.

When it comes to calculations, computers are superb. They can complete thousands, if not millions, of computations per second. Furthermore, computers seldom make errors, like forgetting to carry when adding long columns of numbers. Cumbersome statistical computations can be completed in minutes, and professional-looking graphs can be created in a flash. Importantly, the reliability of computers means that the same results will be achieved time after time. Specialized computer applications have saved the criminal justice system many man-hours of time; California's AFIS system, for example, speeded up fingerprint processing so much that twelve people could do the work of 46 to 50, and with increased accuracy (Wilson & Woodard, 1987).

Computers also have valuable storage capabilities. Reducing text and other data to electronic files can save immense storage space. For example, an entire encyclopedia can be recorded onto just one compact disk (CD-ROM) with room to spare. Due to this capability, a number of criminal justice agencies have replaced their "dinosaur files" with computer files that take up less space and from which duplicates can easily be made in case any originals are lost.

As an added plus, computer files can often be searched by keyword. For example, the National Criminal Justice Reference Service recently released *Firearms Evidence Sourcebook (FES)*, a software program that assists with examinations of firearms evidence. Should someone need information on, say, Colt Cobras, the program will supply text and graphics associated with the keyword "Colt Cobra" in a few seconds. One can also search by a variety of other firearms characteristics, including groove impression width and ejector position. Through relying on search capabilities, many hand-held, ticket-issuing computers alert officials when they are ticketing stolen vehicles or cars on a tow list (Roberts & Peters, 1992A). This function allows for more effective identification of scofflaws and stolen cars. That computer files are searchable means that information can more readily be accessed and report writing time reduced substantially.

It is probably the widespread availability of computers that has had the most impact on their population explosion. It is now possible to buy a computer for less than it costs to buy a good camera or television. And, you can now buy them everywhere, including department stores. Most importantly, however, is the availability of easy-to-use software packages. Without software, the computer is nothing more than an expensive paperweight unless one knows how to program it. User-friendly software, on the other hand, turns the computer into a tool—a powerful tool that can help criminal justice professionals do their jobs better and more efficiently.

TECHNOLOGY IN LAW ENFORCEMENT

Beginning with the detection of crime, innovative technologies can be of assistance to law enforcement. From robots and other computerized devices that detect security breaches to software programs that help detect financial fraud, technology is rapidly infiltrating the crime detection field.

Computers also help detect crime through the use of databanks that contain important information with respect to criminal identification. The National Crime Information Clearinghouse (NCIC), for example, can alert patrol officers if individuals encountered during routine stops or license plate runs have any outstanding warrants. NCIC operates 24 hours a day and can provide information within seconds of a request; before NCIC, agencies had to contact jurisdictions individually to obtain such information. This service has reduced the number of suspects who essentially escaped apprehension by crossing state lines or who were able to surprise officers who were unaware of their violent pasts. And, some systems can transmit actual photos of suspects across the country into moving squad cars (e.g., Nemecek, 1990).

One of the things for which new technologies are best suited are the completion of investigations. New fingerprint technologies can generate or narrow down lists of suspects in a few hours, whereas hand sorting often took months (Wilson & Woodard, 1987). Photo composite software can help police identify suspects; some of these programs have also been used to locate missing children by "aging" childhood photos to show what the children probably looked like years after their disappearance (e.g., Roberts & Peters, 1992B). Some software programs help detectives by "leading" them through investigations with

cues like "request information from ____" or "monitor all contacts of
____" (Bayse & Morris, 1990). Other expert systems, like Harlequin's
Watson software, establish possible links between suspects and evidence. Statistical software has been used by some police agencies to
predict future crime sites by plotting earlier offenses; some years ago,
the Dallas Police Department successfully tracked both an auto burglar and a serial rapist using this approach (Dallas Police Department,
n.d.).

Some police departments now have computer terminals in their
squad cars. In addition to displaying information requested from various databanks such as NCIC, these mobile units also allow officers to
communicate with one another through messages presented on the
computer monitors. Instead of deciphering and remembering information shouted across radio lines, officers can consult their screens to
refresh their memories regarding important details such as addresses
and names. As an added plus, the computer communications can't be
"overheard" by unauthorized scanner listeners. As mentioned earlier,
some mobile units even allow photos of suspects to be displayed
onscreen.

Technology has also affected documentation of police efforts.
Report writing, once an onerous and mistake-filled process, has been
automated through laptop computers. In some jurisdictions, the
reports are pre-formatted to save officers time and energy. The reports
can then be checked by software programs for spelling and common
grammatical errors, thereby increasing the usefulness of the record at
later stages of the justice system. Even traffic and parking ticket writing has been affected by battery-operated devices, like TicketTrack,
that generate completed tickets. At the end of the day, the information
can be downloaded into an agency's computer databanks, thus avoiding the all-too-commonplace data entry error.

Noninvestigative functions have also felt the impact of technology.
Time sheets and other clerical tasks are often completed using a variety of software programs. Electronic mail (email) is finding itself more
and more common in the criminal justice system; some agencies use
it to update personnel on new policies or important information. The
Internet, first used on a large scale by libraries, provides a plethora of
information to anyone with a computer and a modem. There are
many criminal justice-related items available to Internet "surfers";
SEARCH Consortium's National Clearinghouse Internet site, for

example, has a variety of publications and criminal justice shareware programs for agencies to download and use as they wish.

TECHNOLOGY IN COURTS

Innovative technologies are a boon to those in the court system. Mail merge programs have streamlined the process of juror selection and management. If a hearing must take place, scheduling software has helped ease the burden of juggling courtrooms, personnel, and available time slots. During hearings, computer-aided transcription allows court reporters to generate transcripts within seconds of keystroking the words. Computers may also make the courts more accessible as well; the ability to generate onscreen transcripts allowed two deaf litigants in a divorce proceeding to "better understand what was happening" (Moss, 1989). And, at least one software package translates the reporters' notes into other languages.

Some devices allow attorneys to scan courtroom exhibits into electronic files and present visual aids onscreen, rather than forcing them and other court staff to rely on cumbersome flip-sheets. Accident reconstruction software, in addition to aiding in the investigation of automobile accidents, can also serve as a visual aid to help jurors understand what took place. In some jurisdictions, facsimiles of traffic tickets can be quickly and easily pulled up during trials; judges can then verify signatures and other important information without adjourning to find the original ticket. Attorneys have found computer animations to be safe alternatives to using stuntpersons to re-enact accidents (Reuben, 1995), and useful in illustrating to juries complex medical injuries (Meyer, 1993).

Technology also plays a role after the rendering of judgements. Software packages have been developed to help judges determine sentencing options; one expert system identifies possible intermediate sanctions for offenders (Copen, 1991). Another useful package determines parental support payments based on data entered into its banks. After all is said and done, the records can be saved as electronic files that take up a fraction of the space and can be text-searchable.

Computers have transformed the practice of law. Even small-office attorneys regularly use Lexis-Nexis or WestLaw to get legal information from their offices. Due to their popularity and usefulness, law schools often include instruction on the databases in their curriculum. Information can be downloaded onto an office computer or printed, depending on the user's preference. Online databanks, such as Online Searches, allow attorneys (and others) to track the whereabouts of witnesses and other individuals, conduct background investigations, or generate business searches. Finally, office management software packages have helped attorneys run their offices with minimal clerical assistance (e.g., Davis, 1996), and avoid malpractice suits by tracking appointments and court hearings (Alberts, 1994).

Another courthouse organization, the victim's assistance office, can use software to track court dates, offender release dates or whereabouts, and other information. Mail merge software can then be used to generate and send update letters to victims informing them of this information. In some jurisdictions, these capabilities have helped the staff better serve victims of crime. And, like other criminal justice organizations, they can use statistical programs to graph their current and projected caseloads.

One interesting innovation worth mentioning is QuickCourt. This interactive computer system was designed to help "create an environment in which courts are accessible and responsive to the needs of society" (Wiletsky, 1994, p. 2). The system allows citizens to seek and generate information by touching the computer screen on a stand-alone kiosk. Among other things, QuickCourt can generate and print the forms necessary to file for divorce. Although it probably won't replace human interaction in the courts, QuickCourt is certainly a move towards making courts accessible to the general public.

TECHNOLOGY IN CORRECTIONS

Corrections has found ways to incorporate technology into its daily workings. From intake to sentence completion, computers are used to monitor and track offenders' progress. One of the first systems jail and prison inmates may see is a software package designed to facilitate the logging of personal items. The program eliminates the need for using index cards that can be misplaced or damaged. Other programs store information about inmates including special needs (e.g, medication,

counseling, educational), visitors, good/bad time calculations, classifi-
cation, and history. A multitude of high-tech devices monitor the facilities for fires and other anomolies not detected by the staff observing
the inmates through cameras.

One intermediate sanction, electronic monitoring, has been made
possible due to the advent of computers. Once fastened around an
offender's ankle, the device automatically alerts probation staff if the
offender strays too far from a base unit. A related product
(JurisMonitor) alerts officials when an offender gets too near a base
unit; this product is useful for keeping offenders away from victims of
domestic violence or stalking. Probation officers can also have computers call and verify that offenders are following curfew orders. These
devices have greatly reduced the ability of offenders to violate with
impunity orders to remain in their homes or away from victims.

Probation offices have used software packages for some years now
to track fine and probation payments. Some jurisdictions have specialized software that alerts probation officers when their clients are in
arrears on payments; the program is easy to use and has "definitely
helped to increase collections–probably by 30 percent" (Finn &
Parent, 1992: 7). The increase in collections may be due, at least in
part, to people feeling that "Big Brother" is monitoring their compliance, making it harder for them to slip through the cracks and avoid
having to pay their fines (e.g., Roberts & Peters, 1992A). Other packages can be used to track whether probationers have satisfactorily
completed the conditions of their sentences.

One package, written and developed by Posey County (Indiana)
probation officer Sam Blankenship, deserves special mention. His
comprehensive probation program allows for direct entry of information gained from official records and interviews with probationers.
Based on this data, the program then generates a presentence report
acceptable by the court. Probation officers can easily edit the reports
before submission to the court if they wish. Due to the data-based
nature of the program, the automated pre-sentence reports are very
thorough and often include items that may be overlooked by probation officers who write the time-consuming reports manually. The program also composes letters to victims and others on an as-needed
basis. One interesting feature is the automatic computation of a probationer's risk assessment score for departments that use this information.

Kiosk-based systems have also appeared in corrections. One system, VISCON Jail Visitor Control, tracks inmate visitors and generates passes; corrections staff register eligible visitors, who may use the kiosk for future visits. In addition to regulating the number of visitations per inmate, the system generates reports on who is visiting whom. A second system, Check In, allows corrections staff to monitor parolees and probationers whose identities are verified by the fingerprints they provide at the check in kiosk. The system can also request breath alcohol samples if an optional unit has been installed in the kiosk, and can ask questions of clients. While Check In may not be able to fully replace face-to-face meetings, the alternative in some jurisdictions that now utilize Check In would be minimal monitoring, sometimes through monthly postcards.

Computer technology has allowed law enforcement, court, and corrections systems to function efficiently, while simultaneously dealing with reduced budgets and increased caseloads. Further, high-tech systems have increased productivity without reducing the attention paid to security. Of course, the proliferation of technology has had negative affects as well, including modern criminals who employ computers to commit their crimes.

COMPUTER CRIME: CRIMINAL JUSTICE'S NEWEST NEMESIS

With the coming of computers came new forms of crime that took advantage of their capabilities or targeted their vulnerabilities. Computer crime quickly followed the appearance of computers, but was exacerbated when inexpensive desktop models were introduced into mainstream society (e.g., Albanese, 1988; Rosenblatt, 1995). The costs are enormous; estimates are that the loss to businesses from computer crimes is many times greater than losses due to any other form of theft or robbery (e.g., Nickell, 1991).

There are two general categories of computer crime: computer "as tool" or "as target" (Sessions, 1991). The first category of criminals uses the computer as a tool to commit other offenses, usually to gain access to computerized accounts to facilitate the commission of fraud. The second category includes both hackers who are motivated by "simple curiosity" and often want to merely examine the contents of files

(United Nations, 1994, p. 9), and intentionally malicious criminals who seek to destroy or steal computer data.

Unfortunately, the criminal justice system has to adapt to computer crime. As one author has argued: "Credit card numbers, passwords, and access codes are replacing the gun, pry bar, and jar of nitroglycerine as the classic tools of crime" (Stites, 1991, p. 20). First, investigators must be at least somewhat familiar with how computers operate and how to gather evidence from them. Then, the courts have to be able to process the cases in a smooth manner. Of course, neither situation describes the reality found in most jurisdictions.

As investigators, law enforcement faces a host of problems: a general lack of adequate knowledge and training in their field, a near absence of up-to-date equipment to assist in detecting and tracking computer criminals, and the unique challenges of investigating crimes where the offenders are often one step ahead of the justice system (e.g., Meyer and Short, 1998). Changes are happening so fast that investigators are having trouble keeping up-to-date. The specialized skills that are needed to effectively investigate this type of crime have led law enforcement to lament that "it takes one to know one."

The courts must also adapt to computer crimes. First are thorny issues about jurisdiction; who has the authority to investigate crimes that cross over jurisdictional boundaries? Should jurisdiction be based on where the harm took place, where the offender was at the time of the offense, or where the computer system resided? The three locations may be very different, and may cross over international borders. Jurisdictional and other issues must be resolved before criminal justice can effectively handle computer crime.

Next, are the use and interpretation of existing statutes (e.g., Nugent, 1991). Prosecutors are sometimes wary of test-driving computer crime statutes (if they even exist), preferring instead to charge the crimes under common larceny statutes. Questions have been repeatedly raised, however, regarding whether one can steal computerized data, especially when only copies of the data are taken. Over time, the courts will have to refine what constitutes a computer offense and when one can be recognized.

The criminal justice system will also have to decide the best way to address evidentiary concerns. When can copies of computer files or mirrors of hard drives be admitted as evidence in place of the actual computer system itself? The courts will also continue to play an important role in privacy issues. Should electronic mail (email) be treated the same as regular postal mail? What is the proper approach to "searching" a computer for evidence? Should the strict chain-of-evidence requirements be altered somehow for computer evidence? What if a third party (e.g., a large corporation that depends on its computer system) cannot release the computer system used by a criminal; can the third party be ordered to surrender its computers for purposes of searching for evidence of crime? And, what constitutes evidence and how should the criminal justice system safeguard the data evidence it has seized? There are many questions that must be answered before the criminal justice system is ready to tackle computer crime.

Computer crime is not the only negative aspect of technology. Other, less nefarious, obstacles make technology difficult to implement.

THE NECESSARY EVILS

It would be naive to contend that computers and technological advances are without their drawbacks. The first obstacle to their adoption is cost. Computers and other high-tech equipment are very expensive and the optional supplies are seldom cheap. Software packages can be even more costly than the equipment that supports them. Some such packages cost $250,000 or more, a hefty price tag for small or underfunded agencies. Of course, this problem has been circumvented by some resourceful agencies like the Jicarilla Apache tribal police, who call a nearby city that has access to services outside their budgetary means. Other agencies are forming regional partnerships so that they can share the costs of new technologies. A few agencies have been able to tap private businesses for funds to acquire technological equipment; the Austin-Metro High Tech Foundation, for example, is a partnership between law enforcement and local businesses that donate money and in-kind services to help the investigation of high-tech crimes.

The costs of technology are not only monetary in nature. Training staff to use computers and other equipment can be a long, frustrating process. Often, users and tools seem to be at odds with one another; some staff complain that computers and other innovative technology are "stubborn" or otherwise unpleasant officemates. Training also means additional expenditures; funds must be used to teach staff to master new technologies, and trained personnel command higher wages.

Large amounts of time must also be invested in setting up the newly purchased contraptions. Setup of computers or complex software may require on-site assistance from manufacturers. Often, new technologies must be customized to an individual agency's needs. One common process, computerized databanks, requires huge amounts of data entry, by hopefully quick and accurate typists. One author notes that selecting, installing, and learning new systems gives even computer-literate users "the shudders" (Davis, 1996, p. 49).

An ironic weakness of new technologies is their constantly changing nature. Of course, replacing old (and not so old) equipment can be costly at best, and to compound problems, operation of new components must then be mastered. Sometimes new units are obsolete within a few months of their release, adding to some agencies' reluctance to enter the world of high-tech. Another irony is that some agencies underutilize a package's capabilities; one typical law office uses only a third of the capabilities of their office management suite (Davis, 1996).

One of the most persistent drawbacks to innovative technologies is the risk they present to criminal justice. Critical data can be lost or destroyed with one keystroke, power surge, or computer virus. Natural and man-made forces (e.g., sunlight, heat, microwaves, and electromagnetic fields) may jeopardize the ability of high-tech gadgets to function properly (e.g., Roberts & Peters, 1992A). Confidentiality of sensitive data may be compromised by computer hackers or unethical staff. And worst of all, criminals often have access to the same equipment and information as the criminal justice field and have recently discovered the potential of computers to make their criminal careers more productive.

Lastly, useful innovation often generates dependency. Staff sometimes choose to use computers rather than "good old-fashioned street work," which might mean that personnel rely on outdated or incorrect information rather than obtain new data. Computer downtime, battery failure, or equipment malfunctions may essentially stagnate entire agencies while repairs are completed (e.g., Russell, 1993). More importantly, increased reliance on items like computer databanks means that strict standards of quality must be maintained. Increased attention must be paid to the importance of complete, accurate data entry, lest some offenders be accidentally released due to incorrectly entered social security numbers or other errors, or that innocent citizens are detained due to their information matching that erroneously entered into a databank somewhere.

CONCLUSIONS AND SUGGESTIONS FOR THE FUTURE

Computers and other technologies can increase the amount of work that can be completed in a single shift. The devices can add speed and reliability to agency work. Besides, computers are very good at staying up all night working on tasks without complaining. While investigators once had to write or call individual agencies for information, systems like NCIC provide quick responses to inquiries. Innovative technologies help others in the criminal justice system, from courts to corrections officials handle the often crushing caseloads they face on a daily basis.

New technologies are not without their drawbacks, however. Costs, setup time, training, constant changes, and the possibility for data loss prevent some agencies from moving into the rapidly changing world of high-tech. Computer crime represents a new challenge for criminal justice, and may essentially change the demographics of crime and criminals in America.

While the future is never completely known, it is certain that computers and technology will play an increasingly important role in criminal justice. It is important that agencies consider all their options before acquiring a new system, and that all potential effects are explored before committing to the selected system.

Computers have begun to transform the face of crime in the United States, and will undoubtedly continue in this direction. Whereas most thefts were once committed by young men who could "outrun the law," the next generation of thief need not be physically endowed. Rather, a quick mind and a few passwords will open up whole new worlds of very profitable crimes. As society becomes more dependant on computers, it is likely that terrorist acts against computer systems will increase.

Computers can be very useful in society, but their limitations must be recognized. Improperly used, computers can wreak havoc and undermine even the most competent programs and personnel. In the end, increased attention to planning and policy will be key.

REFERENCES

Albanese, J. (1988, September-October). Tomorrow's thieves. *The Futurist, 22,* 24-28.

Alberts, A. (1994, November). Keeping track of clients, deadlines on a computer. *California Bar Journal, 12.*

Bayse, W.A., & Morris, C.G. (1990, June). Automated systems' reasoning capabilities a boon to law enforcement. *The Police Chief,* 48-53.

CEMA. (1997). *U.S. consumer electronics industry today.* Arlington, VI: Computer Electronics Manufacturers Association (CEMA).

Copen, J. (1991, June). Courts of the future. *ABA Journal,* 74-78.

Dallas Police Department (n.d.). *Date, time and day: Offense analysis.* Dallas, TX: City of Dallas Police Department.

Davis, S.E. (1996, September). All systems Go. *California Lawyer,* 49, 50, 59.

Finn, P., & Parent, D. (1992). *Making the offender foot the bill: A Texas program.* Washington D.C.: National Institute of Justice.

Meyer, J.F. (1993, December). Body of evidence. *ABA Journal,* 88.

Meyer, J.F., & Short, C. (1998,). Investigation of computer crime: Concerns voiced by local law enforcement agencies. *Police Chief,* 65, 28-35.

Moss, D.C. (1989, February). Computers can aid deaf lawyers. *ABA Journal,* 26.

Nemecek, D.F. (1990, April). NCIC 2000: Technology adds a new weapon to law enforcement's arsenal. *The Police Chief,* 31-33.

Nickell, D.B. (1991, December). Networked for crime. *Security Management,* 25-29.

Nugent, H. (1991). *State computer crime statutes.* Washington D.C.: National Institute of Justice.

Reuben, R. (1995, November). Stuntpersons add drama to cases. *ABA Journal.* 14.

Roberts, D.J., & Peters, K.J. (1992A, March). Hand-held ticket-issuing computers. *Technical Bulletin* number 1. Sacramento, CA: National Consortium for Justice Information and Statistics.

Roberts, D.J., & Peters, K.J. (1992B, June). Optical imaging in criminal justice. *Technical Bulletin* (number 2). Sacramento, CA: National Consortium for Justice Information and Statistics.

Rosenblatt, K.S. (1995). *High-technology crime: Investigating cases involving computers.* San Jose, CA: KSK Publications.

Russell, M.J. (1993). *Toward the paperless police department: The use of laptop computers.* Washington, DC: National Institute of Justice.

Sessions, W.S. (1991). Computer crimes: An escalating crime trend. *FBI Law Enforcement Bulletin,* 60, 12-15.

United Nations. (1994). United Nations manual on the prevention and control of computer-related crime. *International Review of Criminal Policy, 44,* 1-47.

U.S. Census. (1994). *Statistical abstract of the United States.* Washington, DC: Bureau of the Census.

Stites, C.M. (1991). Unveiling the new face of computer crime. *Interface,* 15(1), 20, 43.

Wiletsky, L. (1994, Summer). QuickCourt–An automated information system for the public. *SJI News,* 5(2), 2,4,7.

Wilson, T.F., & Woodard, P.L. (1987). *Automated fingerprint identification systems: Technology and policy issues.* Washington, D.C.: Bureau of Justice Statistics.

PART I

CRIMINAL JUSTICE EDUCATION AND TECHNOLOGY

INTRODUCTION

Part I, Criminal Justice Education and Technology, contains three chapters written by criminal justice educators. The issues explored include integrating computers in the classroom, teaching statistics in the 21st century, and criminal justice students' attitudes toward distance learning. Chapter 2, written by Laura and Larry Myers, serves the function of providing a baseline of information for the discipline regarding the current level of faculty computer literacy development across the discipline. Criminal justice educators are surveyed about their attitudes about computer use; their computer knowledge, skills, and abilities; and perceived barriers to the use of computers. The results of this study serve to illustrate the needs of the discipline regarding faculty computer literacy and provide the knowledge necessary for criminal justice programs and educators to plan for the future.

The next two chapters relate to the Myers' chapter. In Chapter 3, the role technology plays in teaching statistics is explored, while in Chapter 4, distance learning is evaluated as a function of student demographics. Specifically Chapter 3, written by Janet Hutchinson, James Mays, and Laura Moriarty, provides a summary of the current considerations in teaching statistics, with emphasis on supplemental materials and technological advancements. Traditional teaching methods have for some years been supplemented with workbooks and computer software programs. These tools serve more as methods for "producing" statistics, as opposed to tutorial for "learning" statistics. Computer-based supplements, such as the use of the Internet and CD-ROMs, are gaining momentum as tutorial devices. Current development of these sources is discussed, including a review of the small number of actual completed projects. The multimedia capability of the Internet and CD-ROMs provides enormous flexibility for more effective and entertaining tutorial devices. The chapter concludes with a proposed CD-ROM project designed by the authors to address the limitations of the other resources.

In Chapter 4, James Wells and Kevin Minor focus on distance learning conducting an assessment of this method of teaching. The authors collected data from students enrolled in distance learning courses concentrating on the relationship between attitudes toward this mode of learning and student demographics and learning styles. They found that such attitudes are explained by the interactive combination of demographics and learning styles.

Chapter 2

INTEGRATING COMPUTERS IN THE CLASSROOM: A NATIONAL SURVEY OF CRIMINAL JUSTICE EDUCATORS

Laura B. Myers and Larry J. Myers

As the next century approaches, criminal justice educators must develop appropriate curriculums that will make graduates of their programs successful in the workforce. The traditional curriculums of typical criminal justice programs may no longer be best suited to the needs of the twenty-first century criminal justice graduate.

Many criminal justice agencies have already integrated computers into the daily tasks of personnel and other agencies are on the brink of such integration (Myers & Myers, 1995). Basic computer skills learned in a required computer science course are no longer sufficient for new employees. Self-learned computer skills are especially insufficient.

Basic computer skills are common among most criminal justice graduates, but are not enough for the highly applied computer tasks taking place in many criminal justice agencies (Myers & Myers, 1995). Larger agencies are using sophisticated data management systems that all personnel must interact with from remote stations. Probation officers, court personnel, and even law enforcement officers are finding they must communicate using such systems on a daily basis. Numerous law enforcement agencies, for example, have installed mobile data terminals (MDTs) or mobile data computers (MDCs) in their patrol vehicles (Sharp, 1991).

If criminal justice educators are to assist their graduates in becoming better prepared for such activities, then traditional curriculums and methods of teaching must be analyzed. Critics would suggest that this issue is not something criminal justice educators should be concerned with, but in fact agencies should provide their own training on such computer applications (Parra, 1992). The response to such criticisms is

21

that agencies would provide the training if they could, but often they cannot. Basic training academies have extensive curriculums that must be covered with limited time left for teaching computer skills. In-service training is even more limited, especially when so many agency veterans must be trained.

To reduce this strain on criminal justice agencies, criminal justice educators find themselves in a position to make a difference. Traditional curriculums and methods of teaching can be modified to better prepare graduates for the technologically sophisticated criminal justice workplace. The question is whether criminal justice educators are in a position to provide the leadership necessary to make the needed changes. Criminal justice educators must possess the right attitudes regarding the use of computers by students and then they must have the knowledge, skills, and abilities that will allow them to teach their students. Finally, they must have the equipment, resources, and support that will permit them to make these changes.

This chapter reports on the results of a national study of criminal justice educators regarding their attitudes on computers and their use of computers. The data were analyzed to determine the leadership potential of current criminal justice educators in the field that will permit the needed changes in traditional curriculums and methods of teaching. The implications of the results are discussed to help criminal justice educators and administrators prepare for the twenty-first century needs of criminal justice graduates.

COMPUTER LITERATE CRIMINAL JUSTICE GRADUATES

Computer technology is being integrated in all facets of the workplace. It is no longer possible to ignore the acquisition of computer skills if one wishes to be marketable in the workforce. Even veteran employees find themselves in a position to learn such skills or they risk becoming obsolete (Thornburg, 1992).

Criminal justice is no exception. The daily tasks of criminal justice practitioners are only becoming more complex and computer technology can enhance and make such tasks more efficient and effective. Society demands such efficiency and effectiveness and criminal justice is responding as quickly as resources will allow.

Believing that criminal justice agencies will prepare their employees for these computerized tasks is naïve. Most agencies find it difficult to train their employees on the basic skills needed to accomplish required tasks. Teaching required tasks is essential and training resources are always limited (Parra, 1992). Teaching computer skills becomes secondary.

LEARNING COMPUTER SKILLS ON THE JOB

Because agencies are not in a position to properly train their employees on the use of computers, many employees find themselves having to learn on the job. Criminal justice college graduates should not have to learn computer skills on the job. Without adequate computer skills, criminal justice graduates are just like other employees. So why should agencies hire them? A criminal justice degree should be meeting the needs of criminal justice agencies, not just providing more bodies who may or may not become good personnel down the line.

CRIMINAL JUSTICE EDUCATORS AS LEADERS

Criminal justice educators are in a position to teach criminal justice undergraduates computer skills and the application of those skills. However, criminal justice educators must be willing to use computers in the teaching of criminal justice knowledge. The teacher education literature contains numerous studies on the potential of educators to use computers in the teaching process. These studies indicate that teachers are more likely to use computers in their teaching under the following conditions: if they have the right attitudes about computer use, if they have the appropriate knowledge, skills, and abilities, if their administration supports the use of computers, if adequate computer training is available, if equipment and resources are sufficient, and if they have the time to explore how to use computers in their teaching (Baron & Goldman, 1994; Mahmood & Hirt, 1992; Sheingold & Hadley, 1990; Topp, Mortensen, & Grandgenett, 1995).

Criminal justice educators are not unlike other educators. They face many of the same problems faced by those educators in the teacher education literature. In addition to their primary goal of balancing teaching, research, and service (Myers, 1994), they must also find innovative ways to enhance the learning process. Because of the heavy demands placed on criminal justice educators, developing new, innovative teaching methods can be difficult. Developing teaching methods that incorporate the use of computers is even more complicated.

Attitudes

Criminal justice educators must first possess the attitudes conducive to using computers in the classroom. Many educators already use computers in the administration of their own courses, in their data analyses, and in the article production process. To make the leap to classroom use means that they must see the utility of students learning with computers. Not only must they think educators should be computer literate, but students should be as well. They must also think that the computer literacy of students must extend beyond the typical courses which rely on computers, such as math and science. They must believe that computer skills are essential for criminal justice students within their major curriculums (Mahmood & Hirt, 1992).

Computer Knowledge, Skills, and Abilities

According the Sheingold and Hadley (1990), educators must be comfortable with the use of computers. Educators who are not familiar with what computers can do, as well as with particular forms of software, cannot make the transition into the classroom. They do not have the necessary repertoire of computer tools to be successful.

Administrative Support

As the turn of the century approaches, many educators are facing the demands to use computers in the classroom. Administrators often recommend that the use of such technologies is going to be essential and that educators should be prepared. However, such recommendations may not be backed with the appropriate resources, training, time to prepare, and rewards (Baron & Goldman, 1994; Topp et al., 1995).

THE PRESENT STUDY

This chapter discusses the results of a national study of criminal justice educators and their role as leaders in computer-based teaching. A current membership list of the Academy of Criminal Justice Sciences was obtained and using the designation of each member, those who were clearly not educators were excluded from the sampling frame. A total of 1544 members remained in the sampling frame. A sample of one-half was then selected by choosing every other member in the frame. A total of 772 surveys were mailed in the Fall of 1997. A total of 377 surveys were returned of which 354 were useable for a response rate of 47 percent. The return of 377 surveys results in an oversampling that guarantees the use of a five percent error in estimating the parameters of the population (Hagan, 1989).

Results

Three-quarters of those surveyed have had a home computer for five or more years. Two-thirds have had an office computer for five or more years. However, less than ten percent have had computers in the classroom for five or more years. Over two-thirds of those surveyed do not have computers in their classrooms. The largest proportion (15%) of respondents who have had computers in the classroom have had them for less than two years.

To demonstrate the potential of these educators to use computers in the classroom, respondents were asked to indicate how often they use selected educational technologies (see Table 2-1). The use of overhead projectors and videotape players were the most commonly used educational technologies. Older, outdated technologies, such as tape players and film projectors, were used less often. Computers were used occasionally or very often by just a third of those surveyed and less than a quarter used computers with overhead projection systems. The traditional use of overhead projectors and videotape players indicates the desire of educators to use forms of media to enhance the learning process. This desire can easily be channeled into using computer technologies if several factors are present. One, computers must be placed in the classroom. Two, faculty need training opportunities to learn about these technologies.

Table 2-1. Use of Educational Technologies (Percentage responding in agreement)

Use of Educational Technologies	Occasionally or Very Often
Videotape Player	85%
Overhead Projector	69
Computer	33
Computer with Overhead Projection System	23
Slide Projector	21
TV or Satellite	21
Video Camera	14
Audiotape Player	13
Film Projector	11
Video Conferencing	10

Respondents were asked about the nature of computer tasks they performed at home or in their offices (see Table 2-2). The most common tasks were document creation and the use of e-mail. Nearly three-quarters performed data analysis and over half used computers for record keeping and exploring prepared data bases or information services. The computer tasks most likely to be used in the classroom, such as presentation development, multimedia development, and Web Page construction, were not common tasks among the respondents. Forty-two percent did do some form of presentation development, most likely PowerPoint. Just over a quarter had used their computers for the construction of Web Pages. Less than 10 percent used telecommunications equipment for distance learning.

Table 2-2. Computer Tasks (Percentage responding in agreement)

Computer Tasks Performed at Home or Office	
Do not use computer at home or office	2%
Record keeping	63
Document creation	93
Graphics development	39
Presentation development	42
Mulitmedia development	5
Computer-based instruction development	16
Web Page Development	26
Data Analysis	72
Exploring prepared data bases or info services	65
Exchanging data between computers	35
Telecommunications	9
E-mail	90
Entertainment	41
Self-training	28

The tasks for which respondents used their computers indicate a traditional reliance on them for assistance in research and publishing, as well as correspondence. Learning to use computers to enhance the learning process is relatively new and the lower percentages of respondents reporting such efforts is not surprising (Office of Technology Assessment, 1995).

When asked which classroom tasks they performed with computers, over half of the respondents indicated that they did not use computers in the classroom (see Table 2-3). When analyzed by professor rank, associate and full professors were more likely to use computers in the classroom than were assistant professors, adjunct instructors, and lecturers ($p < .05$). Assistant professors most likely have less time to devote to innovative teaching strategies because of the emphasis they must place on the tenure and promotion process.

Of the potential tasks that could be accomplished in the classroom, the most common task was as a presentation tool for lecture support (26%). Some of the newer, innovative uses for the computer in the classroom, such as real-time experiments and distance learning, are being implemented by less than a quarter of the respondents. Such low percentages probably reflect lack of knowledge about these new tasks, training, or perhaps time to explore them.

Table 2-3. Classroom Tasks (Percentage responding in agreement)

Classroom Tasks Performed with Computer	
Do not use computers in the classroom	57%
Tutorial or remedial skills training	7
Presentation tool for lecture support	26
Real-time experiments	3
Telecommunications	6
Internet demonstration/searching	22
Research tool for individualized student work	23
Exploring prepared databases or info services	20
Data analysis	20

To further explore the incongruence between computer use and the lack of usage in the classroom, respondents were asked about their computer experiences (see Table 2-4). It would seem that educators would be less likely to use computers in the classroom if they did not feel comfortable using computers or learning new tasks to be performed with computers. This was not the case with a large proportion of these respondents. Nearly 80 percent indicated they were comfortable working with computers and other technologies. Approximately two-thirds indicated they had had successful instructional technology experiences, they were at ease learning new instructional technologies, and had experienced beneficial technology training.

Table 2-4. Computer Experiences (Percentage responding in agreement)

Computer Experiences	
Successful instructional technology experiences	65%
Comfort working with computers and other technologies	79
Ease in learning new instructional technologies	63
Beneficial technology training experiences	68

Perhaps the problem was whether respondents had the proper attitudes toward the use of computers in the classroom. They might be very good at performing non-classroom activities with computers, but might not believe in their use in the learning process. That was not the case (see Table 2-5). Almost all of the respondents indicated that students should use computers throughout college and that computers should be used by criminal justice faculty to support instruction. Only 6 percent indicated that computers were more suited to math and science than other subject areas. However, less than half indicated they used computers with students for instructional purposes. Educators who responded to this survey have the right attitudes to make the leap into using computers in the classroom, but a much smaller proportion have actually done so.

Table 2-5. Attitudes Toward Computers (Percentage responding in agreement)

Attitudes Toward Computers	
Important all students use computers throughout college	99%
Computers should be used by criminal justice faculty to support instruction	98
Individual access to computers for all students	95
Administrators should be computer literate and use one for admin purposes	96
Faculty should be computer literate and use one on a regular basis	96
Important to have access to e-mail and telecommunications systems	97
Computers more suited to math and science than other subject areas	6
Use computers with students for instructional purposes	45
Use computers for administrative purposes	84
Have access to computer for instructional or admin purposes at college	89
Computer at home that I do not use on a regular basis	15

To further explore the nature of this problem, respondents were asked about their software skill level (see Table 2-6). As expected, criminal justice educators were more familiar with the traditional forms of software such as word processing, spreadsheets, and statistical analysis. Many were also familiar with some of the new, innovative softwares such as presentation software, e-mail programs, and Internet browsers. However, far fewer of the respondents were familiar with some of the newest software to enhance the learning process, such as Web Page development, graphics, multimedia development, computer-based instruction, and distance learning technologies.

Table 2-6. Software Skill Level (Percentage responding in agreement)

Software Skill Level	*Very Familiar*	*Familiar*
Word Processor	82%	15%
Spreadsheets	29	40
Databases	17	33
Charting/graphing software	17	36
Painting/drawing software	11	28
Desktop publishing	11	24
Photo manipulation	5	14
Presentation software	22	33
Authoring software	1	11
E-mail programs	59	30
Internet software	59	33
Web Page development	10	26
Distance learning technologies	5	28
Programming languages	3	17
Statistical analysis	39	37

So if these criminal justice educators appear so willing to serve as leaders in computer-based education, what is the nature of the problem? Primarily it appears to be a lack of time to explore, learn, and use technology (see Table 2-7). With all the other tasks that must be accomplished in the teaching process, little time remains to learn about these new, innovative strategies that can be accomplished with computers. Faculty cannot be expected to use strategies that they have not had time to adequately learn themselves.

Inadequate rooms and facilities, as well as a lack of computer hardware also seem to be issues for many criminal justice educators. Criminal justice educators who worked primarily at undergraduate institutions were more likely than those at graduate institutions to perceive a lack of computer hardware as a major obstruction (p<.05). Graduate institutions are more likely to provide computer hardware and software because of the emphasis on research.

The barriers indicated by the respondents are actually beyond the control of most individual criminal justice educators. These are problems better solved by administrators and faculty governing bodies than individual educators.

Table 2-7. Obstacles to Technology Infusion (Percentage responding in agreement)

Obstacles to Technology Infusion	Major Obstruction	Minor Obstruction	Not an Obstruction
Lack of computer hardware	48%	23%	27%
Lack of computer software	35	34	28
Inadequate rooms and facilities	51	24	22
Lack of media assistance	38	37	23
Lack of encouragement or rewards	29	35	34
Lack of information on hardware and software	24	44	29
Lack of time to explore, learn, and use technology	58	30	11
Lack of guidance about media integration in general	35	43	19
Lack of hands-on technical training in particular	34	43	21

DISCUSSION AND CONCLUSION

For criminal justice educators to serve as leaders in computer-based teaching, three factors must be present. Criminal justice educators must first have the right attitudes about the use of computers in the learning process. Overwhelmingly, the educators who responded to this survey indicate they have the attitudes conducive to using computers in the learning process. They believe that both educators and students should use computers and for more than just traditional computer-based courses.

In addition, these educators must possess the knowledge, skills, and abilities to use computers in the learning process. The results of this study reveal that many criminal justice educators possess the more traditional skills and abilities and do not have a familiarity with some of the newer, innovative technologies available. Those educators in this analysis appear to be relying on the word processing and data analysis skills they learned in their own educational experiences and have not had the benefit of learning much more.

Lastly, criminal justice educators must have the academic support to use computers in the learning process. The respondents in this survey indicate major obstacles in the use of computers in the learning process. They do not have the necessary hardware and software in many cases, they do not have the right facilities conducive to such learning, and finally, administrators appear to be sending mixed messages about expectations regarding the use of computers in the classroom. Criminal justice educators are being told that computers should be used, but there is little time to learn and prepare for using computers. In addition, in many instances, there are no reward structures for enhancing learning with the use of computers.

The results of this study indicate a great potential for criminal justice educators to serve as leaders in the use of computer-based teaching within criminal justice curriculums. This potential can only be realized if administrators provide the support necessary to enhance the skills and abilities of criminal justice educators and if these educators are provided the time and resources necessary to use those skills and abilities. The criminal justice discipline cannot expect educators to do this on their own time and with their own resources.

The solution is to allow criminal justice educators to reorganize the way they do their jobs. The traditional balance of teaching, research, and service must be modified to allow for the needed changes to occur. Many methods exist for doing so. Faculty evaluation systems could be changed to include credit for developing innovative teaching strategies using computers. Evaluation credit could also be supplemented with other financial incentives for developing new courses and with awards for implementation of innovations that prove worthwhile.

Sabbaticals and release time could be given to provide more time to acquire skills and abilities and to put that knowledge to use. Such time releases have typically been given for educators to pursue research efforts, but modifications could be made to include innovative teaching solutions as part of the research effort.

Administrators must take the initiative and provide faculty development for the learning of knowledge regarding computer use in the classroom. They must also secure the resources needed to pursue these efforts. The proper hardware and software must be made available, along with the technical support needed to maintain such equipment. Classrooms must also be modified to permit the use of computers in them.

Finally, the climate of the university or college must be modified such that the use of computers in the classroom becomes a normative function. Many schools, including Stanford and Ohio State University, have initiated teacher development institutes that are designed to support any educator who wishes to acquire new, innovative skills and put them to use. Such institutes could be started at schools with criminal justice programs.

With such efforts in place, the criminal justice educators who responded to this survey might well realize their fullest potential as leaders in computer-based teaching. The consequence would be criminal justice graduates with the skills and abilities that will set them apart from criminal justice practitioners without degrees. They might then have the potential to affect changes within the criminal justice system that can only be achieved with the use of technology.

REFERENCES

Baron, L.C., & Goldman, E.S. (1994). Integrating technology with teacher preparation, *Technology and Education Reform* (B. Mean, ed.), Jossey-Bass, San Francisco, 81-110.

Hagan, F.E. (1989). *Research Methods in Criminal Justice and Criminology*, Macmillan, New York.

Mahmood, M.A., & Hirt, S.A. (1992). Evaluating a technology integration causal model for the K-12 public school curriculum: A lisrel analysis, *EDRS Report*, ED 346847.

Myers, L., & Myers, L. (1995). Computer literacy for the twenty-first century, *Journal of Criminal Justice Education, 6*, 281-297.

Myers, L. (1994). The evaluation of criminal justice programs: assessment of evolving standards in context, *Journal of Criminal Justice Education, 5*, 31-48.

Office of Technology Assessment (1995). *Teachers & Technology: Making the Connection. OTA Report Summary*, U.S. Government Printing Office, Washington, DC.

Parra, J.E. (1992). *What Special Pre-Academy Training Programs Will Be Required by the Year 2001 in Order to Prepare Applicants for Law Enforcement Academies?* Report, California Commission on Peace Officer Standards and Training, Sacramento.

Sharp, A.G. (1991). Computers are a cop's best friend, *Law and Order, 39*, 41-45.

Sheingold, K., & Hadley, M. (1990). Accomplished teachers: Integrating computers into classroom practice, *EDRS Report*, ED322900.

Thornburg, D.D. (1992). Learning alternatives: technology in support of lifelong Education, *Learning Technologies Essential for Educational Change* (Council of Chief State School Officers), Council of Chief State School Officers, Washington, DC.

Topp, N.W., Mortensen, R., & Grandgenett, N. (1995). Building a technology-using faculty to facilitate technology-using teachers, *Journal of Computing in Teacher Education, 11*, 11-14.

Chapter 3

TEACHING STATISTICS IN THE 21ST CENTURY: TECHNOLOGY IN THE CLASSROOM

Janet R. Hutchinson, James E. Mays and Laura J. Moriarty

INTRODUCTION PRIVATE

Teaching statistics in criminal justice (as in other disciplines) in the 21st century offers new challenges and opportunities for both instructors and students. One such challenge is expanding traditional teaching to incorporate technological advancements such as micro-computer applications and multimedia instruction. In this chapter, we explore the methods used to teach statistics and identify the strengths and weaknesses associated with each. We explore the role played by technology in advancing student learning and comprehension of difficult statistical concepts and review a selected sample of products designed to aid student learning. We conclude by presenting a product the authors believe will address the limitations identified in the other computer products.

TEACHING STATISTICS

It is not unusual for both undergraduate and graduate students to complain about taking statistics courses. These complaints often arise

---

1 The authors are equal contributors to this chapter. Please note that the web sites mentioned in this document may have changed since publication of this chapter.

from their fear of math (sometimes referred to as "math anxiety," and in the case of older, so-called nontraditional students, "math atrophy") caused by inadequate high school preparation in mathematics (Royse & Rompf, 1992, p. 271), or the forgotten math skills that often trouble the nontraditional students (adult learners). The challenge for the statistics instructor is to find a way to abate student anxiety without compromising the integrity of the course. The effective use of technology will help to meet this challenge.

A review of the literature on teaching statistics results in a variety of articles from many disciplines focusing on teaching methodologies, computer-assisted learning, and strategies to increase the quality of instruction. Betsy Becker (1996) examined the print and electronic literature focusing on teaching statistics using three electronic databases. Her review yielded well over 1,000 articles from ERIC, PsycINFO, and ACAD (Extended Academic Index). Becker combined the references, eliminated duplicates, and discarded irrelevant sources, resulting in 501 references to examine. She then sorted the articles into five categories: computer use, teaching materials, teaching approaches, individual differences, and discussions. She further divided the material into empirical and nonempirical references.

Becker found a total of 209 articles addressing computer usage and teaching, of which only 56 were empirical studies. Further, she found that 53 sources focused on computer-assisted instruction with 35 being empirical sources. She identified 71 sources on the topic of software with only 6 being empirical. Lastly, she examined sources that focused on simulation activities/exercises and found 44 such articles of which only 4 were empirical sources. To summarize, Becker describes the vast majority of the literature as nonempirical, largely representing anecdotal information, and providing the reader with suggestions and recommendations from the experiences and intuition of the instructors in an effort to improve the quality of teaching statistics. We do not review all the works cited by Becker because most are not appropriate for our purposes. We do, however, present the literature focusing on improving the quality of instruction through the use of technology.

Some scholars have suggested that using technology will fill the gap in traditional teaching methods associated with teaching statistics (Gordon & Hunt, 1986, p. 66). For example, most statistics teachers demonstrate probability theory by tossing coins or drawing from a fish bowl filled with numbers. Gordon and Hunt recommend enhancing these examples by using technology, especially microcomputers with the appropriate software. They maintain that microcomputers allow for quick calculations with less effort and students find the investigations to be more interesting and captivating. Gordon and Hunt also argue that traditional teaching methods cannot teach intuition to students. They believe that "only by interaction and experimentation ... (can) a student develop intuition ... (and) many students are unable to achieve this by traditional methods suggest(ing) that the microcomputer (with its natural interactive ability) will prove useful" (Gordon & Hunt, 1986, p. 67).

Other researchers have examined computer software to determine the benefits of using such software in teaching statistics (Anderson, 1990; Cohen, Chechile, Smith & Tsai, 1994; Cohen, Smith, Chechile, Burns, & Tsai, 1996; Cohen, Tsai & Chechile, 1995; Dimitrova, Persell, & Maisel, 1993; Fuller, 1988; Halley, 1991; Helmericks, 1993; Persell & Maisel, 1993; Webster, 1992). Elaine Webster (1992) reviewed selected computer software to determine the relative strengths and weaknesses of each in terms of the software's ability to teach difficult concepts in statistics to students. Webster considered random sampling, the Central Limit Theorem, the binomial distribution, hypothesis testing, regression analysis, and analysis of variance as those topics most difficult for students to comprehend and for instructors to teach using the traditional teaching method of lecturing. The five computer software packages reviewed included: *Stat+/Data+*, *Minitab*, *Easystat*, *Mystat*, and *The Data Analyst*. These products were further divided into two categories: software "associated with a statistics textbook" and "student-oriented, general statistical packages, not associated with a textbook" (Webster, 1992, p. 378). Webster concludes that both types of computer software meet the objective of increasing learning, with "Stat+/Data+ and Minitab offering the most comprehensive coverage in meeting the pedagogical and technical needs of the instructor in teaching the six statistical topics discussed" (Webster, 1992, p. 384). However, these computer packages are designed mainly for data manipulation and calculation, and more efficient tools are needed for actually "teaching" and understanding the statistical concepts at a basic level.

For students to comprehend statistics, it is suggested that discipline-specific meaningfulness be attributed to such analysis (Bessant, 1992). It is important to relate statistical procedures to everyday situations in the area of greatest interest for the student. In doing so, the student receives a better appreciation of the practicality of the procedures and should show increased interest in learning the material. For example, Bessant (1992) found that sociology students comprehended statistics more fully when the presentation of the material was carefully imbedded in sociological meaning.

Lastly, researchers have suggested incorporating humor into teaching statistics. For example, cartoons have been found to reduce math anxiety (Potter, 1995; Schacht & Stewart, 1990). Placing students in creative, interactive learning environments that go beyond traditional learning experiences reduces math anxiety as well (Schacht & Steward, 1992). Technological developments are creating vast new opportunities in this area of education.

COMPUTER-AIDS (TUTORIALS) FOR STATISTICS COURSES

A review of the tutorial resources available for statistics courses results in four broad categories of items. They include workbooks with data sets, student versions of statistical software packages, Internet applications, and CD-ROMs. By far, the category with the most selection is the workbooks with data sets. Focusing specifically on criminal justice resources, the following is an abbreviated listing of the materials found in each category.

Several companies including MicroCase Presentational Software, Pine Forge Press, West Publishing Company, and Allyn and Bacon publish various types of workbooks with data sets. Some are specifically designed to accompany a research methods or statistics course, while the others are designed teach a specific class (American government, for example). In either case, the workbook can be used in a statistics course, if the professor so chooses.

The MicroCase products include *Criminology: An Introduction Through MicroCase, 3rd Edition* by Rodney Stark; *American Government: An Introduction Through MicroCase* by David Schultz; and *Research Methods in Political Science: An Introduction Using MicroCase* by Michael Corbett. There are many other workbook products available through MicroCase (see http://www.microcase.com). The Pine Forge Press merchandise includes three workbooks specifically designed to accompany research methods and statistics courses. These are *Adventures in Social Research: Data Analysis Using SPSS for Windows* by Earl Babbie and Fred Halley; *Exploring Social Issues Using SPSS for Windows* by Joseph E. Healey, Earl Babbie, and Fred Halley, and *Adventures in Criminal Justice Research: Data Analysis Using SPSS for Windows* by George W. Dowdall, Earl Babbie, and Fred Halley. The West Publishing Company has one work- book entitled *Your Research – Data Analysis for Criminal Justice and Criminology: Computer Graphics Statistics Package and Workbook, 2nd edition* by Michael B. Blankenship, Gennaro F. Vito, and Kenneth E. Hinze. Allyn and Bacon publishes *Social Research Methods - Qualitative and Quantitative Approaches, 3rd Edition* by W. Lawrence Neuman.

While these resources may increase the students' aptitude regarding computer usage and to a lesser degree increase their mechanical knowledge of statistics (that is, they begin to understand the proper syntax to produce the statistics) in the aggregate they offer only minimal tutorial value. In comparison to the other resources, workbooks with data sets are the least likely to emphasize mathematical principles and computations. There is even less emphasis on the underlying statistical assumptions. Most often, the student follows the instructions and produces the appropriate statistic without being challenged regarding which statistic the student thinks is the most appropriate and why. For these reasons, we feel the workbooks are not the best approach to learning statistics in the 21st century. Workbooks may be helpful, however, in instructing students in the use of statistical software procedures when used in conjunction with other teaching approaches.

The second category of tutorial resources is student versions of statistical software packages. Some of the most popular student versions include *SPSS 7.5 For Windows: Student Version, SYSTAT for Students 6.0,* and *The Student Edition of Minitab 8.* These packages are the actual statistical software offered at a reduced price for students. These packages allow students to analyze data from their own computers, helping commuter students or students who work full-time and cannot take advantage of the university labs. Depending on the specific software package, there are varying degrees of help available through accompanying manuals and help menus. The main purpose of supplementary materials is to teach the students the specific software package, not to teach them the statistics. It should be noted, however, that most of the companies that sell software packages aimed at the student market have separate statistics texts for purchase. For those who view teaching statistics from a more applied perspective, these software packages provide the opportunity for students to learn how to produce the statistics using whichever package they choose. Once again, however, the problem with these statistical packages is the lack of instruction regarding which statistical procedure is appropriate to use given the underlying assumptions of the particular problem. There are some general introduction paragraphs explaining the different statistical procedures, but it is clear that the main purpose of the software is to teach the students that software package. For the purpose of teaching statistics, such a product would need a section on applications, exercises, or problems to be useful as a tutorial.

The third category of tutorial resources includes Internet applications. This is perhaps the fastest growing area for student assisted learning and for access to supplemental course material. Before the 21st century, all students will surely have access to the "web" and its vast supply of learning tools. There are currently three main categories of how the Internet is being used as a teaching supplement for statistics: (1) to provide basic information and announcements for specific courses (syllabus, notes, assignments, links to other relevant sites, ...), (2) to provide complete courses that replace the classroom, and (3) to provide access to supplemental teaching tools in the form of demonstrations of specific topics in a course. The latter two areas are relevant here and are discussed briefly.

A recent technological advancement is the development of statistics courses that are taught entirely over the Internet, allowing access to many potential students who traditionally have been unable to schedule time for such pursuits. Closely related to this is the development of statistics textbooks on the web. For a sample of the many such courses and textbooks being developed, see the site at (http://www.execpc.com/%7Ehelberg/statistics.html). One of the larger scale ongoing projects in this area is the UCLA Electronic Statistics Textbook (UCLA-EST) at (http://www.stat.ucla.edu/papers/preprints/201/html/textbook.html), where the authors have designed an interactive, hypertext online tutorial. Projects such as these may change, or at least add to the approaches to teaching statistics, but they too would benefit from supplemental tutorials developed to help the individual student grasp difficult concepts.

This issue is being addressed by an increasing number of web sources that contain graphical interactive demonstrations of chosen topics. Examples of such demos are applications written in Xlisp-Stat or Java applets.[2] Some of the statistical topics demonstrated by these web sources are histograms, regression, the binomial and normal distributions, and the central limit theorem. These topics include many of the previously mentioned topics considered by Webster (1992) as "difficult to teach." For links to the most popular Java applets, see the web site at (http://www.stat.duke.edu/sites/java.html). These types of graphical demonstrations will be very appealing to the student, whether as an in-class or out-of-class supplement. However, they each address only one specific topic, and by no means do they, even as a collection, comprise a comprehensive statistics tutorial. A combination of such demos with an underlying course structure appears to be a worthwhile goal heading into the 21st century.

Two additional on-line sites with discipline-specific course material are mentioned here. The Social Science Research Methods and Statistics: Resources for Teachers web site (http://www.siu.edu/~ hawkes/methods.html) has embedded web sites including sources of qualitative data, information about statistical software, and resources for qualitative research. The Action Research Resources page (http://www.siu.edu.au/schools/sawd/ari/ar.html) includes an on-line refereed journal, mailing lists for students (and faculty) to discuss theory and practice of action research, an on-line course offered each semester, archives that describe action research processes or discuss action research issues, and links to worldwide action research resources.

The last category of tutorial resources is CD-ROMs. George Cobb and Jonathan Cryer have developed *An Electronic Companion to Statistics* (published by Cogito Learning Media, Inc., 1997). This CD-ROM, with comprehensive workbook, is designed to complement any statistics textbook. It is a tutorial device which provides interactive review and self-testing of key concepts, including over 400 interactive testing questions in a variety of forms. Multimedia is used in the form of animations, user-controlled diagrams, and real-world videos (from the *Against All Odds: Inside Statistics* series (S.1.: COMAP and

---

2 An applet is a self-contained, pre-compiled batch of code that is downloaded as a separate file to a browser alongside an HTML document. HTML (Hypertext Markup Language) is the language used to create web pages.

Chedd/Angier, 1989). The accompanying (optional) workbook contains hundreds of extra problems and very brief overviews of the topics presented, following the same order of progression as the CD-ROM. Many topics are included, ranging from basic statistical concepts to more advanced topics. The web site (http://www.cogitomedia.com/elec_cmp/EC_stat.html) contains more information on this product.

Paul Velleman's *ActivStats* (released July 1997 by Data Description, Inc.) is a CD-ROM that contains a full introductory statistics course integrating "video, animation, narration, text, pictures, interactive experiments, web access, and a full screen statistics package." The computer display takes the form of a lesson book that guides the student through the course. The student may select from the Contents tab to visit lessons in any order, allowing this product to serve as a tutorial or a source for review of basic statistical concepts. However, the lessons do build upon one another (using previously created data, for example), and the best use of this product appears to be for the student to chronologically complete each lesson, much like the progression of a traditional course. Quizzes, review activities, and homework assignments are included to test and increase the student's learning. *ActivStats* also provides access to the statistics software program Data Desk (also by Data Description, Inc.), which provides the data analysis and graphics capabilities for the course. The web site for Data Description, Inc., which contains information and links to both Data Desk and *ActivStats*, is located at (http://www.datadesk.com).

Both of these CD-ROMS are excellent resources. One major problem, however, is the inability of these products to adapt to the specialized interests of students in diverse disciplines. As Bessant (1992) maintains, in order for students to grasp statistical concepts, the examples and tutorial aids must be discipline-specific. For the CD-ROMS listed above, the instructor does not have the flexibility of adding his or her own data sets to be analyzed, which would add to the discipline-specific effectiveness of the products.

It is clear from the above discussion that the statistics instructor must expend considerable effort to compose a course that incorporates many of the tools described. The vast number of technological advances that have occurred over recent years have the potential to considerably enhance our ability to convey difficult concepts to students of statistics, yet the time and energy requirements for (1) learning the technology, (2) incorporating the technology into the classroom, (3) accommodating these new course designs to continuous software upgrades, and (4) assisting students who have not caught up with the technologies cannot be discounted. What may have been considered timesaving devices have become for many diligent instructors more time-consuming than the traditional textbook/lecture approaches which prepared many of us for our current roles. Ideally, the medium used will help, not hinder, the instructor's ability to provide individualized instruction to those students who are struggling, while facilitating learning for their more advanced classmates. The CD-ROM discussed in the next section will, in our view, accomplish these objectives and others as well.

PROPOSED CD-ROM

CD-ROM production has greatly increased over the last five years, augmenting traditional teaching strategies in many disciplines. The CD-ROM has the "potential to enhance student learning, motivation, and metacognition" (Adams, 1996, p. 19). According to Adams, the CD-ROM has many educational benefits including "its quick random access of information which enables the learners to control the pace and direction of learning, ... (providing) more opportunities for cognitive processing," its ability to present a large body of knowledge from many perspectives, which leads to a robust understanding of content by students, and its creation of more positive student attitudes toward learning (Adams, 1996, p. 20). With the merits of CD-ROMs or hypermedia (Adams, 1996) well established, we put forth our design.

Our CD-ROM is a multidisciplinary effort by faculty from the Departments of Mathematical Sciences, Political Science and Public Administration, and Criminal Justice, with technical support from the College's Information Technology Support Services and the School of Fine Arts. The program envisioned will be designed in a self-contained, modular format. Unlike other tutorial programs, it will incorporate several discipline-specific data sets of interest in applied settings, including public and private management and policy making, social policy issues of interest to students in criminology, health and social services, environmental and other public services, and business.

In addition, it will have the capability of incorporating personal data sets, overcoming a major limitation of the products currently available.

The program will rely heavily on visualizing statistical concepts, using only minimal explanatory text on principal screens. Links to detailed textual and computational definitions will be incorporated into the program. We reason that the adult learner, in particular, prefers to visualize the operations first, attempting to "puzzle through" the material being presented before reading a detailed explanation of what he is seeing. Further, link-based definitions may be avoided by those who are revisiting the program.

The program will incorporate a multimedia approach. Animation, digital photographs, cartoons, graphs, music, and voice-overs will be used to clarify principles and enliven the presentation. Mnemonic devices will accompany visual presentations as learning aids. Each module will be self-paced, taking the average reader approximately 20 minutes to complete if all definitional and computational links are used. An appropriate reading level will be targeted.

CONCLUSIONS

According to Schacht (1990), students taking statistics courses feel introductory statistics textbooks must: "review basic algebraic operations, discuss summation notation, include and explain exercise answers, use computational rather than definitional formulas, use examples relevant to students' statistics/mathematics anxiety" (Schacht, 1990, p. 393). Schacht found that not one of the textbooks reviewed addressed all the issues outlined by the students.

We feel that our proposed CD-ROM will meet these criteria in addition to incorporating most of the suggestions found in the literature. This sophisticated yet inexpensive CD-ROM will focus on the adult learner who may have minimal or rusty mathematical skills, while maintaining appropriateness for the traditional student. Because most anxiety regarding statistics is associated with a fear of math, both groups of students, traditional and non-traditional, will benefit from this product. Perhaps the most innovative and creative aspect of the CD-ROM is its capability to incorporate personal data sets to increase the overall relevance of statistics to students in different disciplines. Both instructors and students who are well versed in computer technologies will find the ingenious, interactive learning environments, framed in their own disciplines, quite effective, practical, and even fun.[3]

REFERENCES

Adams, P.E. (1996). Hypermedia in the classroom using earth and space science CD-ROMS. *Journal of Computers in Mathematics and Science Teaching, 15* (1/2), 19-34.

Against All Odds: Inside Statistics. Santa Barbara, CA: Intellimation. 1989 (video-recording)

Anderson, R.H. (1990). Computers, statistics, and the introductory course. *Teaching Sociology, 18* (2), 185-192.

Becker, B.J. (1996). A look at the literature (and other resources) on teaching statistics. *Journal of Educational and Behavioral Statistics, 21* (1), 71-90.

Bessant, K.C. (1992). Instructional design and the development of statistical literacy. *Teaching Sociology, 20* (2), 143-149.

Cohen, S., Chechile, R., Smith, G, & Tsai, F. (1994). A method for evaluating the effectiveness of educational software. *Behavior Research Methods, Instruments, and Computers, 26* (4), 236-241.

Cohen, S., Smith, G., Chechile, R.A., Burns, G., & Tsai, F. (1996). Identifying impediments to learning probability and statistics from an assessment of instructional software. *Journal of Educational and Behavioral Statistics, 21* (1), 35-54.

Cohen, S., Tsai, F., & Chechile, R. (1995). A model for assessing student interaction with educational software. *Behavior Research Methods, Instruments, and Computers, 27* (2), 251-256.

Dimitrova, G., Persell, G.H., & Maisel, R. (1993). Using and evaluating ISEE, a new computer program for teaching sampling and statistical inference. *Teaching Sociology, 21* (4), 341-351.

Fuller, M.F. (1988). MIRCOTAB and the teaching of statistics. *Teaching Statistics, 10* (1), 12-15.

Gordon, T.J., & Hunt, D.N. (1986). Teaching statistics with the aid of a microcomputer. *Teaching Statistics, 8* (3), 66-72.

Halley, F.S. (1991). Teaching social statistics with simulated data. *Teaching Sociology, 19* (4), 518-525.

Helmericks, S.G. (1993). Collaborative testing in social statistics: Toward Gemeinstat. *Teaching Sociology, 21* (3), 287-297.

---

3 Authors Note: This is an on-going project in the developmental, funding phase. Contact any of the authors on the status of the CD-ROM project.

Persell, C.H., & Maisel, R. (1993). Developing the ISEE instructional software for sampling and statistical inference: Dilemmas and pitfalls. *The American Sociologist, 24* (3-4), 106-118.

Potter, A.M. (1995). Statistics for sociologists: Teaching techniques that work. *Teaching Sociology, 23* (3), 259-263.

Royse, D., & Rompf, E.L. (1992). Math anxiety: A comparison of social work and non-social work students. *Journal of Social Work Education, 28* (3), 270-277.

Schacht, S.P. (1990). Statistics textbooks: Pedagogical tools or impediments to learning? *Teaching Sociology, 18* (3), 390-396.

Schacht, S.P., & Stewart, B.J. (1992). Interactive/User-Friendly gimmicks for teaching statistics. *Teaching Sociology, 20* (4), 329-332.

Schacht, S.P., & Stewart, B.J. (1990). What's funny about statistics? A technique for reducing student anxiety. *Teaching Sociology, 18* (1), 52-56.

Webster, E. (1992). Evaluation of computer software for teaching statistics. *Journal of Computers in Mathematics and Science Teaching, 11* (3-4), 377-391.

Chapter 4

CRIMINAL JUSTICE STUDENTS' ATTITUDES TOWARD DISTANCE LEARNING AS A FUNCTION OF DEMOGRAPHICS

JAMES B. WELLS AND KEVIN I. MINOR

Distance education is a process in which teachers use audio, video, and computer technology to convey instructional material from one location to students at remote locations. Two variants of distance education are network- and classroom-focused learning (Barker & Dickson, 1994). With the former, students employ such technologies as electronic bulletin boards, databases, listservs, newsgroups, webpages, together with the Internet and e-mail, to collect information and communicate with others as they choose. The classroom variant is meant for groups of students and entails the live transmission of instruction to multiple classrooms through technologies like fiber optics, microwave, terrestrial broadcast, audio-graphics broadcasting, and satellite television. Satellite television is the delivery mode that the largest number of schools (K-12 and postsecondary) have adopted (Hezel, 1996).

Increasingly, public and private organizations are using distance learning technology to enhance access to education and training (Picard, 1996). Distance learning is potentially well suited to criminal justice education. While the number of criminal justice programs across the nation has increased, there are still many people for whom it is not feasible to live on or near a campus which offers a criminal justice curriculum. Distance learning technology can reduce travel time for both students and instructors and can decrease reliance on traditional correspondence study. Also, few existing criminal justice programs cover all the diverse facets of the field (Young, Barnes, &

Lowery, 1995). Some students wish to learn more about facets of the field (e.g., law enforcement, juvenile justice) that are not well represented in programs to which they have access, and distance learning can expand opportunities for these students. This study focuses on the experiences of criminal justice students with distance education.

PREVIOUS RESEARCH

Researchers have compared distance education with regular or traditional instruction in order to address the concern that the former medium is of inferior quality (Perrin, 1995). Studies conducted outside criminal justice (e.g., Batey & Cowell, 1986; Crane, 1984; Hezel, 1996; Johnston, 1987; Moore, 1989; Schramm, 1977) have not reported one medium to be superior to the other. As Rose (1995, p. 5) summarizes, "research within higher education has consistently found that distance education is at least as effective as more traditional classroom (i.e., lecture) approaches." More important than the physical medium of conveyance is the substantive material and the pedagogical process by which it is conveyed (Gagne, 1970; Lane, 1992).

A number of schools are offering criminal justice distance courses, but distance learning has received minimal attention in the criminal justice education literature. Young et al. (1995) present helpful insights on assessing needs and planning for distance education, but no outcome data are provided. In a case study of a single criminal justice course, Peak (1991) found that students were generally positive toward distance learning. The same finding was reported by Wells, Minor, and Snarr (in press), based on analyses of student evaluations from six criminal justice distance courses taught between fall 1993 and spring 1995. However, Wells et al. found that evaluations were significantly lower among students taking televised courses from a main-campus (versus off-campus) location and among those taking a team-taught distance course. These findings suggest that criminal justice students' evaluations can be expected to vary with certain factors, and research needs to identify these factors.

In view of the growth and potential of criminal justice distance education, further research on students' perspectives is needed. This paper addresses that need by examining student attitudes and variations in attitudes by demographic factors.

A SUMMARY OF THE DISTANCE EDUCATION PROGRAM

The Department of Correctional Services at Eastern Kentucky University (EKU) has been employing satellite television technology in an effort to serve various extension programs throughout the state. Select courses in the curriculum are offered via one-way video and two-way audio, so that students at the main-campus site and all extension sites can view their instructors teaching from a university-based studio. Students at a particular site can converse with their classmates at the site, with students at other sites, and with the instructor. The equipment necessary at each site includes a downlink, television sets with video cassette recorders, press-to-talk audio units, dedicated phone lines, and facsimile machines.

Each site must also have a paid facilitator who acts as a liaison between the instructor and the students. Facilitators are not enrolled in the courses. Their duties consist of operating equipment, receiving class materials mailed from the instructor and distributing these to students, stimulating class participation, as well as proctoring examinations and returning these to the instructor. Library staff at the main campus are responsible for fulfilling requests for books and articles.

High levels of interactions among students, and also between students and the instructor, are essential to avoiding monotony during distance education (Haaland & Newby, 1984; West, 1994; Young et al. 1995). Therefore, the lecture material delivered by instructors is supplemented with such things as individual and group exercises at each site, intersite exercises (e.g., student debates and presentations), panel discussions, and guest speaker question and answer sessions. Instructors are able to present text, graphics, and digitized photos on an "electronic blackboard" through the use of authoring and presentation software.

RESEARCH METHODS

Participants

The participants in this study were undergraduate students enrolled in a total of 10 distance courses over six consecutive semesters, beginning summer 1995. Courses included introductory corrections, correctional counseling, juvenile delinquency and justice, community corrections, institutional corrections, judicial processes, and research methods. The last three courses in this list were offered twice each, and the others were offered once. The total enrollment in the 10 courses was 466 students. Enrollments per course (across sites) ranged from 21 to 75, with a mean of about 47 students.

Attitudinal instruments were received from 346 (74.2%) of the 466 students. Fully completed quantitative portions of the instrument were received from 319 students. For the 27 students who failed to respond to an item(s), mean values were inserted for missing values. Analyses were then repeated using only complete cases. Results with and without the missing data were very similar.

Of the 340 students providing data on gender, 153 (45%) were male, and 187 (55%) were female. Ninety-seven percent of the 346 students provided data on age. Ages of students ranged from 18 to 52, with a mean of 27.0 years. Just under two-thirds (64.7%) of the students had taken satellite television courses before. Among these students, the number of courses taken varied from one to nine, with a mean of 2.9 courses.

Instrumentation and Procedure

The instrument used to measure attitudes toward distance learning was an expansion and refinement of the one used by Wells et al. (in press). Eighteen Likert-style items comprised the quantitative portion of the instrument, and these were designed to measure both technical (i.e., audio and visual) and nontechnical aspects of distance learning on five-point rating scales; higher scores indicated more favorable attitudes. Off-campus students were also asked to provide data on miles commuted to the distance class and miles that would have been commuted to the main campus. The qualitative portion of the instrument contained open-ended items asking students what they liked best about the class, what they liked least, and their recommendations for class improvement.

A factor analysis (oblique rotation) of the instrument's quantitative portion resulted in two major factors and one minor factor. Factor 1 (eigenvalue = 8.34) contained seven items and measured nontechnical aspects of the course. These aspects are instructor-related and include areas such as instructor-student interaction, provision of academic assistance, interest in the course, and enjoyment of the course. Factor 1 exhibited high internal reliability (Cronbach's alpha = .93). Factor two (eigenvalue = 1.89) contained eight items and measured technical aspects of the course (e.g., visual aids), as well as overall satisfaction with televised presentations and assistance provided by site facilitators (Cronbach's alpha = .88). Factor 3 (eigenvalue = 1.49) consisted of three items assessing the promptness with which materials were returned and whether student-to-student interaction was deemed sufficient (Cronbach's alpha = .74). The strongest inter-factor correlation is between Factors 1 and 2 (.51); the correlations between Factors 1 and 3 (.30) and between Factors 2 and 3 (.33) are somewhat lower.

After being mailed to each site toward the end of each course, the instrument was anonymously administered during class after the instructor explained the purpose of the instrument and provided directions for its administration. Completed instruments were placed in sealed envelopes by site facilitators and mailed back to the main campus.

RESULTS

Qualitative Findings

The computer program *The Ethnograph* was used to content analyze qualitative data. The four features of distance classes that the highest number of students indicated liking most were: class location and the convenience of attending class (n = 47); quality of teachers (n = 44); discussion, interaction, and participation between sites (n = 32); and the quality of class (n = 20). The four features that the highest number of students reported liking least were: technical difficulties (n = 30); the teachers (n = 28); time length of classes (n = 23); and class projects (n = 22). The most common suggestions offered for class improvement were to: have a different teacher (n = 16), go back to traditional classes (n = 13), and have more teacher-student interaction.

Quantitative Findings

Those students attending classes at off-campus sites reported saving an average of 54.2 miles one-way by not having to travel to the main campus. According to student responses, a grand total of 12,077 miles were saved as a result of the ten distance classes being offered.

Table 4-1 presents means and standard deviations for items comprising Factor 1 of the instrument. It can be seen that students were generally favorable toward non-technical, instructor-related course components. The lowest means are for items comparing traditional and distance classes. Nonetheless, 61.8 percent of respondents either agreed or strongly agreed that they enjoyed distance courses as much as if the courses been taken through a traditional format. About 64 percent agreed or strongly agreed that they found distance courses as interesting, and 63.3 percent agreed or strongly agreed that they learned as well in distance courses.

Table 4-1. Student Ratings of Non-Technical Components

Factor 1 Items	Mean	S.D.
Sufficient instructor-student interaction	4.05	.93
Received adequate academic assistance from instructor	3.98	1.03
Enjoyed course as much as I would have if I had taken it as a traditional class	3.65	1.26
Found course as interesting as I would have if I had taken it as a traditional class	3.58	1.24
Learned as well from this course as I would have if I had taken it as a traditional class	3.68	1.20
Positive aspects of this course outweigh its negative aspects	3.87	1.13
Would take another television course if it was offered	4.29	.96

Table 4-2 presents data on Factor 2, which addresses technical course components. As in the case of non-technical aspects, students' attitudes were generally favorable in the technical area. The remaining items from the instrument, which loaded on Factor 3, appear in Table 4-3. Here again we see that, in general, students were favorable toward the promptness with which materials were received/returned and toward the level of student-student interaction.

Table 4-2. Student Ratings of Technical Components

Factor 2 Items	Mean	S.D.
Ease of interaction in using phone instrument	3.87	.91
Ability to hear other students via television	4.01	.82
Audio portion of the television instructor	4.12	.81
Video portion of the television instructor	4.19	.79
Television visual aids (charts, graphics, etc.)	4.12	.79
Television visual aids (films, videotapes)	4.12	.78
Overall satisfaction of television presentations	4.04	.95
Satisfaction with site facilitator's assistance	4.04	.86

Table 4-3. Student Ratings of Other Components

Factor 3 Items	Mean	S.D.
Syllabus & other materials received in timely manner	4.16	.94
Homework, assignments, exams returned promptly	3.75	1.07
Sufficient student-student interaction	4.11	.90

Because of the smaller number of items and lower reliability of Factor 3, this factor was omitted from the analyses reported below. Nontechnical and technical composite indexes were formed for each student by summing the seven items in Table 4-1 and the eight items in Table 4-2 respectively. The possible point range on the nontechnical index was 7 to 35, and the range on the technical index was 8 to 40. Composite scores were employed in the comparisons presented below.

Comparisons

We computed Pearson Correlations between the number of distance courses taken previously and both indexes to check for any confounding influence of prior experience with distance learning. The relationship between the number of prior courses taken and non-technical index scores was positive but weak ($r = .20$); the same was true for the technical index ($r = .17$).

Distance classes are taught from a television studio, where no students are present, to multiple remote classrooms. This means students taking a distance course offering on the main campus also receive televised instruction (unless another section of the same course is being offered through regular format the same semester). An important question is how the attitudes of these main-campus students compare with the responses of students taking courses at off-campus locations.

Table 4-4 addresses this question and also provides data on gender and age differences. As is apparent, off-campus students displayed higher means than on-campus students for both indexes. The data reveal minimal gender and age differences in attitudes toward distance learning.

Table 4-4. Index Comparisons for Location, Gender, and Age

	Index			
	Non-Technical		Technical	
Variable	*Mean*	*S.D.*	*Mean*	*S.D.*
Location				
Main Campus	24.18	7.16	31.64	4.92
Off Campus	28.56	5.45	33.53	4.85
Gender				
Male	27.37	5.91	33.38	4.37
Female	26.82	6.86	32.47	5.40
Age (median = 24)				
Under 24	26.90	6.80	33.44	4.91
24 and Over	27.21	6.12	32.43	5.04

Variable combinations are presented in Table 4-5. This table shows that on the non-technical index, off-campus students (both males and females of different ages) have the highest scores, and main-campus students (both males and females of different ages) have the lowest scores. On the technical index, younger students (both males and females) at off-campus sites have the highest scores, whereas students on the main campus (both males and females of different ages) have the lowest attitudes.

Table 4-5. Index Comparisons for Age by Gender by Campus Location

Variables	Non-Technical		Technical	
	Mean	*S.D.*	*Mean*	*S.D.*
Age				
<24				
Male				
Off Campus	29.45	4.17	35.17	3.13
Main Campus	24.59	7.52	31.97	5.45
Total	27.15	6.44	33.65	4.65
Female				
Off Campus	28.89	5.98	34.87	4.73
Main Campus	23.56	7.62	30.97	4.96
Total	26.66	7.17	33.24	5.17
Total				
Off Campus	29.15	5.18	35.01	4.04
Main Campus	24.10	7.53	31.50	5.22
≥ 24				
Male				
Off Campus	28.39	4.78	33.48	3.67
Main Campus	25.40	6.34	32.10	5.10
Total	27.59	5.37	33.11	4.11
Female				
Off Campus	28.05	6.14	32.10	5.95
Main Campus	22.79	7.03	31.52	4.02
Total	26.98	6.64	31.98	5.60
Total				
Off Campus	28.19	5.62	32.65	5.19
Main Campus	24.07	6.75	31.81	4.53

To determine if the variables singly affect index scores, or whether the effects of one variable are conditional upon another, factorial analysis of variance (ANOVA) procedures were used. Since scores on both indexes were moderately negatively skewed (nontechnical index skew = -1.18, technical index skew = -.78), scores were "reflexed" prior to square root transformations (Tabachnick & Fidell, 1983). In addition, adjustments were made for unequal cell sizes by weighting cell means. Two separate ANOVAs were conducted because the two indexes are conceptually independent. The ANOVA results are summarized in Table 4-6.

Table 4-6. Factorial ANOVA of Nontechnical and Technical Indexes
by Age, Gender, and Campus Location

Source	df	Sum of Squares	Mean Squares	F ratio
Nontechnical index				
Main Effects				
Age	1	1.060	1.060	.928
Gender	1	.759	.759	.665
Campus	1	41.370	41.370	36.222*
2-Way Interactions				
Age X Gender	1	.099	.099	.087
Age X Campus	1	.428	.428	.375
Gender X Campus	1	1.326	1.326	1.161
3-Way Interactions				
Age X Gender X Campus	1	.346	.346	.303
Technical				
Main Effects				
Age	1	6.732	6.732	8.840*
Gender	1	1.444	1.444	1.897
Campus	1	14.299	14.299	18.777*
2-Way Interactions				
Age X Gender	1	.372	.372	.489
Age X Campus	1	3.898	2.898	5.119**
Gender X Campus	1	.266	.266	.349
3-Way Interactions				
Age X Gender X Campus	1	.227	.227	.297

As Table 4-6 shows, the only significant finding for the non-technical index was a main effect for campus location; off-campus students had significantly higher attitudes than on-campus students. A significant interaction between age and campus location was detected on the technical index. Tukey post hoc multiple comparison tests revealed that that younger students off campus had significantly higher attitudes than both younger ($p < .01$) and older students ($p < .01$) on campus.

DISCUSSION

Our data indicate that the majority of students were favorable toward the nontechnical and technical features of distance learning. This finding is consistent with those of past studies in other fields (e.g., Batey & Cowell, 1986; Crane, 1984; Johnston, 1987; Moore, 1989; Schramm, 1977) and with the limited number of studies conducted in criminal justice (Peak, 1991; Wells et al., in press). The qualitative data suggest that one reason for the generally favorable attitudes of students is the location of distance classes and the convenience this affords. This interpretation is supported by the finding that the average off-campus student saved about 52 miles one-way by not having to drive to the main campus. For many students, such mileage savings translate into substantially less financial expense over the course of a three- to four-month semester.

It is clear from our data that a minority of students displayed either ambivalent or negative attitudes toward the distance learning experience, and such responses were most evident on items asking students to compare distance with traditional classes. The reasons for this finding cannot be discerned with the data at hand. However, we do know from the qualitative data that several students expressed dissatisfaction with technical difficulties.

One of the main findings in this study is that, irrespective of age and gender, students taking distance courses at off-campus locations had significantly more favorable attitudes on the nontechnical index than main-campus students taking televised courses. On the technical index, younger students at off-campus sites were significantly more positive than students of all ages at the main-campus site. Using a different data set generated from an earlier version of the instrument employed in the present study, Wells et al. (in press) also found significantly lower evaluations of distance courses among main-campus students. Collectively, these studies imply that, although main-campus and off-campus students receive identical instruction, the latter students may be more positive toward distance course offerings because of not having to travel to the main campus. Main-campus students have no similar incentive to be positive and, in fact, may disapprove of, or even resent, not having an instructor physically present in their class.

On the technical index, the attitudes of older off-campus students approached those of main-campus students in magnitude; younger off-campus students were the most positive toward distance learning. This finding suggests that instructors should be particularly attuned to concerns about the "hi-tech" aspects of distance education that older, more nontraditional students may harbor. This issue is likely to become very important in the near future, since it is projected that by 1998 the number of college students age 35 and older will exceed the number of those age 18 and 19 (Green, 1997). As a group, older students are probably less likely than younger students to have experienced the utilization of current technologies in their formal education.

On the basis of our research on student attitudes, we would certainly not recommend that distance classes be considered as a replacement for traditional classes; this applies especially to main-campus settings. As the results of our study demonstrate, educational institutions should be cautious in offering distance education courses to main-campus students. Distance learning remains today what it started out being, namely a means of providing opportunity and access to education where these would otherwise be restricted or nonexistent. Where opportunity and access cannot serve as justification, distance learning may be less well received by students.

It is estimated that in the very near future, the demand for distance education classes will substantially increase. The nontraditional college cohort is increasing with changes in the labor market. Similarly, the traditional college cohort is expected to increase due to both a growth in the proportion of students attending college right after high school and a rising number of college-age students (Green, 1997). Few states will be able to meet this demand solely by constructing new campuses and expanding existing ones. As a result, Green notes, educational institutions may be forced to transfer the content of distance education from short-cycle extension classes into long-term mainstream course offerings. Furthermore, distance learning is significantly expanding the service region of educational programs. The boundaries of any program's service region are potentially limitless.

Perhaps the greatest barrier facing the growth of distance education is funding. A substantial investment is required for capital start-up costs, as well as for annual recurring costs (Hezel, 1996). Short-term grants and extramural funds alone cannot support distance learning beyond the start-up phase, and alternative sources of operating funds will have to be planned. New resources are required if distance education programs are to be established or expanded. Otherwise, traditional instructional programs may lose resources through budget reallocation, and faculty can expect a higher workload without any proportional increase in rewards.

Our experiences with distance education teach us that the success of educational technology depends on an institutional vision and comprehensive strategy. However, only 17 percent of the nation's two-year and four-year colleges and universities have a formal plan in their distance education strategy (Green, 1997). Given the current ad hoc distance education planning of most educational institutions, individual programs will often have to adopt their own comprehensive planning strategies. According to Green, these strategies should include, at minimal: a business plan (concise definition of markets, products, consumers, and producers); content development plan (a team effort requiring faculty, code writers, curriculum specialists, and others); and recognition and reward for faculty who integrate technology into their classrooms, syllabi, and instructional activities. Over the last 15 years, there has been little reward or recognition for faculty who have invested in developing technology-enhanced courses. Young et al. (1995) provide further detail on how criminal justice programs can plan for distance education.

Further research is needed in this area so that additional conclusions can be drawn. More information is needed on why some students are ambivalent or negative toward distance education, and variables besides those studied here (e.g., student learning styles) need to be examined for their relationship with attitudes toward distance learning. Finally, other outcome measures (e.g., student performance indicators) must be used, ideally comparing distance with regular courses. With a foundation of research findings in place, we will be in a position to improve distance course offerings.

REFERENCES

Barker, B. O., & Dickson, M. W. (1994). Aspects of successful practice for working with college faculty in distance learning programs. *Ed Journal, 8* (2), J-6 - J-7.

Batey, A., & Cowell, R. N. (1986). *Distance education: An overview.* Portland, OR: Northwest Regional Educational Laboratory. (ERIC Document Reproduction Service No. ED 278 519).

Crane, V. (1984). *Student uses of the Annenberg/CPB telecourses in the fall of 1984.* Chestnut Hill, MA: Research Communications, Ltd.

Gagne, R. M. (1970). *The conditions of learning* (2nd ed.). New York: Holt, Rinehart & Winston.

Green, K.C. (1997). Drawn to the light, burned by the flame? Money, technology, and distance education. *Education at a Distance, 11*(5), J1-J9.

Haaland, B. A., & Newby, W. G. (1984). Student perception of effective teaching behaviors: An examination of conventional and teleconference based instruction. *Teleconferencing and Electronic Communications III,* 211-217.

Hezel, R.T. (1996). Coordinated statewide telecommunications: An essential ingredient of distance learning. *Ed Journal, October 10*(10), J-4 - J-8.

Johnston, J. (1987). *Electronic learning: From audiotape to videodisc.* Englewood Cliffs, NJ: Lawrence Erlbaum Associates.

Lane, C. (1992). Distance learning. In P. S. Portway & C. Lane (Eds.), *Technical guide to teleconferencing & distance learning* (pp. 255-268). San Ramon, CA: Applied Business telecommunications.

Moore, M. (1989, May). *Effects of distance learning: A summary of the literature.* Washington, DC: Office of Technology Assessment Contractor Report, Congress of the United States.

Peak, K. (1991). Criminal justice in the outland: The methods and promise of distance education. *Journal of Criminal Justice Education, 2*(1), 133-137.

Perrin, E. (1995). The continuing battle in distance learning. *Education at a Distance, 9*(3), 6-9, 13.

Picard, D. (1996). The future is distance training. *Training, 33*(11), S3-S10.

Rose, A. (1995). Expanding the potential of distance education. *Adult Learning, 7*(1), 5, 8.

Schramm, W. (1977). *Big media, little media: Tools and technologies for instruction.* Beverly Hills: Sage.

Tabachnick, B. G., & Fidell, L. S. (1983). *Using multivariate statistics.* New York: Harper and Row.

Wells, J. B., Minor, K. I., & Snarr, R. W. (In press). Distance education in criminal justice: Student evaluations of interactive satellite television courses. *The Justice Professional.*

West, G. R. (1994). Teaching and learning adaptations in the use of interactive compressed video. *T.H.E. Journal, 21* (9), 71-73.

Young, D. B., Barnes, F. M., & Lowery, B. R. (1995). Distance education: How to begin. *Journal of Criminal Justice Education, 6*(2), 299-309.

PART II
LAW ENFORCEMENT TECHNOLOGY

INTRODUCTION

Part II, Law Enforcement Technology, contains five chapters written by criminal justice scholars, educators, and practitioners. It begins with an assessment of the levels of software adoption among city agencies and is contributed by Kenneth Mullen. Chapter 5 distinguishes the significant variables that characterize agencies that have adopted numerous policing software from agencies that are operating their computer system at lower levels. Using ordinary least squares (OLS) regression, Mullen finds agencies with a smaller police to citizen ratio, agencies that are innovative in other areas, and agencies with a high percentage of civilian staff, are computerized at higher levels.

In Chapter 6, Timothy O'Shea examines how police officers manage data and evaluates their usage relying on quantitative and qualitative data. Interviews with unit managers indicate that data are primarily stored in a mainframe computer and are generally analyzed and reported to provide indicators of unit performance for mid- to upper-level managers. Little activity is observed that would indicate efforts to systematically analyze the data set for patterns and relationships useful for tactical purposes.

The next two chapters focus on two specific technology implementation strategies: the Problem-Solver and the Centralized Data Entry System. Lorraine Green-Mazerolle and Robert Haas describe a computer-based problem-solving tool that seeks to enhance problem-oriented policing activities. Chapter 7 begins with the premise that implementation of problem-oriented policing should be tightly integrated with the design and implementation of information technology. Without integration, information technology may be underutilized and efforts to implement problem-oriented policing may flounder or not be sustainable. The "problem-solver" was created through a partnership between a private sector public safety computer company, a consortium of fifty-two New England Police Departments, and a university-based researcher. The "problem-solver" provides a basis for integrating information technology for the purpose of implementing and building a problem-oriented policing capacity in police departments.

Chapter 8 evaluates one county's attempt to manage burdensome paperwork utilizing the Centralized Data Entry (CDE) system. Laura Moriarty and Thomas Dover conduct both quantitative and qualitative assessments of the system. Variables assessed measured who uses the CDE, the frequency of use, and perceptions regarding the CDE. Data were collected using a self-administered questionnaire. All officers using the CDE for the 13-month study period were surveyed. Qualitative data were collected at a site visit. They conclude with overall recommendations for the specific county and for others in similar situations.

In Chapter 9, Keith Haley and Robert Taylor conduct content analysis on law enforcement homepages. In this chapter, the authors describe, analyze, and discuss the common and unique contents found in a sample of federal, state, county, and municipal police web pages. The presentation is centered on more than 30 variables that were examined, including aesthetic quality, web page autonomy, mission statements, organizational hierarchy, useful news and information, community policing issues, police-citizen communication opportunities, recruiting information, and hyperlinks to other web pages. A final discussion focuses on future issues confronting police web sites and the Internet, as progressive steps to virtual reality and digital domination become a reality.

Chapter 5

LEVELS OF SOFTWARE ADOPTION BY CITY POLICE AGENCIES

KENNETH MULLEN

INTRODUCTION

Computers are not, by their design, a dichotomous technology. They allow the owner to increase and change the capabilities of their computer system by adding new software applications and hardware as needed or desired. Hardware systems ranging from IBM mainframes to Hewlett/Packard minicomputer and the Tandy (Radio Shack) TRS 80 personal computers can be found in American police agencies (Bush & Cooper, 1991).

Software applications are also in abundance. Currently, there are software applications for helping police agencies in making and tracking arrests, case disposition, case management, citation control, computer-aided dispatch (CAD), crime analysis, crime labs, criminal associates, evidence control, Automated Fingerprint Identification System (AFIS), fleet management, modus operandi, parking tickets, expert systems, traffic accident reports, uniform crime reports, management information systems, decision support systems, and service of warrants (Bacard, 1993; Pilant, 1994).

Regarding the issue of computerization though, by merely having a CPU terminal, and one software application on-line, a police agency could state they are computerized. However, as we can easily see, there is a great difference when comparing the agency described above and one with many software applications serving different administrative, operational, and law enforcement functions. Thus, we should not answer the question of computerization with merely a "yes" or "no."

DESIGN

This study will focus on the in-house computer systems of city police agencies. Operationally the in-house computer refers to a computer system that the agency uses to analyze and maintain its own generated data. Merely having the state provide a computer terminal where they can obtain driver license information and the like will not qualify the agency as computerized. Word processing, as well, will not meet the operational definition of a computerized police agency.

To analyze the issue of level of computer adoption, this study will assess the number of different software applications that the police agency has on-line. Software applications represent the general category into which a specific software program falls. That is, this study is concerned with whether or not the agency is operating a computerized crime analysis application, not which specific crime analysis software program they have.

The City and County Data Book (Bureau of Census, 1988) lists cities with populations of 25,000 or more and indicates if a police department is present. Only cities with a police department were considered. Based on these criteria, the population was 882 cities. Of these, 593 cities were randomly selected for the sample.[1] A structured questionnaire was used to gather information regarding specific computer issues and general police department characteristics. Overall, 303 agencies returned the survey for a 51 percent response rate. Of these, 282 of the city police agencies stated that they had an in-house computer system.

DESCRIPTIVE STATISTICS

In an effort to evaluate the software-adoption levels of city police the research area known as the diffusion of innovations will be applied. One underlying premise within diffusion of innovation studies is the importance of understanding how new ideas, products, technologies, and policies are diffused and adopted within a given social system.[2] Understanding the diffusion process will add to one's ability to predict how innovations diffuse, how change agents would best maximize the introduction of an innovation, and how researchers should design their studies when examining innovations within a given social system.

This study's primary research objective is to examine the diffusion of computer software and the levels that different software applications have been adopted within the social system of city police agencies (see Table 5-1). By applying known diffusion models and the common independent variables from other diffusion research, the goal is to identify the diffusion patterns within city police agencies. If police organizations are found to have similar characteristics to other organizations regarding the diffusion process, then comparisons and conclusions can be made regarding the diffusion of innovation within police organizations.

First, in an effort to separate software application based on purpose, the three common divisions of a police agency were used: administration, law enforcement, or operations. Most of the software applications were found directed toward law enforcement needs (see Table 5-1). Thirty-nine percent (1022 of 2591 software applications) of the software on-line falls within the law enforcement category. This compares to 31 percent of the software for operational needs and 29 percent for administration. If one combines law enforcement and operations within the basic police/law enforcement function, 70 percent of the software applications being used by city police agencies are aimed at meeting policing needs as opposed to administration functions.

Software designed to monitor arrests was the most commonly reported on-line application. Two hundred forty of the 282 agencies, or 85 percent, reported having an arrest program online. If placing a software application on line indicates setting priorities then it appears that city police agencies see the monitoring of arrests as their highest priority and need, and that computerization may be the answer to this need. Also, by computerizing arrest, the police could use these data within MO (modus operandi) and crime analysis.

The least common application was the unit locator. This could be explained in two ways. First the unit locator, whose purpose is to monitor the whereabouts of police vehicles, is a large dollar item. The patrol car needs a transmitter, as well as hardware and software at the police department to plot travel and location. The second factor limiting this application is the resistance to monitoring by officers. Officers have been known to sabotage equipment placed on their patrol cars designed to detail their speed, mileage, and location (Arcado & Neithercutt, 1985).

Table 5-1. Computer Software Use by City Police Agencies
(n=282)

System	Agencies Using	Percentage of N
Administration		
MIS	155	55
Budget	100	35
UCR	218	77
Scheduling	65	23
Personnel	154	55
Fleet Management	74	26
Law Enforcement		
Crime Analysis	194	69
Arrest	240	85
Investigation	194	69
Field Interrogation	181	64
Citations	185	65
Traffic Diagrams	27	10
Operations		
CAD	194	69
Calls for Service	222	79
Evidence	153	54
Unit Locator	21	7
Alarms	69	24
Jail Information System	54	19
Booking	97	34

Large and mid-size agencies have the greatest number of software programs on-line. Table 5-2 shows the results of initial software purchase versus software added later. That is, the operational definition of initial software was programs purchased and installed at the original time of computerization. Thus, agencies that added software to their systems are continuing to experiment and explore new areas where the computer might be useful. Large sized agencies (250-999 officers) are the leaders regarding the continued experimentation of software applications.

Table 5-2. Computer Software Initially Chosen by City Police Agencies by Size
(n=282)

System	Megalopolis >/=1,000 (n=20)	Large 250-999 (n=53)	Mid-size 100-249 (n=79)	Small <99 (n=130)
	I/T	I/T	I/T	I/T
Administration				
MIS	5/8	15/37	38/42	57/68
Budget	5/6	7/16	16/28	25/50
UCR	10/14	14/40	50/66	80/98
Scheduling	5/7	6/13	10/20	13/25
Personnel	5/13	10/37	28/45	43/59
Fleet Mgmt	3/8	3/13	10/20	18/33
Law Enforcement				
Crime Analysis	11/15	17/41	42/56	67/83
Arrest	10/14	23/44	58/70	106/112
Investigation	7/12	20/34	41/53	76/95
Field Interrogation	6/9	19/35	40/54	70/83
Citations	7/8	12/30	39/52	81/95
Traffic Diagrams	1/2	2/7	5/9	5/9
Operations				
CAD	8/16	18/48	45/57	48/73
Calls for Service	8/13	19/46	54/66	80/97
Evidence	5/9	6/26	25/42	45/76
Unit Locator	0/4	4/6	2/4	3/7
Alarms	2/9	4/13	16/24	16/23
Jail Information System	2/7	1/14	6/16	9/14
Booking	2/10	3/17	20/31	28/35
Totals	102/184 (55%)	203/517 (39%)	545/755 (72%)	817/1135 (77%)*
Average Software Applications per Agency	5.1/9.2	3.8/9.7	6.9/9.5	6.2/8.7

Note: I/T means Initial/Total *p<.001

The large agencies purchased only 39 percent of their software at the time of computerization. This compares with 55 percent for the megalopolis agencies, 72 percent of the mid-size agencies, and 77 percent for the small agencies. One would expect the agencies that computerized later (laggards) would have added fewer software programs as they have not had as long to experiment. In addition, the laggards would also have had the opportunity to learn from earlier adopters what works and what does not. Nevertheless, the large agencies, having started their computerization with the lowest percentage of software applications (39 percent) and the lowest number of programs per agencies (3.8), now have the highest number of programs per agency (9.7) and should be seen as the leaders of computer experimentation. To test for significance across the group an ANOVA was used and the size of the agency was significant to software growth and continued experimentation.

Next, a comparison of the agencies by region was conducted (Table 5-3). The Northeast region appears to be lagging behind in experimentation. When initial software programs were separated by the number of officers, the large agencies were clearly experimenters. Here, however, the Northeast appears to lag behind the other three regions as only 30 percent of their software has been added since computerization. Although the Northeast initially began their computerization with the highest number of software applications (6.2), they now show the lowest number of applications per agency (8.7). However, the ANOVA did not produce significant results and the findings may have occurred by chance.

Table 5-3. Computer Software Initially Chosen by City Police Agencies by Region
(n=282)

System	Region			
	West (n=80)	Midwest (n=78)	Northeast (n=41)	South (n=83)
Administration				
MIS	16/36	36/47	22/25	41/47
Budget	14/24	24/41	2/7	14/28
UCR	49/65	44/58	16/29	45/66
Scheduling	8/19	8/17	6/11	12/18
Personnel	20/37	24/45	15/25	27/47
Fleet Mgmt	7/17	10/24	6/10	11/23
Law Enforcement				
Crime Analysis	42/65	32/50	21/27	42/53
Arrest	56/66	57/69	29/36	55/69
Investigation	41/58	40/54	18/25	45/57
Field Interrogation	46/51	36/47	18/19	35/54
Citations	37/49	44/58	17/22	41/56
Traffic Diagrams	6/10	4/8	0/4	3/5
Operations				
CAD	37/59	28/45	22/31	32/59
Calls for Service	43/58	45/62	27/34	46/68
Evidence	17/44	22/42	14/22	28/45
Unit Locator	4/7	2/4	0/2	3/8
Alarms	8/19	11/17	10/13	9/20
Jail Information System	4/10	4/13	2/5	8/23
Booking	2/10	3/17	20/31	28/35
Totals	470/727 (65%)	485/725 (67%)	253/360 (70%)	513/779 (66%)
Average Software Applications per Agency	5.8/9.1	6.2/9.2	6.2/8.7	6.1/9.3

Note: I/T means Initial/Total

LEVELS OF COMPUTERIZATION

Rogers (1983) asserts that not all members of a social system adopt an innovation simultaneously, thus most diffusion of innovation studies looking at government agencies have focused on "what causes a government to adopt a new program or policy" (Berry & Berry, 1990,

p. 395). Two general models have been used in the attempts to answer this question. The first is the *Internal Determinants* model. Here it is suggested that states innovate for internal political, economic, and social reasons. In other words, states are viewed as closed systems.

Next is the *Regional Diffusion* model that posits that external influences drive innovation as states emulate their neighbors (Berry, 1987). Here the findings suggest that states adopt innovations primarily influenced by an effort to copy their neighbors. As an example, a state adopts a new policy because a neighboring state has previously undertaken it (e.g., a state lottery or a tax hike).

However, Berry and Berry (1990) suggest that the Internal Determinant and Regional Diffusion models are not mutually exclusive. That is:

> ... it is unrealistic to assume that a state blindly emulates its neighbors' policies without its public officials being influenced by the political and economic environment of their own state. It is also implausible to presume that states are totally isolated from influence by neighboring states, given the context of federalism, active national associations of state officials, and media attention on state innovations (p. 396).

Berry and Berry thus offer a *Unified* Model incorporating factors of both paradigms.

Because city police agencies are being used instead of states (internal or external), the independent variables will be viewed as either organizational or environmental characteristics. Thus, a modification of Berry and Berry's (1990) Unified Model was made to better fit this study.

Commonly found independent variables from the Internal Determinants, Regional Diffusion, and Unified Models were used: size, wealth, communication, region, innovativeness (or the willingness to adopt new policies or technologies), and environmental issues. Other diffusion studies have suggested organization-level variables such as the complexity of the organization, the presence of a crisis, specialization, and job satisfaction also influences the adoption of an innovation (Downs, 1976; Rogers & Shoemaker, 1971; Zaltman, Duncan & Holbek, 1973). However, the organizational-level variables were discarded because of the difficulties of obtaining meaningful data via a survey. These issues, complexity of the organization, and the presence of a crisis would have required a subjective interpretation from the respondent, as one agency's crisis could be another's everyday occurrence. Job satisfaction would have required, at the minimum, a sampling of the agency's employees. Both subjective answers and many per-agency surveys would have been impossible to control for and would have biased the study.

On an individual level, education, social status, intelligence, imaginativeness, and dominance have been noted as possible pertinent variables (Downs, 1976; Elksin, 1991; Loy, 1969; Rogers & Shoemaker, 1971). Again, because this study used a national survey, as opposed to an interview/observational study, the individual level variables that may have influenced the adoption process were excluded.

Organizational correlates consist of issues within and characteristics of the police agency while environmental correlates include issues outside the police organization that would include city characteristics and their regional location. Of the possible general variables listed above, size, wealth, innovativeness, region, and organizational issues will be used.[3] Each has been modified to fit policing and accommodate use of a questionnaire.

Table 5-4. Variable Coding Information for Independent Variables

Variable	Coding	Mean	SD
SIZE			
O-Employees	Sworn officers + civilians	613	2482
O-COP:POP	Ratio: # of police per 1000 civilians	2.0	.75
WEALTH			
E-PERCAP	Per capita spending	$608	$358
O-PEREMP	Agency budget per employee	$61,285	$50,391
INNOVATIVENESS			
O-PROGRAMS	Police programs in operation	13.8	3.8
E--%WOMEN	Percent female officers	8.0	6.0
O-Civilian	Percent civilian	22.0	9.0
REGION			
E-REGION	Dummy coded: 1 = West 2 = Midwest 3 = Northest 4 = South	2.4	1.2
CRIME			
E-CRATE	Crime rate per 10,000	6914	2813

Note: O - organizational variables, E - environmental variables

The size of the organization has been an important variable in past diffusion research (Gow, 1992; Mort, 1959; Rogers, 1983). Here, the total number of employees will define size (EMPLOYEES).[4] This variable is seen as an organizational correlate.

The second size characteristic will account for a police-to-population ratio (COP:POP). Here, comparing the city population to the number of sworn officers establishes a ratio describing how many officers serve 1,000 citizens. Though the city population is part of the agency's environment police-to-population will be seen as an organizational correlate. This was done because it is the police who argue and provide support for police officer positions. Though city government may authorize positions, it is the police who determine how many sworn officers they need to do their job.

Next is the area of wealth. Like size, wealth has been an important factor in diffusion research. Mort (1959) found that per capita spending per student had significant impact regarding diffusion within educational social systems. Rogers (1983) found that farmers with higher average income were more likely to adopt innovations and Gow (1992) reported that government agencies in Canada with greater resources were the leaders regarding policy innovations.

Two measures of wealth were used, one being an organizational and the other an environmental correlate. Like Mort's (1959) diffusion study of school districts, this inquiry used per capita spending (PERCAP) and not merely the size of the agency's budget. This was done to avoid having the larger agencies (number of officers) and the larger cities (population) always possessing the largest budgets. The amount that the city spends based on their population will represent a more accurate picture of both their wealth and their willingness to spend. The question will be whether per capita spending adds to the likelihood of a police agency adopting numerous software applications. Per capita spending, being a city level characteristic, is an environmental correlate.

The second indicator depicting wealth will be spending per police employee (PEREMP). The police agency's budget was used along with the total number of employees (officers + civilians). Because salary and benefits comprise such a large portion of any agency's budget, excluding the civilian employees would present false results. Again, the question will be if increased per employee spending of a police agency adds to the likelihood of being computerized. Per-employee spending is an organizational correlate.

Innovativeness is the next group of variables and again there will be both organizational and environmental correlates. Walker (1969), Savage (1978), and Lutz (1989) all found that an organization's or state's innovativeness, or the willingness to adopt new policies or technologies, has been an important correlate regarding the diffusion process. In other words, when innovative in one area, an organization tends to be innovative in others as well. This study measures innovativeness in three ways. First, is the number of noncomputer-related programs that the agency currently has in operation (PROGRAMS). It is assumed that if an agency has been willing to adopt other policing innovations, such as community policing, Police Athletic Leagues (PAL), and the PR-24 baton, they would be more willing to adopt numerous software applications. Since the programs listed within the questionnaire are, in many ways, unique to the police social system, the variable accounting for these police programs (PROGRAMS) illustrates a level of organizational, or internal, innovation. Because of the nature of these programs, the police would have decided to adopt them themselves and thus is seen as an organizational correlate.

The second variable regarding innovativeness will be the percent of officers who are women (%WOMEN). The increase of women police officers has influenced the traditional policing organization (Ehrlich-Martin, 1980; Horne, 1980; Lord, 1986) and has occurred at different rates among police agencies. Within the study's population, there were eight agencies with no female officers, while one agency had nearly 50 percent women officers. We could see the hiring of women as a policy matter or, perhaps even more accurately, as a social issue. Because of the social implications of hiring women police officers, and the fact that the courts may have mandated some police agencies to do so (Holden, 1994; More & Wegener, 1992; Stone & DeLuca, 1994), this measurement of innovativeness is viewed as an environmental correlate.

The third indicator of innovation is the percentage of civilians within the police organization (%CIVILIAN). Traditionally, police officers have been found in positions of managing records and communications, supervising evidence rooms, and other nonpatrol/investigation functions. However, with an increase in civilian employees these officers are returning to policing duties while civilians assume the administrative slots. The civilian percentage of the agency is seen as an organizational correlate.

The importance of location and region has had mixed findings within the diffusion literature. Researchers such as Walker (1969), Savage (1978), Brown (1981), and Lutz (1989) all found that proximity or region was correlated to the adoption of innovations. However, Gray (1973), Pred (1977), Brown and Malecki (1977), Weiss (1991), and Chi and Grady (1991) found that regional location had no influence on the adoption process, but similar styles or issues are the important correlates; these, in fact, override proximity.[5] Because of mixed findings on the importance of region, and the relationship it may have on the adoption of computer technology, a variable was created representing the four regions of the United States (REGION). The regional location of the agency is an environmental correlate.

The last area concerns the crime issue. Because of the possible concern and pressure by the community for the police to "do something about crime," plus the basic function of a police department to protect life and maintain order (Sheehan & Cordner, 1989), the police and their community often use the crime rate to measure the success of police agencies. Thus, the crime rate is seen as a possible influencing factor in adopting an innovation, especially an innovation that may help the police in reducing crime. Manning (1992) has suggested that computers cannot help the police with their "fight" against crime; however, we cannot ignore that vendors of computer hardware and software promote their products this way.[6] The crime rate as described here is an environmental correlate.

ANALYSIS

Ordinary Least Squares (OLS) analysis was applied using the total number of software applications that an agency has in operation as the dependent variable. The results are presented in Table 5-5. The independent variables representing police programs (PROGRAMS), police-to- population ratio (COP:POP), and the civilian percentage of the police employees (%CIVILIAN) were significant and will be explored in turn.

First, the number of adopted policing programs besides computer software (i.e., D.A.R.E., K-9, etc.) will be examined. Because of the positive relationship one would predict that as the number of policing programs increases one would expect the number of software applications to rise as well. The adoption of police programs are seen as a measurement of the agency's innovativeness, and specifically, its internal innovativeness. This may also be an indicator of organizational complexity. That is, as the number of policing programs increases, the agency is being separated into additional areas of focus; as additional focuses are created, complexity increases. An agency that supports a midnight basketball league, a DARE program, civilian volunteers, and Neighborhood Watch is not only innovative, but by budgeting and logistics alone, has become a more complex organization. Thus, to manage more complex organizations, these agencies have adopted additional software applications.

Table 5-5. OLS Results onthe Levels of Software Use

Variable	Coefficient	Beta	T
SIZE			
O-Employees	2.673	.018	.280
O-COP:POP	-.077	-.164	-2.140*
WEALTH			
E-PERCAP	8.601	.086	1.131
O-PEREMP	-4.352	-.061	-1.027
INNOVATIVENESS			
(O)-Programs	.182	.194	2.805**
(E) %Women	-2.162	-.033	-.501
(O) % Civilian	4.315	.119	1.655*
REGION			
(E) South	.738	.093	1.232
(E) Midwest	.616	.077	.968
(E) North	.236	.023	.786
West-reference category			
CRIME			
E-CRATE	-8.585	-.067	-.969
CONSTANT	7.395		5.557**

Note: *p<.05; **p<.01; R2=.31; F=2.111**

The police-to-population ratio (COP:POP) accounts for the number of officers per one thousand citizens within the city. The ratio was found to have a negative correlation to software levels. That is, as the number of police officers per one thousand citizens declines one would expect an increase in the number of software applications.

Two possible explanations seem appropriate. First, because of the low police-to-population ratio the police may be trying to compensate for the low numbers. In other words, agencies with small ratios may have adopted additional software applications to assist with the management of their agency as they lack sworn personnel. They have been forced to depend on software instead of officers to help perform managerial and policing functions.

The second explanation is that agencies with a small police-to-population ratio may merely be putting their budget priorities toward software/computer technology instead of personnel. This may represent a managerial philosophy, limited funds for new hires, or an effort to justify the initial computer hardware purchase.

The last significant variable was the civilian percentage within the agency (%CIVILIAN). Here, as with past explanations, the percentage of civilian police employees is seen as an example of internal innovativeness. As the percentage of civilian employees escalates, one would expect an increase in the number of software applications that the agency is using when controlling for the other independent variables. One cannot assert that civilians cause computerization or software adoption, but this study found, as did a Canadian study of five American computerized police agencies (Atcheson, Hann, Palmer, Shearing, & Zaharchuk. 1976), a relationship between the percentage of civilian police employees to both computer adoption and the level of software adoption.

SUMMARY

This analysis examined the levels at which police agencies have adopted computer software applications. The dependent variable depicts whether or not the agency is using a general type of software application (yes=1, no=0) and then totaled. Independent variables were used that represented size, wealth, innovativeness, region, and crime issues. Three variables were significant—all of which were identified as organizational variables. Thus, it was the Internal Determinate model that was supported, not the Unified Model (Berry & Berry, 1990).

The number of innovative programs in place, the ratio of officers per one thousand citizens within the jurisdiction, and percentage of civilian employees were all significant and correlated to the level of software use. The environmental correlates, such as region and crime rates, were not significant and do not help explain the level of software applications within a city police agency. The Unified Model is rejected, and the Internal Determinate model appears as the best predictor regarding the level of software applications.

It appears that city police agencies relate the decision to adopt computer software to organizational characteristics of the agency. This may be an indicator of the police culture and its resistance to outside or environmental forces. Though most agencies have adopted computers (BJS 1991), the question is whether they have, or if they will, allow computers to reach their full potential. Toffler (1972) realized more than twenty years ago that the police need to find the skill to manage and evaluate the rapidly changing technology that relates to their field. Obviously, this would include both organizational and environmental forces. However, if agencies base computer software adoption and growth only on organizational police characteristics while excluding environmental forces the true potential of the police computer may be limited at best. The police cannot operate and base technology decisions on internal issues alone. City police departments do not, and cannot, operate in a vacuum or as a "closed" system. The openness to outside factors, especially in the area of computer technology where the expertise lies outside the police social system must be recognized if the computerized police agency is to meet its full technical potential.

REFERENCES

Arcado, A., & Neithercutt, M. (1985, April). Tachographs in patrol cars. Paper presented at the Academy of Criminal Justice Sciences, Las Vegas, NV.

Atcheson, R.M., Hann, R.G., Palmer, J.I., Shearing, C.D., & Zaharchuk, T.M. (1976). *Study of Police Management Information Systems* Ottawa: Solicitor General.

Bacard, A. (1993). Privacy in the computer age. *The Humanist, 53*, 40-42.

Berry, F.S. (1987). Tax policy innovation in the American states. Ph.D. dissertation, University of Minnesota.

Berry, F.S., & Berry, W.D. (1990). State lottery adoption as policy innovations: An event history analysis. *American Political Science Review, 84*, 395-415.

Brown, L.A. (1981). *Innovation diffusion: A new perspective.* New York: Methuen.

Brown, L.A., & Malecki, E.J. (1977). Comments on landscape evolution and diffusion processes. *Regional Studies, 11*, 211-223.

Bureau of Census. (1988). *The city and county data book 1988.* Washington, DC: U.S. Government Printing Office.

Bush, G.L., & Cooper, G.R. (1991). *1990 Directory of automated criminal justice information systems* (Vol. III-Law enforcement). Washington, D.C.: U.S. Government Printing Office.

Chi, K.S., & Grady, D.O. (1991). *Innovators in state government: Their organizational and professional environment.* Lexington: The Council of State Government.

DiLeonardi, J.W. , & Curtis, P.A. (1992). *What to do when the numbers are in.* Chicago: Nelson-Hall.

Downs, G.W. (1976). *Bureaucracy, innovation, and public policy.* Lexington, KY: Lexington Books.

Downs, G.W., & Mohr, L.B. (1976). Conceptual issues in the study of innovations. *Administrative Science Quarterly, 21,* 700-714.

Ehrlich-Martin, S. (1980). *Breaking and entering: Policewomen on patrol.* Berkeley, CA: University of California Press.

Elksin, H.N. (1991). Diffusion of innovation and characteristics of adopters of innovation in school psychology. Ph.D. dissertation, University of Georgia.

Gow, J.I. (1992). Diffusion of administrative innovations in Canadian public administrations. *Administration and Society, 23,* 430-54.

Gray, V. (1973). Innovation in the states. *The American Political Science Review, 67,* 1174-85.

Holden, R.N. (1994). *Modern police management.* Englewood Cliffs, NJ: Prentice-Hall.

Horne, P. (1980). *Women in law enforcement* (2 ed). Springfield, IL: Charles C Thomas.

Lord, L.K. (1986). A comparison of male and female peace officers: Stereotypic perceptions of women and women peace officers. *Journal of Police Science and Administration, 14,*83-92.

Loy, J. (1969). Social psychological characteristics of innovators. *American Sociological Review, 34,* 73-82.

Lutz, J.M. (1989). Emulation and policy adoptions in Canadian provinces. *Canadian Journal of Political Science, 22,* 147-54.

Manning, P.K. (1992). Information technologies and the police. In M. Tonry and N. Morris (Eds.), *Modern policing: Crime and justice, a review of research, 15.* Chicago: University of Chicago Press.

More, H.W., & Wegener, E.F. (1992). *Behavioral police management.* New York: MacMillan.

Mort, P.R. (1959). *Public School Finance.* New York: McGraw-Hill.

Pilant, L. (1994). Information management. *Police Chief, 61,* 30-42.

Pred, A.R. (1977). *City systems in advance economics: Past growth, present processes and future development option.* New York: Halsted Press.

Rogers, E.M. (1983). *Diffusion of Innovation.* New York: Free Press.

Rogers, E.M., & Shoemaker, F.F. (1971). *Communication of innovations: A cross-cultural approach.* New York: Free Press.

Savage, R.L. (1978). Policy innovativeness as a trait of American states. *The Journal of Politica, 40,* 212-219.

Sheehan, R., & Cordner, G.W. (1989). *Introduction to police administration.* Cincinnati, OH: Anderson.

Stone, A.R., & DeLuca, S.M. (1994). *Police administration* (2nd ed). Englewood Cliffs, NJ: Prentice-Hall.

Toffler, A. (1972). *Future shock.* New York: Bantham Books.

Walker, J.L. (1969).The diffusion of innovations among the American states. *The American Political Science Review, 63,* 880-899.

Weiss, A. (1991). *The adoption of innovation in American police: A test of a diffusion hypothesis.* Paper the meeting of the American Society of Criminology, San Francisco, 1991.

Zaltman, G., Duncan, R., & Holbek, J. (1973). *Innovations and organizations.* New York: John Wiley and Sons.

ENDNOTES

1. Six hundred cities were chosen of which seven were used to pretest the survey tool.

2.The diffusion of innovation literature has defined a "social system" as individuals, organizations, or agencies with a shared culture (Rogers 1983).

3.The questionnaire attempted to gather information on the variable dealing with communication. This called for the agencies to list the law enforcement organizations (national, state, county) that their officers belonged to. That is, these organizations present the opportunity for officers to exchange information by both formal channels (newsletters, magazines) as well as informal channels at their meetings. Rogers and Shoemaker (1971) suggest that formal communications are effective in creating knowledge regarding innovations where interpersonal channels are important in changing attitudes towards new ideas. Unfortunately, the responding agencies all but ignored this question and the rate of missing data made use of this variable impossible.

4.There was multicollinearity between the variable representing the total number of employees (officers + civilians), the size of the city population, and the number of sworn officers. Because multi-collinearity confounds multivariate statistical procedures (DiLeonardi & Curtis, 1992) the variable EMPLOYEES was used as it represents sworn officers and civilian staff. The variables accounting for officers and city population were dropped.

5.This instability of findings regarding region is not uncommon in diffusion research. Downs and Mohr (1976) cite this variance within diffusion literature as alarming and problematic. As they state:
> Factors found to be important for innovation in one study are found to be considerably less important, not important at all, or even inversely important in another study. This phenomenon occurs with relentless regularity. One should

certainly expect some variation of results in social science research, but the record in the field of innovation is beyond interpretation (p. 700).

6.*Police Chief* and *Police Magazine* contain examples of the computer software advertisements targeting police administrators.

Chapter 6

ANALYZING POLICE DEPARTMENT DATA: HOW AND HOW WELL POLICE OFFICERS AND POLICE DEPARTMENTS MANAGE THE DATA THEY COLLECT

TIMOTHY C. O'SHEA

INTRODUCTION

Police organizations operate in a decision making environment characterized by uncertainty. The organization, in an effort to manage uncertainty, collects data; yet, simply collecting it is insufficient; the data also must be transformed into useable information and then disseminated to the appropriate personnel. Archambeault and Archambeault (1984) maintain that an organization's survival is dependent upon its ability to access information. Police managers, since the turn of the century, have recognized the importance of maintaining records and using them for effective planning. August Vollmer, who developed the foundation for what we today call the professional policing model, was the first to establish formal records management while he was Chief of the Berkley, California Police Department in the early twentieth century. Police departments devised numerous, and at times elaborate, manual filing systems to store crime information, e.g., incident reports, nickname files, modus operandi files, field contacts, criminal histories, fingerprint cards, etc. In large departments, files proliferated as specialized units found it useful to maintain separate files; for example, the auto theft unit would likely have a file of known auto thieves. As time passed, the number of files increased, as did uses for the data. The problem with manual files was that access to the data was difficult by virtue of its central location and the awkward, complex, and cumbersome methods used to retrieve hard copy records (Levine, 1979). In 1965, the Federal Bureau of Investigation undertook development of the National Crime Information Center, the purpose of which was to provide an automated, centralized, national repository for crime data easily accessible by local police departments (Marchand, 1980). Similar automated data bases, which included criminal histories and vehicle information, began to appear at the state level. Larger local police agencies that had access to municipal or county mainframe computers also began to utilize automated systems to store and retrieve data formerly contained in the manual crime files. With the advent of the inexpensive personal computer, smaller local police agencies were able to build and use automated data bases to replace many of their manual files. At present, there are a vast array of technology-based solutions that have been applied to the tasks of collection, collation, analysis, and dissemination of crime information.

Police agencies have advanced considerably in the storage and retrieval of crime data. After the data are collected, stored, and the means for querying the data set is developed, police departments are faced with the problem of transforming that data into useable information. The theory and practice of police data analysis, particularly crime data captured by the police in the variety of reports they complete, has been the subject of academic inquiry. Gottlieb, Arenberg, and Singh (1994); Peterson (1994); Eckblom (1988); and Reuland (1997) have provided both students and police practitioners with a basic overview of the crime analytic process. The nature, quantity, and quality of data collected by the police and a comparison of the Uniform Crime Report and National Incident Based Reporting System data collection methods have been studied (Coyle, Schaaf, & Coldren, 1991; National Institute of Justice, 1995; Reaves, 1994). The use of the microcomputer in the field of crime analysis has been the subject of several works (Craen, 1991; McEwen, 1990; Search Group, Inc., 1988; Spelman, 1988). Ratledge and Jacoby (1989) and O'Shea and Muscarello (1997) probed the use of advanced hardware and software technologies to perform complex analytic tasks, e.g., expert systems and neural networks. Manning (1992) examined the crime analysis process in the organizational context. Anthony's (1986) interest centered on forecasting the directions crime analysis will take in the future. Some have debated whether the analytic function should be centralized and practiced by specialists or decentralized throughout the organization and practiced by individual officers (Peterson, 1997; Lewin, 1997). Others have worked at developing a conceptual framework making a distinction between strategic and tactical crime analysis (see Gottlieb et al., 1994). Strategic crime analysis has been described as those analytic functions that focus on long-range planning, resource allocation, and productivity measurement (Campbell, 1972; Chaiken & Dormant, 1975; Danziger & Kraemer, 1985; Farris, 1987; Smith, 1973; Stallo, 1997). Tactical crime analysis has been described as those activities and support technologies used to execute day-to-day patrol and investigative field operations. Examples of tactical crime analysis include geographical information systems (Block, Dabdoub, & Fregly, 1995; Eck & Weisburd, 1995; Fitch, 1996; Harries, 1990; ICJIA, 1987; Maltz, Gordon, & Freman, 1989; Sherman, 1989), pattern recognition (O'Shea & Muscarello, 1997), Computer Assisted Dispatch (National Criminal Justice Information and Statistics Service, 1978), and Automated Fingerprint Identification Systems (Lee & Gaensslen, 1991; Wilson, 1987).

Research activity at the micro-level, i.e., the analytic behaviors of the individual police officer, has not received academic attention. Under the professional policing model, police executives, in an effort to control the actions of subordinates, compiled elaborate standard operating procedures which constrained police officer decision making, constraints that progressively increased as one descended the hierarchy. These constraints effectively reduced the analytic demands placed upon a police officer. The community policing model, on the other hand, proposes to move decision making responsibilities downward to the patrol officer, who is asked to exercise initiative, creativity, and analytic skills in order to identify and solve problems. The community policing literature implies that the success of the method rests on the police officer's capacity to analyze the vast array of collected police data (Goldstein, 1990), or, put another way, success is a function of how and how well individual police officers use information. The literature is silent with respect to the ways police officers obtain information, the nature of information available to police officers, the demand among police officers for information, or what sort of information police officers deem useful. We also have no empirical evidence of how data move through the organization, to whom they are directed, or for what purposes. Technology-based solutions to information systems problems require first that we clearly define the problem. Without understanding the factors that explain the information processing operations of the end user, i.e., the police officer, it is likely the problem definition will be misstated. This research seeks to begin to address this gap in the literature by providing a snapshot of information processing operations in a major urban police agency operating under a professional policing model.

RESEARCH DESIGN

This research was originally conducted in 1993 to explore the information processing operations of the Chicago Police Department, which was beginning a massive reorganization from professional to community policing. The total strategic planning task was initially divided into several substantive subcommittees, one of which was charged with exploring crime analysis. The crime analysis subcommittee ordered this study to systematically investigate data collection and analysis issues which the members believed would stimulate policy ideas useful for the strategic plan. Information processing activities were tracked along several paths throughout the organization. The first concerned that information which makes its way from the patrol officer upwards. The second path explored the transmission of information from one patrol officer to another. The third path consisted of the information that makes its way back to the patrol officer from a variety of collation points within the department, points that should transform the bottom-up data into tactically useful information for patrol officers. The final path tracked information captured from the patrol division, collated and analyzed, and disseminated to command level policy makers.

In short, the intent was to focus our attention on the type of data collected, where it made its way, in what form, and for what purposes. Additionally, we were interested in discovering how and in what form the data made its way back to the patrol officer, how and how well it was used for tactical purposes, and the perceived value of the information. To accomplish this goal managers of several key units within the Chicago Police Department were interviewed and several focus groups of patrol officers were conducted.

The units visited were as follows: (1) Data Systems, (2) Records Division, (3) Communications Operations Section, (4) Patrol Division, (5) Detective Division, (6) Youth Division, and (7) Gang Crimes Unit. A mid-level manager of each unit was interviewed, each interview lasted from one to two hours.

Four patrol districts were selected to be the sites of the focus group interviews. The Commanding Officer in each district was asked to choose two groups of patrol officers, each group consisting of from six to ten members, and to select participants based on the following criteria: (1) officers selected should be "working" police officers (Department parlance for productive members) and (2) officers selected should work the "street," in whatever capacity.

The focus groups were conducted in the spring of 1993 at the participants' unit of assignment. Eight focus groups were held, each of which lasted approximately two hours. Fifty-six subjects were interviewed in groups consisting of from five to nine members. Fourteen African-American officers, 38 White officers, and four Hispanic officers were interviewed in all, of which 49 were males and seven were females. The participants ranged in age from 33 to 60 years with an average age of 39 years and in years of service from one to 30 years with an average of nine years of service. The moderator opened each session with a brief introductory statement that advised participants of the purpose of the study and assured them anonymity, after which each group was asked five open ended questions from a prepared questioning route. The interviews were neither audio nor video taped because of concerns that the officers might see this as a threat to anonymity and thereby, for our purposes, a threat to an open exchange. Because there was no verbatim record, a note taker attended each session with the moderator, after which they collaborated to prepare a summary report.

FINDINGS

Unit Interviews

Data Systems was found to be responsible for producing data summary reports to most units of the Department. Field operations units collected the data, after which it was entered into the mainframe computer and a variety of queries were executed. The results of these queries were reduced to hard copy reports that principally consisted of crime totals, e.g., homicides, criminal sexual assaults, burglaries, etc. The reports were then distributed to the commanding officers of all Department units. Managers interviewed pointed out that command staff considered crime totals an indicator of the efficiency and effectiveness of a unit, which explained why mid-level managers were particularly interested in these reports. Other reports included the number of arrests made by unit, cases cleared, etc., also indicators of efficiency and effectiveness of a unit.

The Records Division, as the name implies, was found to be the Department keeper of records. This division maintained hard copies of all police reports and was the proprietor of an exhaustive criminal history data base, both in hard copy and automated. The Records Division did not provide regularly circulated reports to other units of the Department. The Division served two primary functions: the first was to act as the custodian of Department collected reports; the second to search for, retrieve, and distribute copies of these reports, upon request, to Department personnel. The type of reports stored included initial case reports, arrest reports, and traffic accident reports.

All citizen calls for service data were maintained by the Communication Section. These data were forwarded to Data Systems for collation and distribution to other units. Communications Section and patrol district commanders used the Data Systems reports as a measure of unit performance since calls for service provided a useful workload indicator.

The Patrol Division was found to collect most of the data for the Department, since all original complaints were investigated by patrol officers, who reduced the details of an incident to a variety of entry level reports, e.g., the general offense case report, the auto theft report, the vice case report, etc. Civilian employees then entered these data via remote terminals into the mainframe data base, after which it was collated and distributed by Data Systems in the form and for purposes described above. As we will see below, little data collected by patrol officers was returned to them in a form useful for tactical purposes.

The Detective Division's primary role was to provide follow-up investigations pursuant to complaints taken by the Patrol Division. Any additional information developed by detectives was reduced to reports and ultimately entered into the mainframe data base. The Detective Division receives mainframe-generated reports from Data Systems, e.g., cases cleared, arrests made, total crimes, etc., which are primarily used by Detective Division managers for performance measurement. Some Detective Division personnel used the RAMIS Mainframe Data Base System, which permitted detectives to execute a variety of data base queries of the entire data set, i.e., all data collected by all units of the Department. This rich source of information permitted the end user to identify myriad relationships and patterns in criminal activity throughout the city. The downside of RAMIS was that it required both knowledge about an arcane programing language, which was demanding, and a fair degree of analytic ability to detect and flesh out the relationships. For these reasons few officers executed RAMIS searches. Crime analysis was another unit within the Detective Division, one in which all hard copy case reports for all offense categories were manually searched for crime patterns. Given there are approximately 35 reported characteristics per incident and in excess of 500,000 incidents per year, one might reasonably suspect that only the most obvious patterns are likely to be discovered.

The Youth Division was found to conduct follow-up investigations of juvenile matters. Data collected by youth officers ordinarily supplemented data collected by patrol officers. Youth Division collected data was ultimately entered into the mainframe data base, after which it was collated by Data Systems and returned to the Youth Division in aggregated form, such as total juveniles processed by the Youth Division, total juveniles arrested for specific offenses, total juveniles adjusted (i.e., not forwarded to court), total referred to court, total arrests made by members of the Youth Division, etc. Once again, the information was targeted primarily for Youth Division managers and used by them as a measure of unit productivity, with little if any utilized by youth officers for tactical purposes.

Gang Crimes Unit was found to collect aggregate incident-based data. All case reports originating from the Patrol Division that contained any entry indicating gang involvement were reviewed by a gang crimes unit analyst and categorized by a set of gang relevant characteristics, e.g., retaliation, recruitment, etc. The categorized reports were then entered into a stand alone Gang Crimes computer. The Gangs Unit, on a regular basis, requested a standard exhaustive RAMIS report which contained a variety of aspects of gang related criminal activity. This information was mainly used for management evaluations of unit productivity. Data were not analyzed by line gangs officers for purposes of discriminating crime patterns and no reports from Data Systems made their way back to gangs officers for tactical purposes.

Focus Groups

The officers described several problem areas involving the methods used by the Department to transmit information to beat officers, the first of which addressed the accessibility of computer information. Although these officers maintained the computer was potentially useful, they insisted it was often difficult to get the information in a reasonably simple and timely fashion. The most common complaints included too few computers, computers that were frequently down, and when seeking computer information over the radio, difficulties in getting on the air or dispatcher slowness in getting results back to the officers.

> I don't run names or plates on the air anymore. You either get a dispatcher who seems pissed off when you ask for it or it takes all night to get it back and by the time it does come back you've let the guy go. Why bother?

Another problem area focused on the Records Division. While insisting the information was useful, the officers claimed that getting hold of it was frequently difficult and slow because of red tape, thereby reducing its value. As one officer pointed out:

> There are a lot of times when I would like a photo or a rap sheet of someone but it is such a big deal to get it and it takes so long to get something back that I just let it go mostly. Try getting a picture on midnights. The way it goes I usually only call for a sheet or photo when I make an arrest and the dicks want it for Felony Review.

Department member's interactions with community organizations revealed another form of information blockage. Many officers believed that contact with community groups could be useful but current departmental practices often prevented this form of interaction.

I would like to go to a community meeting. I don't mean to kiss ass some political heavyweight community organization leader. I especially don't want that. But I would like to see what people in the community have to say, that is people from the community and not the community organization big shots. I wouldn't mind working with them to do my job. The way it is now community relations goes to these things and we don't hear anything. Why don't beat guys that work those beats go? I went to one and they had me stand outside and keep drunks away. That made a lot of sense.

The respondents believed that specialized units held a wealth of valuable information that members of other units were not given access to. Many felt that the information was intentionally withheld because the Department at least partially rates officer performance according to the number of arrests made, and for officers to give away information jeopardized arrests.

Guys in specialized units like their jobs. They're there because they want to be. They have some good information. But let's face it, if they want to keep those nice spots, they have to come in with heads. They're not going to tell us anything that might screw up their pinch. The only way to get anything is to get it from someone that trusts you and you make sure his name goes on the arrest report. But screw him once and that's the last you'll get from him.

A final element of intradepartmental information blockage concerned simple communication between officers.

You can pick up a lot from other policemen. Most of what you learn about how to handle jobs comes from seeing or hearing other guys talking. The only way I find out about what happened the other watches or when I was off is from other guys. Right now I just don't talk to guys from other watches, even the guys that work my car. When I get out of roll call they're gone. I'd like some way for them to tell me what's been going on.

Officers adapted to the difficulties in acquiring information via Departmental sources in several ways, the first of which was what they considered a primary source, face-to-face communication with district residents. The officers used different approaches depending upon the nature of their relationship with informants. Some officers believed the best way to obtain information from citizens was to develop a personal relationship based upon trust and friendship, while other officers believed that the relationship should be distant and more professional. As one officer that subscribed to the personal technique put it:

I been working a foot post for some time now. I know people on my post by their first name and they know me. I'm not out there looking for information from them. I sit and visit. I don't ask what's going on. People care about where they live and what happens there. They're looking for someone they can trust to help. Once they see you as a person who cares and isn't just passing through you get more information than you can use.

Officers that followed the professional method obtained their information from victims and from individuals referred to as "street people," e.g., prostitutes, drug addicts, etc.

I'm a policeman, not a social worker. I don't have time to shoot the shit. Whores, junkies, and gang bangers are my best source of information. They have a million reasons for ratting. All you have to do is be there when they want to talk or catch them dirty and let them think you can do them some good.

Officers interviewed agreed that another way to become familiar with conditions in the district was through observation. By observation, the officers meant those patterns detected over extended periods of time in day-to-day patrol activities, which included: simple visual observations; taking case reports; and monitoring the radio for car assignments, in-progress calls, etc.

If you listen to the radio you get a good idea of what's going on in the district. You get to know what's going on where and when. It seems a lot easier for me to do it that way than to go and look at the case reports in review. There's just too many of them.

Many officers were dissatisfied with the Department's policy of rotating beats and shifts because, they insisted, conditions in the district varied across beats and shifts. One officer's comments are illustrative:

I've been working the same beat for 4 years. I'd like to get to know the people on my beat, and I think I do know some. But it's hard to develop any kind of relationship with them. You're only around for 4 weeks and then you change watches. On each watch there are different people. And on top of that when I am working I'm rarely on the beat. I get jobs all over the District. The beat assignment is really nothing more than a radio call number.

Participants agreed that the Department did provide some useful sources of information, such as the automated data base queries, e.g., name checks, criminal histories, motor vehicle information, National Crime Information Center (NCIC) wanted individuals and vehicles, etc.

While officers recognized the potential benefits derived from analyzed data, they nevertheless expressed reluctance to incur the costs associated with performing the analysis. This attitude, shared by many officers, is reflected by the comments of one officer:

> You know, we take an awful lot of reports and that stuff goes somewhere downtown. I really don't know what they do with it. When I worked tac (tactical unit) I would try to go to review and look at case reports to see if I could figure out where the patterns were. You figure out quick it's not worth it. It takes too much time to maybe come up with something that might wind up in an arrest and then again might not. The odds of the work paying off just are too low. Like I said, it's not worth it. And if you wait for the dicks to come up with something for you, well that's out too. If they find something worth working they'll do it themselves. You just have to pay attention to what's going on in the district.

Finally, in every group interviewed, to varying degrees, another pattern of frustration emerged in which the respondents expressed pessimism about the value of additional information. As one officer suggested:

> You're going to give us all this great stuff. So what? By the time I answer my jobs and get the silly shit they want me to get, a bus check, a mover, or write something down on a useless ridiculous special attention that they shouldn't have taken in the first place, it's time to go home. And you know what, that's all they want. What's in it for me to go further, even if I did have the time? Catching bad guys isn't what made Rodriguez Superintendent.

CONCLUSIONS

In any given year, the Chicago Police Department generates more than 500,000 reports, each of which holds useful data: victim, witness, and offender information; the date and time of the incident; the location and type of location of the incident; the vehicle used in the commission of the offense; gang information; the proceeds taken; type of weapon used; the method of entrance and exit, etc., in all, approximately 35 different characteristics. From these data we know a good deal about the nature and extent of criminal activity in the city, as well as relevant data about individual incidents. The question posed here is how and how well these data are utilized by patrol officers for tactical purposes.

The primary collation method used by the Department was storage of the data in a mainframe data base, from which straightforward data base queries were executed. The object of the queries were twofold, the first of which was to simply sum the data by crime types (e.g., homicides, criminal sexual assaults, and auto thefts), arrests, cases cleared, etc. The totals were then broken down by unit and distributed to mid- to upper-level managers in hard copy reports, which ultimately were used almost exclusively as indicators of performance. The second objective, and one of some tactical relevance, was a query of the data bases to discover information regarding wanted individuals, vehicles, stolen property, criminal histories, etc. Other than very crude manual methods employed primarily by the Detective Division, the data set was not analyzed to identify tactically useful patterns and relationships.

At the individual level, the evidence suggested that patrol officers engaged in a form of cost/benefit analysis as they shopped for information. Although officers said data searches were potentially useful, they were not routinely executed; quite the contrary, according to these officers, collected data were grossly underutilized. The respondents concluded that the costs to obtain information exceeded the calculated probability that the search would produce beneficial outcomes. All the participants, at one time or another, had manually scanned hard copies of case reports in search of patterns; yet, nearly all agreed that the costs to develop this information far exceeded the expected benefits. Instead, the respondents chose to execute a series of information processing heuristics, or short cuts, which consisted of a variety of low cost information acquisition routines, e.g., patrol observations, radio monitoring, and interactions with residents.

The Chicago Police Department has responded to perceived information processing deficiencies. In 1993, the Department introduced local area networks (LAN) that were later connected to a department-wide area network (WAN). Word processing and data base software was made available to targeted units and members were trained and encouraged to make use of the hardware and software. The LANs permitted a broader access to members of the outlining patrol and detective units to data bases residing on the mainframe. A more user friendly method of querying the crime data base was designed, which when completed will move data from the mainframe environment to one that will permit queries from a PC-based graphical user interface. The Department has also developed a geographical information system interface that permits simple and varied queries of the crime data set for display on a map (Fitch, 1996; Lewin, 1997). In 1996, the Department was awarded a National Institute of Justice grant to develop software that would identify crime patterns in the data set (O'Shea & Muscarello, 1997). Finally, in 1995, the Department installed a state-of-the-art computer aided dispatch (CAD) system that offers a wide range of analytic applications to better utilize the calls for service data collected by the Communications Section. In all, these efforts represent a philosophy held by the Chicago Police Department that the crime data set should be made available to patrol officers in a way that, to the greatest degree possible, reduces the costs of obtaining the information to the extent that it will be analyzed for tactical purposes.

Independent of these efforts, police officer attitudes will pose a challenge for policy makers in their efforts to design information systems to facilitate the analytic behaviors demanded by community policing. We might question the assumption that simply increasing the quantity and accessibility of information will translate into enhanced officer analytic behaviors. More is not necessarily better. In order for information to be tactically useful, it must be used by officers, which will occur only after the information has succeeded in surviving a yet unknown cost/benefit analysis threshold reached by officers. Little is known about the information processing operations of police officers, the consequence of which may be the design of technically flawless information systems (e.g., our recent efforts at geographical information systems development) only to be followed by the end user's calculations that judge the product unacceptable and thereby ignored. Information systems designers must not only consider the question of what information serves tactical purposes (a challenge in itself), but they must also take into account these rather complex rational calculations performed by police officers.

REFERENCES

Anthony, J. E. (1986). *Future of crime analysis in California law enforcement, year 2000.* Sacremento, CA: California Commission on Peace Officer Standards and Training (POST).

Archambeault, W. G., & Archambeault, G. J. (1984). *Computers in criminal justice: Administration and management.* Cincinnati, OH: Anderson.

Block, R., Dabdoub, M., & Fregly, S. (Eds.). (1995). *Crime analysis through computer mapping.* Washington, D.C.: Police Executive Research Forum.

Campbell, G. L. (1972). *A spatially distributed queuing model for police sector design.* Cambridge, MA: MIT Press.

Chaiken, J., & Dormant, P. (1975). *Patrol car allocation: Users manual.* Santa Monica, CA: RAND Corp.

Coyle, K.R., Schaaf, J. C., & Coldren, J. R. (1991). *Futures in crime analysis: Exploring applications of incident-based crime data.* Washington, D.C.: National Institute of Justice.

Craen, A. (1991). Information processing and automated crime analysis by the municipal police of Genk, Belgium. *Police Studies, 14* (1), 36-49.

Danziger, J., & Kraemer, K.L. (1985). Computerized data-based systems and productivity measurement among professional workers: The case of detectives. *Public Administration Review, 45,* 196-209.

Eck, J., & Weisburd, D. (Eds.). (1995). *Crime and place.* Washington, D.C.: Police Executive Research Forum.

Ekblom, P. (1988). *Getting the best out of crime analysis.* London: Home Office Crime Prevention Unit.

Farris, J. R. (1987). Translating theory to practice: A strategic matrix for police planning. *Journal of Crime and Justice, 10,* 23-43.

Fitch, T. (1996). *The Chicago police department's information collection for automated mapping (ICAM) Program.* Washington, D.C.: National Institute of Justice.

Goldstein, H. (1990). *Problem-oriented policing.* New York: McGraw-Hill.

Gottleib, S., Arenberg, S., & Singh, R.. (1994). *Crime analysis: From first report to final arrest.* Montclair, CA: Alpha.

Harries, K. (1990). *Geographic factors in policing.* Washington, D.C.: Police Executive Research Forum.

Illinois Criminal Justice Information Authority. (1987). Spatial and temporal analysis of crime. *Research Bulletin,* April.

Lee, H.C., & Gaensslen, R. E. (1991). *Advances in fingerprint technology.* New York: Elsevier.

Levine, E. H. (1979). *Information science: Law enforcement applications.* Cincinnati: Anderson Publishing Co.

Lewin, J. (1997). Decentralized crime analysis by the beat officer. In Melissa Miller Reuland (Ed.), *Information management and crime analysis: Practitioner's recipes for success.* Washington, D.C.: Police Executive Research Forum.

Maltz, M. D., Gordon, A. C., &. Freidman, W. (1989). *Mapping crime in its community setting: A study of event geography.* New York: Springer-Verlag.

Manning, P.K. (1992). Information technologies and the police. In Tonry, M. and Morris, N. (Eds.), *Modern policing.* Chicago: University of Chicago Press.

Marchand, D. A. (1980). *The politics of privacy, computers, and criminal justice records.* Arlington, VA: Information Resources Press.

McEwen, J. T. (1990). *Use of microcomputers in criminal justice agencies.* Washington, D.C.: National Institute of Justice.

National Criminal Justice Information and Statistics Service. (1978). *Application of computer-aided dispatch in law enforcement: An introductory planning guide.* Washington, D.C.: Department of Justice.

National Institute of Justice. (1995). *The nations two crime measures.* Washington, D.C.: National Institute of Justice.

O'Shea, T., & Muscarello, T. (1997). *Using technology to enhance police problem solving.* (Technical Report). Washington, D.C.: National Institute of Justice.

Peterson, M. (1994). *Applications in criminal analysis: A sourcebook.* Westport, CT: Greenwood Press.

Peterson, M. (1997). Criminal analysis. In Dantzker, M.L. (Ed.), *Contemporary policing.* Boston: Butterworth-Heinemann.

Ratledge, E.C., &. Jacoby, J.E. (1989). *Handbook on artificial intelligence and expert systems in law enforcement.* Westport, CN: Greenwood.

Reaves, B. (1994). *Using NIBRS data to analyze violent crime.* Washington, D.C.: Bureau of Justice Statistics.

Reuland, M. (Ed.). (1997). *Information management and crime analysis: Practitioner's recipes for success.* Washington, D.C.: Police Executive Research Forum.

Search Group, Inc. (1988). *The criminal justice microcomputer guide and software catalogue.* Washington, D.C.: Department of Justice.

Sherman, L. (1989). Hot spots of predatory crime: Routine activities and the criminology of place. *Criminology, 27,* 27-56.

Smith, S.B. (1973). *Superbeat: A system for the effective distribution of police patrol units.* Chicago, IL: Illinois Institute of Technology.

Spelman, W. (1988). *Beyond bean counting: New approaches for managing crime data.* Washington, D.C.: Police Executive Research Forum.

Stallo, M. (1997). Crime analysis: The administrative function. In Reuland, M.M. (Ed.), *Information management and crime analysis: Practitioner's recipes for success.* Washington, D.C.: Police Executive Research Forum.

Wilson, T.F. (1987). *Automated fingerprint identification systems: Technology and policy issues.* Washington, D.C.: Bureau of Justice Statistics.

Chapter 7

"THE PROBLEM-SOLVER": THE DEVELOPMENT OF INFORMATION TECHNOLOGY TO SUPPORT PROBLEM-ORIENTED POLICING*

Lorraine Green Mazerolle and Robert C. Haas

INTRODUCTION

The advent of community policing has increased the need for information. Police executives need information to define priority problems, design and implement solutions, and assess the strategic impact of their departments' efforts to control crime problems. Community groups demand information about crime and quality of life problems in their neighborhoods. Street-level problem-solvers need routine access to information to scan for problems, analyze these problems, and subsequently implement and assess problem-oriented policing efforts. Indeed, information technology is a critical ingredient for successful implementation of community policing in general and problem-oriented policing in particular.

Over the last decade, police departments across the nation have invested considerable resources into implementing and upgrading their police information systems. Many police departments have

* This chapter was supported by the Inter-Police Agency Informational Sharing Grant # 95-IN-15B-029 from the Massachusetts Department of Public Safety. An earlier version of this paper was presented at the Academy of Criminal Justice Sciences conference in Louisville (March, 1997). We would like to take this opportunity to thank Ms. Margret K. Streckert and Mr. Jerrold H. Streckert of MICROSystems Integrated Public Safety Solutions Inc.(Melrose, MA), Ms Julie Schnobrich, and the New England Police Consortium of fifty-two Police Departments for their support in the development of "The Problem-Solver." Address all correspondence to Lorraine Green Mazerolle, University of Cincinnati, PO Box 210389, Cincinnati, OH 45221.

worked closely with their vendors to customize their dispatch systems and create reporting systems that allow regular access to basic police data. At the same time, many departments have made serious attempts to implement community and problem-oriented approaches to policing. However, efforts to upgrade information systems are often divorced from organizational plans to reform police agencies, creating deficiencies in departmental capabilities to access information to facilitate problem-solving activities. Our partnership activities began with the premise that implementation of problem-oriented policing should be tightly integrated with the design and implementation of information technology. Without integration, information technology may be underutilized and efforts to implement problem-oriented policing may flounder or not be sustainable.

Police departments spend considerable amounts of time, effort, and resources collecting and storing vast amounts of information. For example, most police departments these days systematically collect and store all emergency calls for service, arrests, incidents, property records, citations, traffic infringements, and field interviews. These data are typically aggregated at the end of each month and used to report demands on police resources, analyzed to identify emerging crime problems, and examined to track those problems that are on the decline. Beat officers use this type of information to communicate crime trends in their neighborhoods to community groups. The COMPSTAT process initiated in the New York City Police Department uses detailed crime trend information both as a management tool and as a method for developing more strategic responses to crime problems at the local level.

While demand for police information is high, most police departments have struggled to develop their information systems to enable easy (and up-to-date) access to information to support problem-solving activities. Departments have extensive amounts of data, yet these data are often inaccessible to line officers, rarely accessed to support police efforts to scan and analyze the locations of hot spots of crime, and typically not well integrated with community-based information (such as census data and local social service resources) to augment problem-solving efforts.

Our chapter describes a computer-based problem-solving tool ("The Problem-Solver") that was designed and developed to make police data accessible to line officers (and supervisors) with the idea of enhancing problem-oriented policing activities department-wide. "The Problem-Solver" was developed through a collaboration between a private public safety computer company (MICROSystems Inc.), a university-based researcher (Professor Lorraine Green Mazerolle), and a consortium of fifty-two New England Police Departments. Chief Robert Haas of the Westwood Police Department assumed the facilitation and leadership role for our consortium.

We begin our chapter by introducing the partners that were involved in developing "The Problem-Solver." We then describe the key components of "The Problem-Solver" and we conclude with a discussion about the utility of information technology in augmenting problem-oriented policing activities.

PROJECT PARTNERS AND PARTNERSHIP BACKGROUND

"The Problem-Solver" is a tool that was developed to augment the problem-oriented policing efforts of a consortium of fifty-two police departments in New England. A private computer company (MICROSystems) and a university-based researcher (Professor Lorraine Green Mazerolle) worked extensively with the New England consortium to design "The Problem-Solver" software.

The consortium of police departments involved in the project comprise primarily suburban police departments located in the Greater Metropolitan Boston area, Western Massachusetts, New Hampshire and Vermont. Fifty-two police departments agreed to participate in the consortium covering ten congressional districts.

Our partner departments comprise an average of about 35 full-time sworn officers, ranging from three sworn officers in the smallest department to 110 officers in the largest department in our consortium. There is an average of about seven non-sworn officers in our consortium departments. The departments serve populations ranging in size from about 5,000 people to nearly 50,000 people in larger jurisdictions (mean is nearly 20,000), covering an average area of about 20 square miles. Operating budgets for the participating departments range from $330,000 to $6.4 million (mean is $2.2 million). From our survey of participating departments, an average of about $23,000 is spent on training and officers are provided with an average of 49 hours of in-service training each year.

The New England police departments participating in our project are fairly typical of police departments in the US: about 91 percent of local police departments in the US employ fewer than fifty sworn officers and the average annual operating expenditure for local police departments is around $1.7 million (Reaves, 1991).

The police departments making up the consortium averaged 430 Part I crimes in 1995. The most common Part I crimes reported to police during 1994 across our consortium of departments was larceny (mean of 284), followed by aggravated assault (mean is 247) and burglary (mean is 108). The police departments recorded a total of 8 homicides and nearly 100 rapes. On average, the departments recorded about seven robberies and 58 motor vehicle thefts during this one year time period.

Most of the departments in the consortium do not have what they themselves would call a community policing plan. For those that do, the nature of their plans vary considerably. One department initiated a professional development program, increasing their training budget by 900 percent in tuition costs alone. Another department sought to build coalitions among various municipal departments within the community. Other departments have no clear plans for implementing community policing and have traditionally been isolated from federal and state money to reform their organizations.

The common element that forms the basis to our consortium of fifty-two police departments is their CAD/MIS systems: over the last twelve years all departments in our consortium purchased a Computer Aided Dispatch (CAD) and Management Information System (MIS) called CrimeTRACK from a private computer company called MICROSystems Integrated Public Safety Solutions, Inc. The CrimeTRACK system provides several attractive features among its many system modules. For example, the records management module allows users to request locations of addresses with multiple arrests for specified time periods. Additionally, a series of "queries" have been created that allow users to predict potential crime fluctuations by varying the numbers of patrol units assigned to particular beats as a means to facilitate resource allocation decisions.

In early 1995, MICROSystems Inc., Chief Robert Haas of the Westwood Police Department, and Professor Lorraine Green Mazerolle of the University of Cincinnati began working together in an effort to develop CrimeTRACK in such a way to encourage, augment, and enhance the problem-solving efforts of the partnership departments. From the outset, Chief Haas assumed a facilitation role for the consortium by encouraging and mobilizing the consortium of Police Chiefs to work together in building a problem-oriented policing capacity within their respective agencies. Through a small State of Massachusetts Byrne Block Grant we worked together to develop "The Problem-Solver."

We have involved the consortium police departments throughout the developmental phase of building "The Problem-Solver:" meeting monthly with representatives from each department through MICROSystem's hosted "Users=Group" meetings and by providing regular formal and informal updates on "The Problem-Solver" progress to the police chiefs in the consortium.

"THE PROBLEM-SOLVER": A PROBLEM-ORIENTED POLICING TOOL

"The Problem-Solver" was originally envisaged as an operational tool for both police managers and street-level problem-solving police officers. We wanted to create a system for accessing information already collected within the *CrimeTRACK* environment to allow easy access to the system data for problem-solving activities.[1] We also believed that "The Problem-Solver" itself could reform the way police went about their day-to-day activities by using information technology to lead officers through a SARA approach to problem-solving (see Eck & Spelman, 1987; Goldstein, 1990). We imagined that police not versed in the SARA methodology (or problem-solving in general) could change the way they responded to local crime and quality of life problems by using "The Problem-Solver." In essence, we understood "The Problem-Solver" in particular, and information technology in general, to be a medium through which we could change the way police do business. As Manning (1992) suggests: "technology is embedded in social organization; it shapes organizations and is shaped by them" (1992, P. 349).

---

1 "The Problem-Solver" is also commercially available as a Windows '95 PC compatible software application. This PC-based application comprises four components: a database manager that includes all question, answer and response libraries; input databases (such as calls for service, arrests, field contacts, etc); a master file; and a geocoded master address file.

The main menu of "The Problem-Solver" invites users to select a stage of the problem-solving process—scanning, analysis, response, or assessment—and offers users the option of approaching their problem-solving efforts either through identifying problem people or problem places. From this main menu, users are led through a series of screens that allow problem-solvers the ability to access data, identify and analyze hot "people" or hot spots of crime, input answers to specific questions about scanned problems, identify appropriate types of responses at different types of hot spots or different types of problem people, and assess the impact of the implemented responses.

The initial "scanning" option of "The Problem-Solver" draws from police calls, arrests, incidents, citations, field interviews, traffic citations, restraining orders, warrants, and suspended licenses. Depending on whether the user wants to search for hot people or hot places, the system accesses either the master name file or the master address file. Users can search all types of incidents ("action codes") or they can select groupings of incidents such as domestics, drug, gang activity, burglaries, vice, traffic, or quality of life offenses. These groupings are all user-definable. Users can group their search in several different ways: by using existing UCR codes, existing NIBRS codes, or they can develop their own groupings (e.g., roller-blading incidents, all gang activity, mental health involvements, etc). The groupings can be as specific or as general as what users choose. The flexibility within the system to group incidents in any manner they desire is an important aspect to the "The Problem-Solver." We imagine traffic enforcement officers, for example, will use the system in very different ways to general patrol officers. Similarly, we expect DARE officers to use the system and create very different problem groupings to the groupings that would be of interest to vice squad officers.

After choosing the types of incidents to search on, users can pick from a range of other search criteria: they can search between particular date ranges, they can choose specific beats or precincts to search within, they can pick the types of involvements (e.g., arrests, emergency calls, citations) from which to search from, and they can weight the involvements to search on. We created an internal weighting system to generate lists of hot people or hot places after analyzing samples of data from several participating departments. These weightings, however, can be overwritten temporarily to allow for user-defined weightings. The weightings option can also be turned on or turned off as the user chooses. Finally, users can request the system to generate any number of hot people or hot places, they can request that the scanned places or people be ordered by location or frequency of involvement, and users can request a minimum threshold of activity to be met before the system displays the list of hot people or hot places.

After the system generates lists of hot people or places, users can pick and choose the places or people they wish to "keep" in their problem file. They can then either re-scan or save their groups of people or places. The saving option allows users to give the problem groupings a "common" description (e.g., "Top 10 gang involved people" or "Top 20 traffic accident locations"). The system then generates a unique problem number.

The "analysis" option of "The Problem-Solver" allows users to systematically analyze each case listed in the "scanned" data. Users can, at the analysis stage, request which problem question group they would like to attach to their problem. For example, if a user has identified the top 20 drug hot spots in their town, they will want to request the "drug" set of problem-solving questions; if they have identified the top 10 youths involved in quality of life problems, they will probably want to request the "Quality of Life" set of problem-solving questions. The question sets are all user-definable: system administrators can cut and paste different questions to different question sets depending on how specific they want the question groups to be (or, conversely, how general they want the question groups to be); system administrators can create their own question sets; place specific questions can be adapted to ask questions about hot people and person-specific questions can be adapted to ask questions about hot places.

Our decision to allow for flexibility in the analysis phase of "The Problem-Solver" stems from a number of practical and theoretical concerns. On the one hand, research suggests that the problem-solving process is more likely to succeed when problems are specifically delineated one from another (see Clarke, 1992; Goldstein, 1990). For example, problem-solvers need to differentiate between different types of burglaries: commercial burglaries are found to require fundamentally different response strategies to residential burglaries. With crime prevention and problem-oriented policing research in mind, we wanted "The Problem-Solver" to reflect a degree of specificity in the analysis phase that would lead the system to generate tailor-made responses. On the other hand, however, we did not want to discourage police officers who were new to the concept of problem-solving by overcomplicating the problem-solving process. As such, the analysis component of "The Problem-Solver" currently provides less specificity than more experienced problem-solving officers would want, yet the flexibility of the system allows system administrators to modify the question groupings, question answers, and suggested response libraries in ways that will allow for more specificity as officers become more experienced.

In developing the question library for each problem group, we met with officers with specific expertise in solving different types of problems. Our initial process for developing the analysis questions and responses allowed individual departments and individual officers to be earmarked as the consortium "experts" for different types of problems, creating "centers of problem-solving" expertise.

The second strategy used to develop the problem-solving questions and responses was through an extensive literature search of both the academic and practitioner-based literature to glean all the different types of interventions that police have used to tackle different types of problems across the country. A list of interventions appear in our "response library" and each response is systematically linked to a specific analysis question.

The better and more extensive the questions and responses (and the linkages made between the questions and responses) the better the system will facilitate problem-solving efforts. We expect, however, a degree of tailoring of the supplied questions and responses to local environments. For example, if a jurisdiction using the "The Problem-Solver" has a particularly serious domestic violence problem, then they may want to develop the question and response libraries in such a way to enable more precise interventions for domestic problems than the interventions that are provided in the base library. Similarly, jurisdictions can tailor the response library to accommodate idiosyncratic names of service organizations, local help groups, or local ordinances. Importantly, the linkages between the question, answer, and response libraries are user definable: users can add, delete, and modify all questions, answers, responses, and linkages in a way that will suit their own individual departments and jurisdictions.

"The Problem-Solver" also allows users to modify and update the base question and response libraries periodically to customize the libraries to reflect new approaches to solving problems. By allowing the questions and responses to be customized and updated, all departments can benefit from the trials and tribulations of the departments that have tried different responses to specific types of problems.

The "analysis" phase of "The Problem-Solver" prompts users to request a question grouping from a list of more than 20 different types of problem types.[2] Based on the question group that the user requests, the system generates a series of analysis questions. For example, for the gang set of questions, the system asks the user to find out how much gang activity a person is involved in; whether the person uses violence in the gang context; or whether they are known to use graffiti to "tag" their territories (among many other gang specific questions). The purpose of the analysis stage of "The Problem-Solver" is to encourage and suggest that officers research the causes of the problem rather than simply assuming they know the answer to the question.[3] The prompted questions cannot generally be answered without making additional inquiries about the problem person or problem place. In this regard, we aim to close the gap we have found in problem-solving: that officers typically do not spend enough time on quality analysis of the problem (see Eck & Spelman, 1987). While our system is designed to encourage officers to complete answering all analysis questions, the system does not break down if some questions are skipped or remain unanswered: the responses will only be based on the questions answered.

Based on the answers to the specific questions generated by "The Problem-Solver," the system generates a series of "suggested responses." These responses are generated from a response library that is systematically linked back to the analysis questions. The response library contains weighted responses based on what we would consider "urgent" or the most important responses to the least or not so vital responses. The responses are specific to the problem groupings selected by the user. For example, the gang responses are specifically designed to tackle gang problems; the youth responses are specifically designed to tackle youth problems, and so on and so forth.

---

2 While 20 question groupings have already been identified, the system is built in such a way to allow system administrators to add up to 999 different question groupings.

3. "The Problem-Solver" should not be viewed as a substitute for training in problem-oriented policing in particular or community policing in general. Indeed, we suggest that as a tool that is designed to facilitate problem-solving activities, "The Problem-Solver" should be implemented in concert with a major training program in problem-oriented policing techniques. This is especially apparent in teaching officers to conduct in-depth analysis of target problems.

Once the system has created a list of "suggested responses," officers enter four pieces of information for each activity they carry-out for each suggested response: they enter the date that they undertook action to resolve the problem; a short description of what action they took; a self-assessment as to the effectiveness of the action (on a four point scale); and the approximate number of minutes they spent on the action. It should be noted that the decision to include this type of action accounting system in "The Problem-Solver" was the subject of considerable debate during the developmental phase. On the one hand, we did not want to "turn-off" officers from "The Problem-Solver" if they saw the module as a way their supervisors could "get them." On the other hand, we believed that many police activities go unnoticed (or at least unaccounted for). For example, phone calls made to a city agency to request the boarding of an abandoned building is rarely counted in police performance measurements. Similarly, the hours that some officers spend in conversation with parents of troublesome youths or in chasing-up background information on a suspected drug dealer typically go unrewarded. After carefully balancing the advantages and disadvantages of documenting the time officers spend on police problem-solving responses, we believed that for the majority of officers, the capacity to record their range of problem-solving activities and the time taken to resolve the problem would outweigh any fears that the system was a "management tool" out to undermine a problem-solver. Moreover, many of the officers we consulted with during the process of building "The Problem-Solver" saw the ability to create a "paper trail" of problem-solving activities as an advantage for them, particularly when they needed to go to court over an issue.

"The Problem-Solver" contains a considerable degree of flexibility in all aspects of the system. For example, our system allows departments to customize the questions and answers to their unique sets of problems in their own town or city. For example, a town by-law (or city code) may carry with it a particular identification number. Our system allows each department to specify the town by-law number rather than use a generic reference to a town by-law from the response library. Users can add questions, add responses, reweight the questions and responses, relink the responses to the questions, and regroup the questions by problem-type.

Finally, the "The Problem-Solver" includes an "assessment" option. This option runs some basic analysis on the numbers of calls, arrests, traffic violations, incidents or any other type of involvement data included in the system by month of the involvement. The assessment part of "The Problem-Solver" allows officers to examine the number of hours spent on a problem against the number of incidents recorded either against the problem person or problem place both before and after the intervention began. Moreover, the system allows users to examine their self assessments regarding the effectiveness of their interventions against the time spent on solving the problem. The system also compiles an "audit trail" to track all entries made in "The Problem-Solver." The audit trail thus allows more than one officer to work on a defined problem at any one time and also tracks changes in the entries made to the system. Appendix A contains selected "screen dumps" of "The Problem-Solver" options.

DISCUSSION AND CONCLUSION

"The Problem-Solver" is a tool for organizing police information and is designed to facilitate police problem-solving activities. By better organizing police data, "The Problem-Solver" seeks to augment and enhance problem-solving activities. By offering an on-line approach to problem-solving, the software assists officers in identifying and responding to problems either in terms of those individuals who pose the greatest concern relative to specific issues or problems (hot people), or in terms of those places in the community that may require the greatest amount of police interventions (hot places). The new technology is designed so that it may be used by officers who may want to target specific problems (e.g. traffic, drugs, public drinking, assaults) or by officers who are seeking information to target general problems (or even clusters of problems).

"The Problem-Solver" draws heavily from two inter-related bodies of research: the software is designed to step officers through the SARA approach to problem-oriented policing (see Eck & Spelman, 1987) and it focuses police attention on hot places or hot people. A significant body of research demonstrates that only a small number of individuals (e.g., see Wolfgang, Figlio, & Sellin, 1972) or locations (hot spots) consume a disproportionate amount of police resources (e.g., see Pierce, Spaar & Briggs, 1988; Sherman, Gartin & Buerger, 1989;

Sherman & Weisburd, 1995; Weisburd & Green, 1985). "The Problem-Solver" seeks to assist line officers, or those officers who specialize in any aspect of policing (e.g., traffic enforcement, narcotics, juvenile matters, domestic violence, burglaries, etc.), in focusing on those people or places that place the greatest demand on police services. Once these chronic people or places are identified, "The Problem Solver" provides officers with a tool to analyze the problem in a structured fashion, develop tailor-made responses to the problem, and assess the effectiveness of their interventions. By presenting information in a format that highlights those individuals or locations that place the greatest demand on police services, "The Problem-Solver" allows street officers to look at the "root causes" of a problem or issue, rather than simply repeatedly responding to the symptoms.

The "Problem-Solver" not only assists line officers in dealing with identified issues or problems in a systematic way, but it also provides information for both supervisory and administrative levels of the police department to assess the impact of their investment of resources on hot people or places. We propose that "The Problem-Solver" (in concert with a problem-oriented policing training program) can promote organizational structural change by pushing operational decision-making to line level officers and developing accountability for the identification, analysis, and response undertaken by line officers to alleviate pressing crime issues and quality of life problems.

REFERENCES

Clarke, R.V. (Ed.) (1992). *Situational crime prevention: Successful case studies.* New York: Harrow and Heston.

Eck, J., & Spelman, W. (1987). *Problem solving: Problem-oriented policing in Newport News.* Washington DC: Police Executive Research Forum and National Institute of Justice.

Goldstein, H. (1990). *Problem-oriented policing.* New York, NY: McGraw-Hill.

Manning, P. (1992). *Information technologies and the police.* In M. Tonry and N. Morris (Eds.), *Modern policing: A review of research* (pp. 349-398). Chicago: University of Chicago Press.

Pierce, G.L., Spaar, L., & Briggs, L.R. (1988). *The character of police work: Strategic and tactical implications.* Boston, MA: Center for Applied Social Research, Northeastern University.

Reaves, B. (1991). *State and local police departments, 1990.* Washington, DC: US Department of Justice, Bureau of Justice Statistics.

Sherman, L., Gartin, P., & Buerger, M. (1989). Hotspots of predatory crime. *Criminology, 27*(1), 27-56.

Sherman, L., & Weisburd, D. (1995). General deterrent effects of police patrol in crime hot spots: A randomized controlled trial. *Justice Quarterly, 12,* 625-648.

Weisburd, D., & Green, L. (1995). Policing drug hot spots: The Jersey City drug market analysis experiment. *Justice Quarterly, 12,* 711-736.

Wolfgang, M., Figlio, R., & Sellin, T. 1972. *Delinquency in a birth cohort.* Chicago: University of Chicago Press.

Chapter 8

THE CENTRALIZED DATA ENTRY (CDE) SYSTEM: ONE COUNTY'S ATTEMPT AT MANAGING BURDENSOME PAPERWORK WITH INNOVATIVE TECHNOLOGY

Laura J. Moriarty and Thomas J. Dover

INTRODUCTION

Policing agencies are constantly looking for means by which reporting can be facilitated quickly and efficiently. Computerized strategies have been implemented in many jurisdictions. In 1975, Mount Morris, Minnesota; Wheaton, Illinois; and Whitefish Bay, Wisconsin equipped officers with portable dictating units. This reduced the time necessary to complete incident reports (Swanson, 1982, p. 329). In 1988, Cincinnati, Ohio began experiencing a backlog of police records (Arkenau, 1990, p. 16) because of the antiquated reporting method which relied on using log books and index cards to track accident reports. This labor intensive activity was too time consuming. In an effort to solve this problem, the department began exploring alternatives:

> . . . the division began to examine alternative methods of managing files. Record-keeping personnel considered several microfilm-based, computer-assisted retrieval systems before selecting the optical disk image retrieval system. This system proved to be the solution to a critical problem (Arkenau, 1990, p. 16).

The Boston police department is using computers to store the thousands of restraining orders issued by the eight district courts throughout the city (Ellement, 1992). And cities like St. Petersburg and Ocala, Florida (Swanson, Territo, & Taylor, 1993); Schaumburg, Illinois (McMahon, 1991); and Diluth, Georgia (Johnson, 1992) are experimenting with officers using lap-top computers to complete preformatted police reports in the field.

Not only in these specific examples but throughout the United States, there has been a "tremendous increase in computer automation in law enforcement" (Swanson et al., 1993, p. 509; see also Lansinger, 1992; Lieberman, 1989; Pilant, 1993). Archambeault and Archambeault (1982, p.4) recognized almost 15 years ago that the future of law enforcement technology included computers. Officers must be "computer-literate" in order to function in law enforcement today. Police work involves managing data in such demand that Taylor (1989) states that "an automated records and communications system is no longer viewed as a luxury but [as] a necessity" (Taylor, 1989, p. 258).

Such automation in police work results in five benefits to police departments: (1) a reduction in time spent on police reports; (2) instant on-line management of information; (3) a reduction in need for office space to store hard copies; (4) improved quality, accuracy, and timeliness of information; and (5) improved quality, accuracy, and legibility of police reports (George & Kleinknecht, 1985).

In this chapter, the authors examine one specific type of police technology used to reduce burdensome paperwork: the Centralized Data Entry (CDE) system. We begin with an explanation for why the system was needed and how it was selected. Then we describe and evaluate it. We conclude with recommendations for improving the CDE.

IMPETUS FOR CHANGE: THE PAPER CRISIS

A rural county in North Carolina began experiencing an increase in drug-related arrests in 1991 that lead to the immediate need to examine alternatives to traditional police reporting systems. Information regarding such arrests was captured in diverse sources including "police records, arrest reports, citations, warrants, court dispositions, and jail intake reports" (Seay, 1992, p. 2). All levels of the criminal justice system in this county attempted to maintain handwritten records to assist individuals within the criminal justice system with information sharing and offender tracking. Because of the increase in drug-related arrests, the handwritten system was literally being pushed to its limit. As a result, the increase in paperwork had become virtually unmanageable and it was obvious that a new system of data management needed to be investigated.

It was found that the majority of the paperwork was produced by the felony caseloads that, by their nature, required most of the resources and attention of the law enforcement agencies, district attorney's office, and the court system. From 1985 to 1991, the number of Superior Court criminal felony filings in the county increased nearly 250 percent (Seay, 1992, p. 2). From 1988 to 1991, the number of arrest reports per year increased by 840; the number of offense reports per year increased by 2,159; the number of jail intake bookings per year increased by 1,965; and the number of criminal court cases per year increased by 2,845. These figures indicate a total increase in reports, bookings, and court cases of 7,809 representing a 12.2 percent increase over the 1988 figures (Seay, 1992, p. 2).

The increase in data processing uncovered several inefficiencies in the system. First, data were being entered from each department, often being captured first on paper, then being entered into a computer. This duplication was an inefficient usage of manpower. Second, data entry into the computer was usually delayed 48 to 72 hours, resulting in verification problems and curtailing the exchange of information between agencies. Third, not all data entry was performed by trained data entry clerks causing problems with the accuracy of the data because there was no uniformed data entry strategy.

TECHNOLOGY TO THE RESCUE: THE CENTRALIZED DATA ENTRY SYSTEM

County officials were looking for a strategy to decrease the paperwork crisis and to increase sharing of information among state agencies. The centralized data entry system was viewed as a viable option worthy of implementation. Not only does the centralized data entry system provide a pool of information, but it also "unites trained analysts with elected officials and ties productivity improvements to the power of the budget" (Swanson, 1982, p. 330).

No single agency in the county had the resources to staff a data entry office full-time, seven days a week, twenty-four hours a day. The only way to solve the problem was to coordinate efforts among all agencies needing the information collected, and then centralize the implemented system.

It is logical that the first steps for coordinated action came from the agency that would most likely witness the total phenomenal increase in reports and record keeping. As a central repository for arrest records, criminal history records, fingerprint cards, mug shots, and the like, the City-Council ID Bureau, led by Director Ginger Seay, applied for and received state-aid to implement a Centralized Data Entry (CDE) system in the county.

The CDE system was patterned after a program implemented by the St. Louis County, Missouri Police Department. Basically, the CDE offers field officers, the magistrate, the jailer, and even citizens wishing to file complaints or give testimony, a way to be "talked" through the process resulting in an immediate entry of information into the computer. A report can be conducted over the phone or in person. The county's CDE operates in the following manner:

> The computer-aided dispatch module . . . assigns a unique case number to each call for service. This unique number ties together all the information entered into the ... system. When an officer answers a call for service where a report is required, he telephones the CDE from the location of the call, gives his unique case number to the data entry clerk, and advises what type of report he needs to make. The CDE operator takes the case number and enters it into the system. The system displays the reporting screen and pre-fills it with applicable information (location, officer, time, etc.) already generated as part of the computer-aided dispatch record. The CDE operator completes the screen by asking questions of the officer and generates the offense report with the unique case number attached. If an arrest is made, the CDE operator then accesses the arrest report screen with the same unique case number. The system pre-fills the arrest screen with information already generated from CAD (computer-aided dispatch) and the offense report. The CDE operator completes the screen, again by asking questions of the officer, and generates the arrest report. The system automatically conducts a local arrest/wanted check on the arrested person. (Seay, 1992, p. 4)

When the suspect is brought before the magistrate, the magistrate accesses the Automated Wants and Warrants Module using the same unique case number. The computer displays the offense report and the arrest report so that the magistrate can determine probable cause. The computer provides the record check to help the magistrate determine conditions of release. It then displays the release order with previous information already generated from prior reports. When the suspect is booked, the jailer calls the CDE operator and provides the unique case number for the suspect. The system presents the intake forms with prefilled information to the CDE operator who then questions the jailer.

Throughout the entire process, no paperwork has been generated. Once data is in the system, it is immediately accessible to other personnel who need the information. Duplicated information collected on separated forms will already be completed if the suspect is in the computer.

EVALUATION STRATEGY

An impact model (Rossi & Freeman, 1993) was developed to evaluate the CDE system. According to Rossi and Freeman (1993, pp. 120-122), an impact model must contain causal, intervention, and action hypotheses. The impact model for the current research consists of the following two sets of hypotheses:

Set 1

The implementation of a CDE system results in a savings of time for criminal justice professionals. (causal hypothesis)

The implementation of the CDE system will decrease the amount of time needed to complete arrest reports. (intervention hypothesis)

As criminal justice professionals use the CDE, they will indicate they have more time than before the CDE implementation to focus on the primary facets of their job. (action hypothesis)

Set 2

The implementation of a CDE system results in increased sharing of information among criminal justice agencies. (causal hypothesis)

The implementation of the CDE system will increase the availability and sharing of information among criminal justice agencies. (intervention hypothesis)

Those using the CDE system will indicate more sharing of information than was the case with the old system. (action hypothesis)

The current evaluation plan can be labeled as a reputability assessment (Rossi & Freeman, 1993, p. 156). Such an assessment "refers to a systematic effort to obtain from relevant stakeholders . . . data on their experiences with, and assessment of, a program as a basis on which to judge the extent of the program's success in meeting its objectives" (Rossi & Freeman, 1993, p. 156). The main objective of the CDE implementation is to reduce the amount of time needed to complete paperwork and increase the sharing of information among criminal justice agencies.

THE EVALUATION PROCESS

Funding was approved by the North Carolina Governor's Crime Commission, resulting in implementation of the CDE in October, 1992. The authors were asked by the County Court Administer to develop an evaluation plan. That plan was presented to a CDE sub-committee consisting of representatives from the police department, sheriff's office, city-county ID bureau, and county court administration. A questionnaire was developed and approved by the CDE subcommittee to be administered to all personnel using the CDE system.

A self-administered questionnaire was completed by all those using the CDE for a 13 month period from October, 1992 to November, 1993. A total of 156 individuals used the CDE during that time and completed the questionnaire. The authors also conducted an on-site visit of the CDE on January 18, 1994. The survey results were complete at that time and the authors had an opportunity to collect important qualitative data to help understand the comments made by the respondents on the survey. The following are the results of the evaluation.

CDE users

The CDE users can be described in the following manner: 122 were male (80%) and 31 were female (20%). The age ranged from 23 years to 68 years with the average age being 36 years old. Almost half (48.4%) of the respondents had some college education with almost one-third having received a college degree. Almost half (48.1%) of the respondents were patrol officers followed by detectives (14%), patrol supervisors (11%), civil processors (8.4%), lieutenant coordinators (5.2%), probation officers (4.5%), administrators (4.5%), and detective supervisors (3.9%). Most of the respondents either worked for the police department (45%) or the sheriff's office (46.4%). The respondents indicated they were employed in their current position an average of five years.

CDE Usage

Nearly every respondent (92%) was aware of the new CDE system. The respondents used the CDE an average of 33.5 times with the range extending from no usage to a high of 130 times used in the 13 month period. The CDE use per month ranged from no usage to 200 times used with an average of 10.2 times used per month [some of the respondents answered this question but left the "use per month" question blank].

Perceptions Regarding the CDE

Respondents were asked to indicate whether they felt this new system (CDE) served them better or worse than the old system where a report was handwritten. More than three-quarters of the respondents felt the new system was either much better or somewhat better than the old system. In addition, more than half indicated much more time or somewhat more time was saved using the CDE over the old method. About one-quarter indicated no time was saved by using the CDE. The average amount of time saved was 14.2 minutes per arrest. The amount of time saved ranged from 0 or none to one hour.

Respondents were asked if they felt data were more or less readily available to them then was the case prior to the installation of the CDE. Almost 40 percent indicated data were much more readily available and 42 percent indicated data were somewhat more readily available. A small percent, about 17 percent, indicated there was no change in data availability.

Respondents were asked if agencies shared information more freely now with the implementation of the CDE. Almost one-third (32.2%) indicated that agencies were sharing information more freely, while almost 38 percent indicated no change in information sharing. Those who indicated agencies still were not sharing information were asked to elaborate on the reasons for this noncompliance. Although there were 19 valid responses to this question, those responses can be categorized into one overall problem: lack of communication.

The respondents were asked to rate the CDE on a scale of excellent to poor. Only one respondent rated the system as poor. Nearly 50 percent indicated the system was good, about 30 percent said excellent, and 17 percent rated the system as average. The respondents indicated that at least 6 to 9 months is needed for an adjustment period before one can be expected to master the CDE process. Respondents were asked to indicate any problems they personally experienced with the CDE. The list of problems ranged from the CDE being unsecured to information missing in the system. A more detailed discussion of the noted problems is provided below.

DISCUSSION

Overall, the CDE evaluation seems to be positive. In terms of the action hypotheses, the results reveal an average of 14.2 minutes of time saved per arrest and about one-third of the respondents indicated agencies are sharing information more freely. From the perspective of the evaluators and the funding agency, these results are considered "adequate." It is anticipated that more time will be saved and more information will be shared more freely as the CDE system continues to operate.

Some of the problems identified by the respondents must be discussed. For example, over 30 percent of the respondents indicated there are real safety concerns associated with the police booking process. The respondents revealed that some officers are not following procedure resulting in a booking area that is unsafe and nonsecure.

In an effort to understand this concern, the authors toured the Booking Unit. From the visit, it was determined that the officers did not fully understand how the CDE system worked. They were taking the suspects to the CDE office to process them. The better approach is to have the officers detain suspects in a holding tank and call the CDE operator with the pertinent information. The officer can communicate with the offender, if necessary, without creating a dangerous situation. The authors recommend that the county consider combining the Booking Unit with the CDE system. This would alleviate, to a certain degree, the safety concerns of the officers.

Other problems identified included (1) the process takes too long to complete; (2) the data entry staff is underqualified; and (3) information is missing. The authors believe that increasing the number of phone lines into the CDE will decrease the amount of time it takes to complete the process. In addition, the county officials must hire and train additional data clerk operators in order to expedite the process and eliminate technical problems, such as, missing data. Finally, officers should be required to complete the process only by phone. This would enhance the safety issue discussed above because the officers would not be allowed to move the suspect out of the booking area.

The final problem identified by the officers results in less information sharing among criminal justice agencies. This lack of sharing of information is attributed to communication problems. Basically, a lack of communication is seen as the main reason for agencies not sharing information. The authors recommend that more training regarding the CDE system be implemented. Not only should the training include how to use the CDE system but also the goals and objectives of the CDE system must be clearly understood by all who participate.

RECOMMENDATIONS

In an effort to increase the amount of time saved by officers using the CDE system, the following policy recommendations are suggested:

1. Increase the number of telephone lines that feed into the CDE system.

2. Increase the number of data entry clerks.

3. Construct an administrative directive which prohibits arresting officers from making CDE reports in person. All reports should be made over the phone.

4. The CDE should be placed in a secured location in the booking area.

Finally, one other recommendation is offered in an attempt to update the county's CDE system. With advances in technology, it seems appropriate for the County to upgrade the CDE system as much as possible. To that end, the authors suggest that the county consider adding a fingerprinting option to the system (see for example Identix, 1993). This is not considered in the current CDE grant application. However, due to time and space consumed in fingerprint retrieval from stored cards, it is another efficient measure that would complement the CDE system, and speed up the booking process.

CONCLUSIONS

The Centralized Data Entry (CDE) system appears to be successful in reducing paperwork for processing suspects. It also is improving the information flow between agencies. Several recommendations are suggested by the authors in an attempt to resolve the major problems identified by the front-line staff. Security issues associated with the CDE can be resolved by combining the CDE with the Booking Unit. Also, increased use of phone lines via administrative directives may alleviate potentially hazardous situations. Finally, in an effort to increase efficiency and reduce paperwork, a fingerprint system is recommended as an important addition to the CDE system.

As a last note, training on this new system is imperative for all personnel. Even though specialists are to be employed as data entry clerks, a working knowledge of how to retrieve documents and research cases using the CDE system will be useful for investigators, magistrates, the district attorney's office, and even frontline personnel.

REFERENCES

Archambeault, W.G., & Archambeault, G.J. (1984). *Computers in criminal justice administration and management.* Cincinnati, OH: Anderson.

Arkenau, D.L. (1990). Records management in the 1990's. *FBI Law Enforcement Bulletin,* June, 16-18.

Ellement, J. (1992, June 2). Boston police computerized restraining order records. *The Boston Globe,* 7,1.

George, D.A., & Kleinknecht, G.H. (1985). Computer assisted report entry–CARE. *FBI Law Enforcement Bulletin, 54,* 3-7.

Identix (1993). TouchPrint, product information sheet. Identix Incorporated.

Johnson, R. (1992, May 25). Diluth police take byte out of paperwork. *Atlantic Journal Constitution,* XJ, 1:1.

Lansinger, C. (1992). Spotlight on . . . upgrading computerized records. *Police Chief, 59,* 36-37+.

Lieberman, P. (1989, July 21). Taking a byte out of crime. *Los Angeles Times, 1,* 1:1.

McMahon, C. (1991, February 3). Crime in Schaumburg just doesn't compute. *Chicago Tribune,* 2NW, 1-2.

Pilant, L. (1993). Spotlight on . . . computerizing criminal investigations. *Police Chief, 60,* 28-29+.

Rossi, P.H., & Freeman, H.E. (1993). *Evaluation: A systematic approach* (5th ed.). Newbury Park, CA: Sage.

Seay, G. (1992). Centralized data entry. Grant application submitted to the North Carolina Department of Crime Control and Safety, Raleigh, N.C.

Swanson, C.R. (1982). The evolution, practice, and future of productivity. *Journal of Police Science and Administration, 10,* 326-334.

Swanson, C.R., Territo, L., & Taylor, R.W. (1993). *Police administration: Structures, processes, and behavior* (3rd ed). New York: MacMillian.

Taylor, R.W. (1989). Managing police information. In D.J. Kenney (ed.), *Police and policing: Contemporary Issues.* New York: Praeger.

Chapter 9

POLICE STATIONS IN CYBERSPACE: A CONTENT ANALYSIS OF LAW ENFORCEMENT AGENCY HOMEPAGES

KEITH N. HALEY AND ROBERT W. TAYLOR

INTRODUCTION

In the last five years, the explosion of both the personal computer and the Internet have opened up new frontiers for police agencies to interact with the public. Aside from direct communication, the Internet provides an opportunity to actually "tour" a variety of police departments without ever leaving the privacy of your own home. For instance, in Dallas, while you scan department facts and read their community policing magazine, you can listen to real-time police calls (Johnson, 1996). At the Nashville Metro Police Department's home page, the curious can follow a map and vicariously experience an actual car chase north and west across Nashville. The Indian River County Sheriff's Office in Florida will let you listen to the "Man From UNCLE" theme or to one of several more modern law enforcement tunes such as the music from the "X Files" TV show, all while absorbing facts about the department. You can even listen to the "nation's toughest sheriff," the man with the prisoners' tent city in Maracopa County, Arizona, tell you what he is most proud of concerning his department. If not yet exhausted from these virtual experiences, you can travel to the Ulster Northern Constabulary in Northern Ireland and go on a virtual reality tour of their police museum where you decide which way to walk and observe. Be careful, however, you just might walk into a glass display case if your virtual reality motor skills aren't well developed. The nation of Georgia (of the former U.S.S.R.)

will show you their police tanks and ask for help. In Kansas City, Missouri, the department will dazzle you with a marvelous historical, collage painting in the background of their home page.

In fact, cyberspace (Gibson, 1984) can provide us with a myriad of things, not all necessarily positive. Hate groups, porn purveyors, and stalkers abound on the net along with cyber crooks looking to defraud whomever they can (Taylor, 1997). The Internet, in fact, has even brought us a new addiction that is listed in the Diagnostic and Statistical Manual of Mental Disorders (Belluck, 1996). On the other hand, you can find old radio shows, clips from movies, and the results of your searching the world for text, sound, or pictures, and newspapers and magazines from every corner of the planet. Moreover, you can find a new home in cities far from where you are, and for a much smaller, trusting number of people, you can even solicit someone to live in it with you. At the more base level, there is even cybersex, a proliferating enterprise on the World Wide Web. Business and other kinds of meetings (audio and video) are becoming commonplace in cyberspace. The Internet and its World Wide Web is a medium unleashed and its utility in serving people would seem limitless.

THE PURPOSES OF POLICE WEB SITES

It is no wonder that the police, already sophisticated in the use of computer technology, would seize the opportunity to communicate with the public via the Internet. As many as 2,000 law enforcement agencies have active web sites (Maier, 1996). Logically, the question arises as to what exactly are the police trying to accomplish by maintaining a web site? According to Lt. Fran Hart (1996) of the Burlington, Massachusetts Police Department, a web site presentation invites the world to share your department's perspective and provide feedback. Obviously there is the public relations benefit as the police champion their causes, such as low crime rates, community policing activities, biographical statements of the leadership, and international accreditation status. In addition, lots of information can be passed on easily to the public(s) who need it, such as how to file a complaint against an officer, determining employment qualifications and vacancies, requesting a vacation house check, receiving a crime alert, and learning the law on a variety of subjects.

Obviously, the police are not alone in their quest to use the World Wide Web to their advantage. Business and industrial organizations have launched into cyberspace also. New York Times staff writer Steve Ditlea (1996) suggests the significance of the activity for CEO's: "In 1996, the executive's home page on the World Wide Web became a staple of American corporate culture, an online talisman that both decreed top-dog status and marked a company as modern and tuned in." By examining only a few of the large police departments' web pages, you will find that the attitude among law enforcement leadership is similar to corporate thinking. The number of police agencies entering cyberspace is growing while the cafeteria of web page content options offered to the public is also expanding rapidly. In the end, what does all of this mean for the agencies and the public who consume these new police services?

METHODOLOGY

The law enforcement agency web sites selected for this study were drawn from available sites in each of the Federal Bureau of Investigation's reporting regions for the Uniform Crime Reports: Northeast, Midwest, South, and West. Hawaii and Alaska are included in the reporting region for the West. An attempt was made to include at least one Web site from each state, although there are states with no listings in the major World Wide Web directories for police agencies. Sometimes online search engines were employed, such as Alta Vista and Yahoo, to find police and sheriff's departments not yet listed in directories. The goal was to examine some of the web sites of municipal departments, sheriff's offices, and the state police or highway patrol in each state. The capital city police department's web site was studied in almost all states if there was one in existence. Included are some web sites of other peace officer agencies such as departments of natural resources and bureaus of investigation in several of the states. A few others were selected for additional reasons: they were in the news, they had a reputation for being a good site, or they were historically significant.

A descriptive analysis was conducted for each site in the study. The sites were examined and evaluated relative to three areas of focus: (1)

the amount and types of useful information displayed for citizens and the police; (2) the aesthetic and technological qualities of the site, such as art, color, layout, framed displays, audio segments, moving video productions, and virtual reality capabilities; (3) the particularly strong and unique features of the web site

Each site was visited at least once. Some web sites were examined numerous times because of the large amount of information presented or to update this study. The New York City Police Department's web page, for example, contains more than 250 pages and the forecast is that it will grow to more than 5,000 soon (Krauss, 1996). Many of the sites posted notices that their pages were "under construction" and were revisited to assess the degree of progress. Relevant literature sources on the subject were also examined, including works that can be found on the World Wide Web. Finally, several webmasters from the departments studied were contacted, both by E-mail and telephone, for background information on web site development.

RESULTS

A total of 48 law enforcement agency World Wide Web home pages were included in this study. Table 9-1 lists the law enforcement agencies by region of the United States.

Table 9-1. Law Enforcement Web Pages by Agency Category and Region

Law Enforcement Agency	Category
Northeast	N = 9
Reading, Pa.	Municipal
Hanover, N.H.	Municipal
Hudson, N.H.	Municipal
Norwalk, Conn.	Municipal
Kingston, Pa.	Municipal
Boston, Mass.	Municipal
Portland. Me.	Municipal
Biddeford, Me.	Municipal
New York, N.Y.	Municipal

Midwest	N = 9
Kettering, O.	Municipal
Fargo, N. Dak.	Municipal
Cedar Falls, Ia.	Municipal
Hannahville, Mich.	Tribal Police
Indianapolis, Ind.	Municipal

South	N = 19
Little Rock, Ark.	Municipal
Newport News, Va.	Municipal
Charleston, S.C.	Municipal
Charlotte-Mecklenburg, N.C.	County
Hope, Ark.	Municipal
Lawton, Okla.	Municipal
Palm Beach County, Fla.	County
Plano, Tex.	Municipal
Palm Beach, Fla.	Municipal
Key West, Fla.	Municipal
Clarksburg, W. Va.	Municipal
Nashville Metro, Tenn.	Mun./County
Dallas, Tex.	Municipal
New Orleans, La.	Municipal
Jefferson County, Ky.	County
Atlanta, Ga.	Municipal
Baltimore County, Md.	County
Annapolis, Md.	Municipal
Metro Dade	Mun./County

West	N = 11
New Mexico Department of Public Safety, N. Mex.	State
Moscow, I.	Municipal
Anchorage, Alas.	Municipal
Las Vegas Metro, Nev.	Mun./County
Spokane, Wash.	Municipal
Missoula, Mont.	Municipal
Honululu, Hawaii	Municipal
Denver, Colo.	Municipal
Sacramento, Cal.	Municipal
Phoenix, Ariz.	Municipal
San Diego, Cal.	Municipal

TOTAL NUMBER OF AGENCIES = 48

DESCRIPTIVE AND PUBLIC RELATIONS INFORMATION

World Wide Web is devoted to describing the police organization and touting its positive qualities. Those who would take the time to examine all of the content on many of these organizations' web sites would indeed leave the site with a favorable impression of the department. Table 9-2 identifies the prevalence of this descriptive information on the Web sites of agencies in this study.

Table 9-2. Descriptive and Public Relations Information

Type of Information	N	Percent
Mission, Values	32	66.7%
History/Description	20	41.7%
Executive's Message	22	45.8%
Who's Who	22	45.8%
Individual Unit Descriptions	32	66.7%
Community Policing	15	31.2%

Total Number of Web Sites Visited = 48

No doubt affected by the mission writing mania that has been prevalent in private and public organizations over the past two decades, police agencies feel obligated to include their mission and values statements in their Web page content. Thirty-two (66.7%) of the agencies in this study did so. The same number of agencies provided individual unit descriptions which most often included a statement of the units' major functions in policing. Twenty (41.7%) of the web page sites went so far as to provide a history of the police department, including historical documents and pictures. Twenty-two (45.8%) posted a Who's Who section where names of unit commanders and officers in special units were identified, often with accompanying pictures.

Nearly half of the agencies studied (45.8%) had a welcome message from the chief, sheriff, or director. These messages varied considerably from brief "hellos" to intricate discussions of community policing and its impact on crime and other aspects of life in the city. Some "welcomes" were actual audio recordings that could be heard by those equipped to receive sound on their computers.

Community policing has evolved as the predominate mode of law enforcement in the nation and its presence was noted in this study as 15 (31.2%) of the departments devoted some portion of their home pages to identifying and discussing this concept's influence on their community. Apparently police administrators have seen how the Internet might further their community policing objectives (Hart, 1996).

USEFUL INFORMATION FOR CITIZENS

Whether or not an agency has declared a commitment to community policing or not, one of its major functions is to provide useful information to citizens that allows them to make intelligent decisions and choose wise courses of action in their lives. Knowing how to protect your home against burglars, identifying the proper location to go to for vehicle inspections, finding out the cost of your traffic citation, and determining the employment qualifications to become a police officer in one's own community are all routine functions performed by law enforcement agencies. Posting current information on the World Wide Web relative to these issues is an efficient method of making the information available to citizens at their convenience. Table 9-3 below lists the prevalence of useful information found on law enforcement agency Web sites in this study.

Table 9-3. Useful Information for Citizens

Type of Information	N	Percent
Missing Persons	8	16.7%
Wanted Persons/Crime Alerts	25	52.1%
Crime Statistics	23	47.9%
Crime Prevention	27	56.2%
Employment	30	62.5%
Community Affairs	26	54.2%
Administrative and Regulatory	13	27.1%
Hyperlinks Links to Other Agencies	33	68.7%
Training Opportunities	15	31.2%

Total number of Web sites visited = 48

The results of this study reveal that making useful information available to citizens is a prevalent utility of police Web pages. If a web "surfer" were interested in finding information concerning law enforcement employment, such as qualifications, salary, job openings, and selection procedures, then the chances are good that it would be found on most police web sites. Thirty (62.5%) of the agencies in this study posted employment information.

Information concerning crime and delinquency and its prevention in the community was also available on police web sites in this study. The number of agencies displaying crime-related information are: 25 (52.1%) wanted persons and crime alerts; 27 (56.2%) crime prevention tips; 8 (16.7%) missing persons; 23 (47.9%) crime statistics. The police undoubtedly believe this is an important concern of their publics and more than half of the agencies have responded.

Some of the information the police have made available on their Web sites concerns activities in the community and learning administrative regulations concerning licensing of one sort or another, such as new speed limits, snow alerts, parking regulations, and procedures for obtaining a variety of permits. Twenty-six (54.2%) of the web sites contained information about upcoming community affairs. Thirteen (27.1%) provided the citizens with useful administrative and regulatory information.

Training opportunities were also mentioned on 15 (31.2%) of the web sites in this study. Available classes were posted mostly for police officers, but citizen academies and other community classes were also present on several sites.

Finally, 33 (68.7%) of the law enforcement web sites in this study had hyperlinks to other law enforcement departments, to other government agencies, or to other web sites related to some aspect of the content found on their own web pages. These links included the web pages of other city or county departments, police officer assistance pages, state and federal agencies, and law enforcement Web page directories.

POLICE-CITIZEN INTERACTIVE OPPORTUNITIES

The need for the police to communicate clearly and efficiently with the citizens they serve is nothing short of paramount. The community policing revolution has been built on the very idea of a citizen/police partnership directed toward improving the quality of life in neighborhoods throughout a political entity. The police web sites in this study were examined to determine what kinds of interactive opportunities they encouraged between the police and the citizens they served. Actual police services, such as vacant house checks, the reporting of crimes, and the filing of complaints and commendations, were some of interactive possibilities located on law enforcement agency home pages. The type and amount of interactive opportunities the police Web pages in this study facilitated are found in Table 9-4.

Table 9-4. Interactive and Service Request Features

Interactive or Service Request Feature	N	Percent
Opportunities to Request Services	14	29.2%
Vacant House Checks	1	2.1%
Report Crime	4	8.3%
File Complaint or Commendation	10	20.8%
Communication Opportunities	43	89.6%
E-Mail	36	75.0%
Phone, Fax Numbers, and Addresses	43	89.6%
Crime Stoppers or Drug Hotline	23	47.9%

Total Number of Web Sites Visited = 48

The police communicate with their constituents most often by telephone and by personal visits. Already strapped with a high volume of emergency requests for service and lots of 911 calls that, in fact, are not emergencies, American citizens in the major cities of the nation, and in some of the smaller ones, wait hours for the police to arrive. Having a Web page with police-citizen interactive capabilities allows the people to make some requests and file complaints at their convenience. Fourteen (29.2%) of the agencies did provide some kind of way for those viewing the police department's Web page to communicate with the police and, in some instances, gave the public a means to request services, lodge complaints, or make commendations concerning the department or its officers. More specifically, one (2.1%) allowed citizens to request a vacant house check while they were away on business or a vacation; 4 (8.3%) actually allowed citizens to report crimes, including felonies; 10 (20.8%) gave citizens the opportunity to submit either a complaint or a commendation concerning the department or its personnel by means of a predesigned, hyperlinked E-mail form.

E-mail communication was available by either a hyperlink to a form or by listing E-mail numbers. Sometimes the addressee was the chief of police. Thirty-six (75%) of the web sites studied facilitated E-mail communication. Forty-three (89.6%) of the agencies in the study provided phone numbers, fax numbers, or addresses of one or more units of the law enforcement agency. Twenty-three (47.9%) allowed some kind of confidential communication concerning the reporting of drug offenses or the submission of information to a Crime Stoppers program.

AESTHETIC AND TECHNICAL QUALITIES

When you consider that just two presidential elections ago in 1992, there was no national Internet Service Provider (ISP) and that today there are hundreds, it is not surprising that additional police agencies are coming online on almost a daily basis. Likewise, it is easy to understand that the web pages in existence differ substantially in their degree of technical sophistication and aesthetic attractiveness. For instance, some locations were one-page and one-color sites where it didn't seem to matter much if the site existed or not; on the other hand, several had full color backgrounds and text, dozens of pictures, entertaining graphics, video enhancements, and even virtual reality features. Table 9-5 presents a tabulation of the aesthetic and technological features identified on the police agency home pages examined in this study.

Table 9-5. Aesthetic and Technological Qualities

Web Page Feature	N	Percent
Pictures/Art Work	39	81.2%
Easily Readable Layout	44	91.7%
HyperText Mark Up Language	45	93.7%
Frames	10	20.8%
Audio	9	18.7%
Video	8	16.7%
Virtual Reality	1	2.1%
Variety of Colors	35	72.9%

Total Number of Web Sites Visited = 48

Thirty-nine (81.2%) of the police web sites in this study contain photographs or artistic drawings. Some agencies had dozens of photographs of personnel, offices, and geographic settings on their web pages which did give the reader a sense of having "been there." Contrast the experience of reading about a law enforcement agency in most magazines or even a book with visiting its well-developed web page and you begin to see the value of these pages in projecting a positive and graphic image of the department to those who are willing to take the time to make a cybervisit. Nine (18.7%) of the web pages allowed the site visitors to actually hear welcomes delivered by the police executive, listen to music, or select talks and lectures by agency personnel on a variety of subjects. Eight (16.6%) of the web pages provided some kind of video feature on their site, meaning something on the web pages moved either by means of animation or through one of the several video formats available. One agency (2.1%), the Nashville Metro Police, employed virtual reality technology which allowed the site visitor to tour various buildings and outdoor venues belonging to the department.

Nearly all of the web pages examined in this study were easily read and well organized. Forty-four (91.7%) displayed an easily readable layout while 45 (93.7%) used a HyperText Mark Up Language (HTML) format which allowed the reader to "click" on highlighted items in the web page text and go to other locations to examine a related subject or obtain in-depth information on the original topic. Frames were used to organize the web page content in 10 (20.8%) of the sites in this study. Finally, a key feature in drawing and retaining attention on the World Wide Web is to have a lot of color in the display. Thirty-five (72.9%) of the police web pages in the study displayed two or more colors.

SPECIAL FEATURES

One of the joys of "surfing the Web," including the exploration of law enforcement agency Web sites, is being surprised, diverted, and even shocked over what you have discovered. Studying law enforcement agency web pages is, among other things, an entertaining experience because you are witnessing the police department laying out its best features, much as artists and writers build portfolios of their best works. True that none of the police agencies in this study posted discussions or clips of the latest case(s) of corruption or labor discord in their departments, but it would be illogical to expect that. Table 9-6 below lists some of the special and unique features found on some of the police web sites included in this study.

Table 9-6. Interesting and Unique Features on Law Enforcement Web Sites

Feature	Law Enforcement Agency
Northeast	
Table of organization includes race and sex	Reading. Pa.
Explains Japanese pagoda on uniform patch	
Advertises for student interns	
Identifies agency as first police department in U.S.	Boston, Mass.
Posts officer and civilian of the month awards	Portland. Me.
Video and sound welcome by city's mayor	New York, N.Y.
Attractive magazine, *Spring 3100*	
Detailed police history and museum pages	
Midwest	
Posts law enforcement and corrections accreditation	Kettering, OH.
Posts Robert Peel quote, "The police are the public and the public are the police."	Fargo, N.Dak.
Has section for the humane (animal control) officers	
Has ICAM (Information Collection for Automated Mapping) feature	Chicago, Ill.
Posts many links to attract citizen involvement	
Has "Beep a Beat" program description - merchants beep beat officers and get cellular phone calls	
Posts purple ribbon campaign to protest violence against women	
Describes tough anti -"boom box" law enforcement Strategy	
Has "Ask an Officer" section	Kansas City, Mo.
Attractive historical background for home page	
Bagpipes play "Amazing Grace" while ticker tape displays fallen officers' names	
Posts a Kansas City Police spouses' home page	
Has sound on its E-mail page	

Extensive online, contact-specific survey for citizens to complete	Fon Du Lac, Wis.
Online procedure to report police abuse to citizens' review board	Minneapolis. Minn.
Posts two poems: DARE program poem; Poem " No Good Cop," written by a good cop at Pine Ridge Reservation	Hannahville, Mich. Tribal Police

South

Lists key issues the department faced in 1995 and 1996 Notes that department reduced sick leave by 35% in 1996	Little Rock, Ark.
National Incident Based Reporting format for crime statistics	Newport News, Va. Charleston, S.C.
Page for citizen killed helping to direct traffic Links to Police Hall of Fame and police video	Charlotte-Mecklenburg, N.C.
Details on President Bill Clinton's home and past Notes that Hope is site of the world's largest watermelon (260 lbs.)	Hope, Ark.
Noted for being state's first municipal Web site List police radio codes Has vehicle ticker tape on vehicle accidents Has DWI Blood Alcohol Estimator	Lawton. Okla.
Has victims' rights section Requests citizen volunteers	Palm Beach County Sheriff's Office, Fla.
Section on condo security and crime prevention Has swimming test as part of selection process	Palm Beach, Fla.
Notes chief will be President of IACP in 2,000 Eleven fraud scams are described Salary goes to $42,614 after 36 months	Plano, Tex.
Notes it is the southern-most police department in the United States Site plays jazz and reggae music	Key West, Fla.
Audio self-defense lectures by Ken Pence Displays map and audio recording of car chase across Nashville Uses Virtual Reality for witnesses and jurors to view violent crime scenes A virtual textbook of information on domestic violence	Nashville Metro, Tenn.

May test to receive a civilian training certificate
from the academy on the web site

Can listen to police department radio dispatches   Dallas, Tex.
while viewing the Web site (no direct link on Web page)
Posts a particularly attractive community policing
magazine
Posts a "Top Cops" weekly magazine

May listen to "The Heat" rock band and Gloria   Baltimore County, Md.
Estefan sing "The Rhythm is Going to Get You"

Extensive "Wanted Persons" lists   Metro Dade, Fla.
Detailed history of the events leading to metro
government

West
Hyperlinks to the Polly Klass Foundation   Public Safety, N.M.

Current Weather Report   Moscow, I.
Chaplain's Page

Black-taped badge and memorial to Officer   Anchorage, Alas.
Dan Seely
Posts interview with a "Traffic Cop"
Posts two sections for children with links to
Disney's "Toy Story" home page
Links to Professor Darryl Woods' Justice Page and
class lectures

Overview of the department's budget   Las Vegas Metro, Nev.
Notes "best dressed" award for the department

"Happy Holidays!" greeting with Santa's sleigh   Spokane, Wash.
"Happy New Year!" greeting
Music on various pages
Award winning pages on robbery
Side show with music introducing officers
Extensive radio button selection menu
Automated slide show of police personnel

Menu button for Spanish-speaking visitors   Sacramento, Cal.

Detailed hate crimes section   Phoenix, Ariz.

Outstanding crime analysis maps   San Diego, Cal.
Historical charts on UCR crimes back to 1950
Neighborhood-oriented site

INTERESTING AND UNUSUAL FACTS

Pursue any topic of interest on the World Wide Web and you are going to discover things you didn't know. Police web pages are loaded with interesting, if not readily useful, facts and discoveries. Below is a brief, select list of such findings:

1. The Kansas City, Missouri Police Department tells of their involvement in the arrest and the subsequent lynching of an innocent black man;

2. The Hannahville Tribal Police in Michigan explains the effects of two legal systems, tribal law and state law, on their community;

3. Numerous web pages display the talents of police officers who have become webmasters extroardinaire;

4. Reading, Pennsylvania Police have a Japanese pagoda on their patch because a wealthy resident wanted to construct such a building and make it an exclusive resort. The idea went bust and the city got the building for a dollar;

5. Chicago Police have walking officers carry beepers in order that merchants can notify them of problems;

6. A person can get a citizen's training certificate from the Nashville Metro Police by passing an online examination;

7. At the Hope, Arkansas Police site you can see where the world's largest watermelon was grown there and I saw on a map the exact location (601 East Second Street) of President Bill Clinton's elementary school;

8. The attachment to the community policing concept is far stronger than imagined;

9. Virtual reality technology is establishing a presence on police web sites;

10. Innumerable crime prevention tips were available on many sites, many of which are quite novel or new.

DISCUSSION

Public Relations

Perhaps the most prominent function of the police web site is public relations. Nearly all of the sites, excluding one large city police department, left the viewer with a positive image of the law enforcement agency. In short, these Web pages are advertisements to enhance the agency's image in the community. The pages are most often colorful, clever, and carefully edited. Smiling, helpful police executives and line officers are prevalent. Only the positive appears. This is one more manifestation of the proposition that the police have learned to manage their image. Unfortunately, a couple of the web sites appear to be "temples" in homage to the chief, while most of the others were tributes to the citizens of the community and the police officers in their service.

Useful Information

Clearly much of the information found on law enforcement agency web pages is useful. Numerous sites displayed detailed information packages on domestic violence, crime prevention, wanted persons, missing people, and local weather alerts. We noted that there were no sites in this study that contained any information about disaster procedures.

Even more specific was the community and neighborhood information available. If the Internet-sophisticated citizen begins to acknowledge the local police web site as a valuable location for finding "news they can use" in the community, the traffic on these sites is likely to increase substantially.

One of the reasons for a World Wide Web presence is to distribute information obviously that helps to extend the "eyes and ears" of the police department, hoping to locate wanted criminals and missing persons. On the web pages included in this study, we saw no mention that a criminal was caught or a missing person found as a result of information posted on the police department's home page. We suspect, however, that citizens have responded to opportunities to contact the police via posted telephone numbers, fax numbers, and E-mail addresses.

The search for talented police applicants continues to be difficult. Most of the police agencies in this study posted recruiting and application information on their web sites. Not only can interested browsers find out the job qualifications and application procedures, but they can download much of this information for further study or request application packets by means of E-mail. Moreover, a number of agencies have chosen to advertise their police employment vacancies on one or more of several well-known law enforcement employment sites on the web. If interested applicants notice this posting, they can then visit the police department's World Wide Web page and obtain or request additional employment information, representing a substantial savings of time and money in the job hunting process.

Interactivity

The police agencies in this study have provided new opportunities for police and citizens to communicate with each other. Citizens can report crimes, file complaints and commendations concerning department personnel, and notify the police that they will be away from their home for a number of days by E-mail, fax, or phone. Posting on the web sites the phone numbers and E-mail addresses of specific units and officers within the department is also likely to enhance citizen-initiated communication. In many cases when citizens call, they will also be able to put a name with a face they saw on the police department's web site. This might be particularly effective in increasing communication from minorities who have noticed officers from their community on the police department's Web site.

Also obvious from this study is the fact that web page technology has made it easier for the police agencies to communicate with each other. It was noted by several departments that the alert concerning the date rape drug, Rohypmol, traveled through police web pages nearly a year before the major media began to disseminate the information. Moreover, most agencies now provide direct links to other law enforcement web sites.

Citizens may not be too far away from being able to contact an officer via two-way video technology which is just now starting to emerge on the Web. Can a software agent police officer named Mary or Hector, delivered by means of virtual reality technology, be far off?

Community policing thrives on citizen involvement. The rudiments of virtual communities and neighborhoods are already present on the web. Common to all members of these communities is the ability to afford a computer. With recent price drops, the cost is well under $1,000 for an Internet- ready computer. The police will no doubt use the World Wide Web to establish and maintain a relationship with these "communities" if doing so brings them vital information and enhances their reputation.

World Wide Web Technology

This study included law enforcement agencies that were in the primordial stages of using web technology and some departments that were on the leading edge. The Clarksburg, West Virginia page is simply a statement that we are there and building. Avant-garde police departments such as New York, Dallas, Lawton, Nashville Metro, Kansas City, and Spokane are clearly experimenting in terms of what is possible. These leading law enforcement agencies will soon know whether the effort is worth it. It would be difficult to envision a retreat on the use of web technology when the digital/multimedia revolution and integration are just beginning. Palmtop and wallet computers are already being used in work venues, including law enforcement, and there is no reason to believe that the police will not continue their implementation.

Finland's citizens already carry hand-held computers the size of original cellular phones capable of connecting to the Internet. The United States cannot be too far behind and the police will be a part of this new mobile method of communicating with people and organizations.

Based on the findings in this study, the most logical perspective to take on the phenomenon of law enforcement sites on the World Wide Web is to see them as works in progress. The police stations in cyberspace are "under construction" and as is the case with any building site, you may return a few weeks later and be amazed at the progress. The World Wide Web itself provides the means to share progressive construction plans with other police agencies rapidly. As police departments, other organizations, and citizens themselves continue to construct home pages at a rapid pace, the possibility to share useful and interesting information among all of the parties appears limitless.

CONCLUSIONS AND IMPLICATIONS

We have only begun to see the first steps in the digital domination of the communication world. Police web pages are only a miniscul part of this revolution. What is possible may not even be imaginable at this point in time. But the police are in cyberspace, a virtual world, or what some have called "an extension to dwell in fiction" (Benedict, 1996). Frankly, the citizen visitor to a police web site is not likely to know if fiction is present. Visiting law enforcement agency web pages, however, will allow you to see law enforcement in its most favorable light. Clearly, this study has shown that some of the nation's police agencies are sophisticated in using the World Wide Web to gild their image and improve their abilities to communicate with the many communities they serve. Cyberspace visits to a police department can also allow you to know your local police or sheriff's department and its personnel, can give you the opportunity to learn of many ways to make yourself and your surroundings much safer, and permit you to request police services at your convenience, not when the police want to get around to you. As a thoroughly delightful aside, you are likely to be entertained by the creativity and humor the department displays on its web pages.

As to the ultimate utility of police stations in cyberspace, Sheriff and Coroner Brad Gates (1997), Orange County, California, commented:

> I am excited about the possibilities of this new medium. Instant communication and exchange of information between individuals, their government, and law enforcement is fast becoming a reality. No one predicts with certainty, the ultimate value of this technology, however, if this Web site succeeds in raising public awareness of criminal activity and enhances our communication with one another, it will become indispensable.

In the last analysis, what you see at present is a lot of experimenting as to the content of law enforcement web pages and their potential for interactivity with citizens in a community. "Throw it all out there" and "see what works" may be the strategy for many police departments in this study. The haste to get something in cyberspace (the "be modern" attitude) has undoubtedly diminished the quality of some police web pages. Keep in mind that the police are on the same developmental path taken by newspapers, businesses, and other government organizations. The technological, aesthetic, and consumer utility features of their Web pages have improved dramatically in a short period of time. It is also important to note that rapid technological changes in digital equipment and service can challenge an agency as a web page leader in a flash if it isn't willing to upgrade regularly.

This study shows that some members of the community use their department's web site, just how many and their degree of satisfaction with a police station in cyberspace has not been determined but should be studied by criminal justice scholars. We can assure you these same scholars will find lots of information about these police departments that can be used in their course preparation, heretofore, virtually inaccessible. CNN Internet (1996) found that 35 million people used the Internet in 1996, up from 27 million in 1995. Students from a variety of disciplines and educational levels are learning the value of the Internet in enriching their personal and professional lives. However, people with the most education are the most likely to use the Internet. In fact, baccalaureate and graduate degree holders are twice as likely to have used the Internet than those without a college education (CNN, 1996).

The degree of interactivity on the World Wide Web is developing at a rapid pace also. E-mail, telephone conversations, live two-way video conferencing, online surveys, and virtual reality tours are all available now as a result of Internet communication. The police are starting to use all of these processes to investigate and prosecute crime. These tools are not just limited to public sector police. There are a variety of novel web sites incorporating private search agencies which are attempting to solve crimes. For instance, there are now web sites (e.g., clues.com and murder.com) which attempt to capitalize on the shear numbers of people visiting a website to help clear unsolved crimes. The entire case history may be presented for assistance in catching the wanted person, finding the missing person, or solving the case. Often, this material includes sketches of the crime scene, autopsy photos, pictures of the missing person, etc. Police agencies offer their entire case histories in an attempt to help solve even the most brutal of crimes.

As Internet technology approaches virtual reality, police are likely to be on the frontier of using that technology to further a sense of community and meaningfulness in people's lives. A police officer software agent indeed will never replace the vitality and presence of an enthusiastic, service-oriented officer, but "he" or "she" will likely become a worthy assistant to the officer. Much on the order of the increasingly popular software agent Headliner, a virtual reality agent at the police department could someday select only the information from the police department that a person has previously expressed an interest in. There are other not so likely uses of such technology, but not beyond imagination or hope. In William Gibson's (1996) latest cyber caper, *Idoru*, a rock musician marries a virtual reality woman that he and his organization created. She can be turned "off" and "on." No spouse would negate the occasional value of such an arrangement.

By means of lightening speed connections, virtual reality technology, and ubiquitous Internet access, we may soon be able to contact the police whenever we want them. Finland seems to have stepped way out front in this regard. Forty-two percent of the nation is wired to the Internet and many carry cellular phones, about the size of the originals in the United States, which gives them the ability to "port" anytime they choose, to include the time they spend commuting on public transportation (Ibrahim, 1997).

In a cybersense, the police also may soon be able to "enter" your home whenever they want if you have left the door "unlocked" or given them a "key" and granted permission to attend to some of your personal affairs while you are out or away for an extended period of time. Of course, "away" in cyberspace may not mean "away" at all. You might also be able to pick the "police agent" you like to respond to your needs, young, old, speaking the language of your choice, or whatever your preferences. Hope you like holograms!

Is there a downside to the techno-progressive forecast? A legion of commentators think so. Some believe it will further dehumanize an already impersonal civilization, while others suggest that the invasion of privacy via technology will eventually lead to domination by the state and loss of democracy. We don't think so! Indeed, information access to mass society may well be the most logical barrier to dictatorships and the key to further democratization of societies. An educated and well-informed society prevents the abuse of power, as well as provides the common forum for individuals to meet and discuss relevant topics. Schools and libraries are already making Internet access available to all in their communities who choose to connect for a reasonable amount of time, and, certainly, people will meet at these "porting" locations (Weeks, 1996). The diffusion throughout society of substantial increases in the number of digital exchanges between people may, in fact, contribute to more human contacts than ever before. Reid Goldsborough (1997) reminds us that "mankind does not live by silicon alone," however, and will continue to seek the human relationship.

Pornography, hate speech, and illicit sex hawked on the World Wide Web are also issues that require resolution. The police are currently involved in these matters and many legal battles are likely to be fought over the control of this content.

Finally, there is the likelihood of computer hacking and cyberterrorism in the form of destroying, stealing, or altering private information in computer databases. Even our military establishments have not been able to escape this kind of assault, so it is probable that police web pages will also fall victim if they have not already been attacked (Babington, 1997; Caragota, 1995; Ravo, 1996; Sussman, 1995; Taylor, 1997).

Far more significant, however, is the delivery to the homes of millions of Americans new entertainment, educational opportunities, and government services that could not be envisioned just a few years ago. We are in the process of "being digital." A critical social agency such as the police will, undoubtably, be a major player in the digital phenomenon of the future (Negroponte, 1995).

REFERENCES

Allen, T. (1997) Personal Interview. January 22.

Babington, C. (1997, January 8). Maryland closed internet site. *The Washington Post*, B1.

Belluck, P. (1996, December 1). Stuck on the web: The symptoms of internet addiction. *The New York Times*, D5.

Benedict, M. (1995, January). Some proposals. *Cyberspace*. Online. Available URL: http://www.audionet.com.

Caragota, W., and Chidley, J. (1995, May 22). Crime in cybercity. *Maclean's, 108*, 50-52.

CNN. (1996, November 15). Poll: Internet grows, online services slow. Online. Available URL: http://www.cnn.com.

Ditlea, S. (1997, January 7). CEO's home pages: Browsing from the top down. *The New York Times*, C1.

Gates, B. (1997, January). Sheriff's message. Online. Available URL: www.ocsd.org.

Gibson, W. (1996). *Idoru*. New York: G.P. Putnam's Sons.

Gibson, W. (1984). *Neuromancer.* New York: Ace Books.

Goldsborough, R. (1997, January 7). Will pc's and net build better people? *Phildelphia Inquirer,* F1.

Hart, F. (1996, December). How and why to implement the world-wide web for community policing. *The Police Chief,* 63, 19-20.

Ibrahim, Y. (1997, January 20). As most wired nation, Finland has jump on 21st century. *The New York Times,* D1.

Johnson, J. (1996, October 24). To protect and surf: DPD's web page captures visitors worldwide. *The Dallas Morning News,* D1.

Krauss, C. (1996, September 3). For New York's finest, it's slow going on internet. *The New York Times,* B3.

Maier, S. (1996, August 6). Long arm of law is going online. *Seattle Post-Intelligencer,* A1.

Negroponte, N. (1995). *Being Digital.* New York: Alfred A. Knopf.

Ravo, N. (1996, September 27). Hacker charged with 25 felony attacks on computer systems. *The New York Times,* A24.

Reingold, H. (1994). *The Virtual Community.* New York: HarperPerennial.

Stoll, C. (1995). *Silacon Snake Oil.* New York: Doubleday.

Sussman, V. (1995, January 23). Policing cyberspace. *U.S. News & World Report, 118,* 54-60.

Taylor, R. (1997). Crime on the internet. Paper delivered at the 18th Annual Contemporary Issues in Police Administration Seminar: Cyberspace and Law Enforcement. Southwestern Law Enforcement Institute, Dallas, Texas, February 27. See also R. Taylor (1996). Computer crime, in C. Swanson, N. Chamelin, and L. Territo (eds.), *Criminal Investigation,* 6th edition, New York: McGraw Hill.

Weeks, J. (1996, November 3) . The future is an open book: Computers seem destined to complement libraries, not replace them. *The Dallas Morning News,* F1.

PART III

CORRECTIONS TECHNOLOGY

INTRODUCTION

Part III, Corrections Technology, contains two chapters written by criminal justice educators, researchers, and practitioners. In Chapter 10, Jeffrey Stone examines the technology used in employment practices focusing on detention officers and the "B-pad." He explains that the hiring process of detention officers entails the use of a series of assessment devices. The B-pad, a video assessment device, is studied as a predictor of employee success in training and job performance in a county detention office in a large southwestern city.

In Chapter 11, Faye Taxman and Stephan Sherman examine strategies to manage the offender in the community. Criminal justice agencies (e.g., corrections, jails, probation/parole, courts, and social service agencies) need to share information on offender progress. New automation technologies offer the opportunity to have multiple agencies sharing a data base which can be used to make decisions about sentencing and sanctions. The Office of National Drug Control Policy is sponsoring a project to implement an automated system to allow criminal justice and treatment agencies to share information including drug test results, treatment placement, treatment attendance, supervision reporting, and offender profiles. This chapter discusses the confidentiality issues in sharing treatment and correctional information in an interactive, real time environment; the steps to implement a multi-agency approach to information sharing; and the operational practices that must be adjusted to accommodate the technology.

Chapter 10

AN EVALUATION OF A VIDEO ASSESSMENT DEVICE FOR SELECTING DETENTION OFFICERS

JEFFREY STONE

INTRODUCTION

Effective employee performance is a concern of every employer. In our nation's prisons and jails, this concern has the highest priority. With facilities strained by soaring inmate populations, as well as increases in corrections personnel,[1] administrators in corrections must employ the most competent person for the job in order to increase efficiency and to reduce legal liability. They often attempt to reach this objective through employee selection, training, and supervision. Though all three methods are important, the selection of effective employees is a critical first step. The selection of jail employees is a complicated process and typically involves the administration of numerous tests.[2] These tests are designed to evaluate a number of qualities and traits. However, one quality that makes a truly outstanding officer—the ability to deal effectively with people (inmates, visitors, fellow officers, and supervisors)—is one that is difficult to measure with traditional written and oral tests and background investigations (Swander, Spurlin & Chapman, 1994).

---

1 In 1988, there were 73,280 corrections officers employed by the nation's jails; by 1993, there were 117,900 corrections officers employed in jails. In 1990, there were 169,263 corrections officers employed by the nation's prisons; by 1995, there were 213,370 corrections officers employed in prisons (Beck, 1997; Maguire & Flanagan, 1991; Maguire & Pastore, 1996).

2 The Maricopa County Sheriffs Office in Phoenix, Arizona utilizes a selection process that contains 5 steps (application evaluation, background investigation, polygraph examination, medical examination, & psychological evaluation).

THE BEHAVIORAL PERSONNEL
ASSESSMENT DEVICE (B-PAD)

One test that attempts to measure this ability is the Behavioral Personnel Assessment Device (B-PAD). B-PAD is a video assessment device which purports to measure the problem-solving and interpersonal skills of applicants. As of August 1996, 16 corrections/detention agencies across the United States were using the B-PAD for Corrections assessment device to test corrections/detention officer applicants' interpersonal skills and judgement. In addition, 92 law enforcement agencies across the country were using the B-PAD for Police to select police officers and deputy sheriffs (The B-PAD Group, Inc., 1995).[3] The rationale and construction of B-PAD is based on the model of test construction developed by Goldfried and D' Zurilla (1969) called the Behavioral-Analytic Model for Assessing Competence (Corey, Wolf, Rand, Rand & MacAlpine, 1995). This model was developed by Goldfried and D' Zurilla on the premise that the greater the similarity between the criterion environment and the measurement environment, the greater the chances were of achieving a high level of validity.

The purpose of the present study is twofold: (1) investigate whether the B-PAD for Corrections has adverse impact against minority applicants applying to the Maricopa County Sheriff's Office, and (2) evaluate whether B-PAD for Corrections is a valid assessment of detention officer applicants.

METHODOLOGY

Data were collected on 380 subjects who were evaluated by the Maricopa County Sheriff's Office Psychological Services Unit in Phoenix, Arizona for detention officer positions between July 1, 1995 and April 30, 1996. The Maricopa County Sheriff's Office employs over 1000 detention officers, and is the fifth largest jail system in the United States (Brashear, 1997). Of the 380 subjects, 78 percent were male (n=298) and 22 percent were female (n=82). Eighty-five percent

---

3 Additional information about the B-PAD device can be obtained from the B-PAD Group, 831 Latour Court Suite A, Napa, CA 94558, 1-800-421-2723.

were Caucasian (n=321), 5 percent were African-American (n=19), and 9 percent were Hispanic (n=32). Eighty- six percent were between 18 and 39 years of age (n=327), and 14 percent were between 40 and 62 years of age (n=52).

The following information was collected on the 380 detention officers in the sample:

- sex
- race
- global score (a score assigned by the Psychological Services Unit based on the applicant's performance on written tests and a structured interview)
- interviewer
- training academy completion
- training academy grade point average (GPA)
- training academy defensive tactics score
- six month probation completion
- six month supervisor evaluation
- B-PAD scores (Task Orientation, Interpersonal Skills, Overall Effectiveness)

For this study, the terms detention officer and corrections officer are used interchangeably. Typically, detention officers are employed by jail facilities, and corrections officers are employed in prisons. Whether the job functions of the two positions are exactly alike is debatable. However, they are generally considered to be analogous.

ADMINISTRATION OF THE B-PAD TEST

During the psychological evaluations (which included psychological examinations and a structured psychological interview), applicants were administered the B-PAD for Corrections. Applicants taking the B-PAD video test were seated before a video monitor and camcorder. After receiving instructions both orally and in writing, they were presented with a series of eight simulations contained on the B-PAD for Corrections videocassette.

The applicants first watched an introduction which again included instructions, and were then allowed to warm up by answering questions such as their name and the date. The actual test then began with the presentation of the first vignette. At the end of each scene, the word "respond" appeared on the monitor and the applicant then had 45 seconds to respond verbally, as if he or she were actually at the scene responding to real people in a real situation. At the end of 45 seconds, the scene faded out and the next scene began. The video camera placed next to the monitor recorded the applicants responses for later scoring by a trained rater (Corey et al., 1995, p.2).

The scoring of applicant responses to the B-PAD video test focused on interpersonal competence as measured by two content scales: task orientation (a measure of the applicant's problem solving ability) and interpersonal skills (a measure of the behaviors used by the applicant to relate appropriately to the subjects in the scene), and a weighted scale, overall effectiveness (a unitary measure of interpersonal competence based on the scores assigned to the two content scales). Each scale was assigned a score of 1-4, with 4 reflecting the highest level of competence (Corey et al., 1995). All three B-PAD scores (task, interpersonal, and overall effectiveness) were collected for use in the study.

According to Rand (1987) and Corey et al. (1995), the B-PAD was designed to realize a high level of content validity. The scenarios used in the B-PAD for Police and the B-PAD for Corrections assessment devices began with a collection of numerous problematic vignettes. These vignettes were collected from a diverse group of subject matter experts (SMEs) from around the country. Efforts were made to include women, ethnic minorities, professionals with urban and rural experience, line employees, supervisors, and administrators. Scripts were then written, and additional SMEs were used to evaluate the realism, importance, and difficulty of the script. The final scenarios on each videotape test were chosen to reflect a wide range of essential job functions in law enforcement and corrections.

Contrary to the suggestion of the B-PAD Group (the producers of the B-PAD tests) who recommend a panel of raters, the Maricopa County Sheriff's Office Psychological Services Unit used only one evaluator to score the B-PAD. However, this evaluator was either the director of the Unit or a doctoral student in psychology, both of whom had extensive experience in evaluating human behavior. The Psychological Services Unit Director believed that this was an acceptable and reliable method of evaluation. To evaluate the reliability of this method, a small sample of B-PAD results that both evaluators independently scored was obtained so that interrater reliability could be determined.

The Maricopa County Sheriff's Office currently utilizes the B-PAD test as a "tiebreaker," using the test results only in cases where the applicant has received a borderline score based on the other aspects of the psychological evaluation. In cases where an applicant receives a score that clearly indicates a recommendation for employment, or in cases where an applicant receives a score that clearly does not earn them a recommendation for employment, the B-PAD score is not considered. In borderline cases, the B-PAD score is evaluated, and if high can result in the applicant getting a recommendation for employment, and if low can result in the applicant not getting a recommendation. It cannot be determined exactly how often the B-PAD score was considered in the current sample, but it clearly was not a factor in the majority of cases. Since it was therefore possible for applicants to have low B-PAD scores and still be given a recommendation for employment, the range of B-PAD scores found in the sample was expanded.

FINDINGS

Adverse Impact

"Adverse impact refers to substantial disparities in the rate with which different groups are affected by personnel decisions involving their employment opportunities"[4] (Manese, 1986, p.107). To assess the significance of disparities in selection rates, the United States Equal Employment Opportunity Commission has adopted the 4/5ths or 80 percent rule. According to this rule, adverse impact is indicated when one selection rate is less than 80 percent of the other. Under Title VII of the Civil Rights Acts of 1964, employment practices which demonstrate adverse impact are presumed discriminatory unless shown to be job-related or justified by business necessity. Therefore, adverse impact must be considered by employers when developing employee selection procedures (Manese, 1986; United States Equal Employment Opportunity Commission, 1978).[5]

---

4 For a philosophical discussion of the concept of 'merit', and its relation to employment testing, the reader is referred to Fallon (1980) and Haney & Hurtado (1994).

5 For further information on the legal context of employment testing, the reader is referred to Frierson (1994) and Manese (1986, 99-131).

For purposes of the study, a B-PAD score of 14 was established as the minimum average score. Individuals scoring below 14 were considered to be below average, and those with scores of 14 or higher were considered average or above average. Tables 10-1 through 10-3 are reviewed in order to conduct an analysis of adverse impact using the EEOC 4/5ths rule.

Table 10-1 - B-PAD Scores and Gender

B-PAD SCORE	MALE	FEMALE
BELOW AVERAGE (B-PAD SCORE LESS THAN 14)	n = 61 20%	n = 17 21%
AVERAGE OR ABOVE AVERAGE (B-PAD SCORE 14 OR GREATER)	n = 237 80%	n = 65 79%

Table 10-1 concerns the gender of applicants. Under the EEOC 4/5ths rule, 80 percent of the male qualification rate of 80 percent yields an adverse impact threshold of 64 percent. The female qualification rate (79%) exceeds this threshold by 15 percent; thus there is no indication of adverse impact by gender.

Table 10-2 - B-PAD Scores and Race

B-PAD SCORE	CAUCASIAN	AFRICAN-AMERICAN	HISPANIC
BELOW AVERAGE (B-PAD SCORE LESS THAN 14)	n = 64 20%	n = 4 21%	n = 9 28%
AVERAGE OR ABOVE AVERAGE (B-PAD SCORE 14 OR GREATER)	n = 257 80%	n = 15 79%	n = 23 72%

Table 10-2 concerns the race of applicants. Under the EEOC 4/5ths rule, the Caucasian rate of 80 percent yields an adverse impact threshold of 64 percent. The African-American qualification rate (79%) and Hispanic qualification rate (72%) exceed this threshold by 15 percent and 8 percent, respectively. As such, there is no indication of adverse impact by race. Sufficient numbers of other protected groups were not available for analysis.

Table 10-3 - B-PAD Scores and Age

B-PAD SCORE	*18 - 39 Years Old*	*40 - 62 Years Old*
BELOW AVERAGE (B-PAD SCORE LESS THAN 14)	n = 70 21%	n = 7 14%
AVERAGE OR ABOVE AVERAGE (B-PAD SCORE 14 OR GREATER)	n = 257 78%	n = 45 87%

Table 10-3 concerns the age of applicants. The Age Discrimination in Employment Act (ADEA) prohibits employment discrimination based upon a person's age if the individual is 40 years of age or older (Frierson, 1994, p.15). In the present study, the qualification rate of the minority group (40-62 year olds) actually exceeds the qualification rate of the majority group (18-39 year olds). Therefore, there is no finding of adverse impact by EEOC guidelines concerning age.

Interrater Reliability

To assess the interrater reliability of the B-PAD scores, Rater One (the Psychological Services Unit Director) and Rater Two (a psychology doctoral student) each scored ten applicant's B-PAD tapes. Previously, both raters had scored five applicants jointly by silently rating each one, then stopping the tape, comparing ratings, and discussing any disagreement. Both raters disagreed most often on ratings of 3 versus 4. The highest level of agreement was on responses that were rated as one. These ratings were conducted during the B-PAD training of the doctoral student.

For this study, a random sample of five applicants that each rater had scored was selected, and scored by the other rater. This resulted in ten applicants that had B-PAD scores from both raters. These ten B-PAD ratings resulted in 80 Task Orientation scores (one for each of the eight scenarios), and 80 Interpersonal Communication scores. It was found that the two raters agreed on 68 of 80 (85%) of the Task Orientation scores and 72 of 80 (90%) of the Interpersonal Communication scores. The Overall Effectiveness scores (mean of Task and Interpersonal scores) for Rater Two were slightly higher than Rater One (18.2 to 17.3). Though based on a small sample of cases, these findings suggest that the agreement between the two raters is high, and therefore the raters appear to be assessing the same skills.

Validity

Another method of evaluating the effectiveness of a personnel selection test is to assess its concurrent validity. Concurrent validity is established by comparing the degree of correlation of the test being evaluated to other instruments which are known to measure similar criteria.

The psychological evaluation, conducted by the Maricopa County Sheriff's Office, provides a measure of the applicant's suitability for detention work. In assessing an applicant, the psychologist employs a structured interview that considers anger management at home and work, chemical usage, psychiatric history, problem solving, ethical alertness, vocational responsibility, non-prejudicial thinking, command presence, empathic responding, instructability, anti-stress skills, and communication skills. An assessment of emotional stability is also conducted based on 16 Personality Factors, Clinical Assessment Questionnaire, and Rorschach Ink Blot responses. The final result is a score ranging from 28 to 81. The lower the score, the more suited an applicant is believed to be for detention work. Applicants with scores greater than 40 are generally not recommended for employment as detention officers. Pearson Product-Moment correlations between the three B-PAD scores and the psychological evaluation global score revealed that a statistically significant negative correlation existed between all three B-PAD scales and the Global Score assigned during the psychological assessment. The Overall Effectiveness B-PAD score correlated at $r = -.26$ (p< .001), the Interpersonal Skills B-PAD score correlated at $r = -.28$ (p< .001), and the Task Orientation B-PAD score correlated at $r = -.17$ (p< .001). The correlation was negative because the Global Score is an inverse scale, with the applicants receiving the most positive rating awarded the lowest score.

Predictive Validity

A third method of evaluating the effectiveness of a testing instrument is predictive validity. Predictive validity is established by comparing the correlation between the instrument being tested and measures of success in the activity for which the test was being utilized.

In this study, the measures of success in the job of detention officer included grade point average in the academy, defensive tactics score in the academy, successful completion of the academy, successful completion of the six month probationary period, and a six month supervisor evaluation. The six month supervisor evaluation consisted of five subscales: quantity of work, quality of work, personal relations, work habits, and adaptability. For each subscale, a detention officer could receive a score ranging from 1 to 5 with five being "superior," 3 being "satisfactory," and 1 being "unacceptable." Adding these five subscales together resulted in a supervisor evaluation score possibly ranging from 5 to 25, with a theoretical average of 15.

Grade point average, defensive tactics, and the six month supervisor evaluation score were continuous variables and were analyzed using Pearson Product-Moment Correlation analysis. Completion of the academy and probation were dichotomous, nominal variables and were analyzed with Spearman correlation analysis. The results from these computations are presented in Table 10-4.

Table 10-4. B-PAD Scores and Measurements of Performance

	B-PAD Score (Overall)	B-PAD Score (Interpersonal Skills)	B-PAD Score (Task)
Academy Grade Point Average.	.16**	.17**	.10
Defensive Tactics Score	.03	.02	.03
Supervisor Evaluation	-.07	-.12	-.10
Completion of Academy	-.03	-.06	.02
Completion of 6 Month Probation	.05	.04	.05

* p< .05
* p< .01

A statistically significant correlation was found between two B-PAD scores (Overall Effectiveness and Interpersonal Skills) and academy grade point average. This suggests that individuals who score high on the B-PAD attain higher grade point averages in the academy. No significant correlations were found between B-PAD and the defensive tactics score or the supervisor evaluation, nor were any statistically significant relationships found between B-PAD scores and completion of either academy training or six months probation.

DISCUSSION

The Behavioral Personnel Assessment Device (B-PAD) is a video test used to assess the interpersonal competence of applicants for positions as corrections officers. As it is believed that interpersonal competence is critical to successful job performance in corrections, the B-PAD test should select better corrections officers. The present study posed two questions. First, the study asked whether the B-PAD has adverse impact against minority applicants. Using a test that has adverse impact can be legally risky for employers. Second, the study asked whether the B-PAD is a valid assessment instrument for detention officer applicants.

The answer to the first research question clearly seems to be no. Three types of protected classes (gender, age, and race) were examined, and no evidence of adverse impact was found. At least one important limitation should be noted. Concerning race, two significant groups of minorities were not included in the analysis: Asian and Native American. These groups were not included because insufficient numbers applied for detention officer positions. For this reason, it is impossible to say whether the B-PAD demonstrates adverse impact for these groups. Other studies of the B-PAD have found no evidence of adverse impact for these groups (Bradstreet 1994; Corey et al., 1995).

Unlike the answer to the first research question, the answer to the second research question is ambiguous. Several measures were used to assess the general effectiveness of the B-PAD test. These included interrater reliability, concurrent validity, and predictive validity.

The interrater reliability between the two B-PAD raters was high. This suggests that the B-PAD can be consistently scored by different raters, and that using skilled individual raters can be effectively used. However, the interrater reliability scores in this study were based on a very small sample, and need to be replicated on a larger scale.

Concurrent validity between the B-PAD and the structured psychological interview was also established at a moderate level. This is an important finding, as the interview has been used by the Psychological Services Unit to successfully select hundreds of detention officers. The interview is a more global assessment, measuring a wide range of attributes believed to be important to successful corrections work. Interpersonal competence is only one of these attributes, and this may have contributed to the finding of only modest correlation between the two measures.

In evaluating the predictive validity of the B-PAD, several measures of job success were collected. These included academy grade point average, academy defensive tactics score, supervisor evaluations, academy completion, and six-month probation completion. Of these factors, the only one that correlated significantly with B-PAD scores was the grade point average in the academy. Again this finding is important as it suggests that people who score high on the B-PAD will do well in the training academy. It might seem logical to assume that these same people would also perform better on the job as they would have a firmer grasp of the required knowledge. However, in this study this assumption was not substantiated.

One interesting observation is the negative correlation between the B-PAD scores and the supervisor evaluations. It may be that the skills and attributes measured by the B-PAD are valued differently by the psychologists who scored the B-PAD and the supervisors who completed the on-the-job evaluations. Thus, while the psychologist may give low scores to a candidate seen as gruff and presenting a tough image, this individual may be evaluated highly by the supervisor who interprets this behavior as professional and detached. However, these correlations were not statistically significant, and any observations derived from them are only speculations.

Several important limitations in the data should be noted. One, the percentage of detention officers who failed to complete the academy or probation was very low. Two, the range of scores on the supervisor evaluations was very restricted, showing a high degree of central tendency. To what extent these limitations impacted the statistical analysis is unknown.

CONCLUSION

The general conclusion reached by this study is that the B-PAD measures important characteristics of detention officer applicants, and does so in an unbiased, reliable manner. However, further testing is needed. Establishing the predictive validity of the instrument should be the priority of future research, and more sophisticated evaluations of employee performance that focus on the situations and skills that the B-PAD assesses are needed.

REFERENCES

Beck, A. J. (1997). An overview of national jail statistics at the Bureau of Justice Statistics. *American Jails, 10* (6), 10-15.

The B-PAD Group, Inc. (1995). *Product literature.* Napa, CA: Author.

Bradsheet, R. (1994, October). *Using video assessment in selecting police applicants.* Paper presented at the meeting of the Society of Police and Criminal Psychology, Madison, WI.

Brashear, J. (1997). The other side of the bars. *Maricopa County Sheriff's Office Roundup, 5* (1&2), 2.

Corey, D. M., Wolf, G. D., Rand, D. C., Rand, R., & MacAlpine, D. S. (1995) *B-PAD technical reports.* Napa, CA: The B-Pad Group.

Fallon, R. H. Jr. (1980). To each according to his ability, from none according to his race: The concept of merit in the law of anti-discrimination. *Boston University Law Review, 60,* 815-877.

Frierson, J. G. (1994). *Preventing employment lawsuits: An Employer's guide to hiring, discipline, and discharge.* Edison, NJ: The Bureau of National Affairs, Inc.

Goldfried, M., & D'Zurilla, T. (1969). A behavioral-analytic model for assessing competence. In C. D. Spielberger (Ed.), *Current topics in clinical community psychology* (pp. 151-169). New York: Academic Press.

Haney, C., & Hurtado, A. (1994). The jurisprudence of race and meritocracy: Standardized testing and "race-neutral" racism in the workplace. *Law and Human Behavior, 18* (3), 223-248.

Maguire, K. & Flanagan, T. (Eds.)(1991). *Sourcebook of criminal justice statistics* – U.S. Department of Justice, Bureau of Justice Statistics, Washington, DC: USGPO.

Maguire. K., & Pastore, A. (Eds.)(1996). *Sourcebook of criminal justice statistics* - 1995. U.S. Department of Justice, Bureau of Justice Statistics, Washington, DC: USGPO.

Manese, W. R. (1986). *Fair and effective employment testing: Administrative, psychometric, and legal issues for the human resources professional.* Westport, CT: Greenwood Press.

Rand, R. R. (1987). Behavioral Police Assessment Device: The development and validation of an interactive, pre-employment, job-related, video psychological test (Doctoral dissertation, San Francisco University, 1987). *Dissertation Abstracts International, 48* (3-A), 610-611.

Swander, C., Spulin, O., & Chapman, M. L. (1994). Hiring corrections officers you want to keep - the use of video testing for preemployment screening. *American Jails,* 3 (4), 11-14.

United States Equal Employment Opportunity Commission, U.S. Civil Service Commission, U.S. Department of Labor, and U.S. Department of Justice. (1978). Uniform guidelines on employee selection procedures. *Federal Register, 43,* 166: 38295-38309.

Chapter 11

SEAMLESS SYSTEMS OF CARE: USING AUTOMATION TO IMPROVE SERVICE DELIVERY AND OUTCOMES OF OFFENDERS IN TREATMENT*

FAYE S. TAXMAN AND STEPHAN SHERMAN

INTRODUCTION

The typical scene. A probationer walks into the probation office straight from court with an order indicating drug testing and treatment. Once an intake is complete, an appointment is set with a probation officer in 30 days, and the offender is given the name of a treatment agency. This begins the brokerage process between the probation and treatment agencies–calls are made, faxes occur, and letters are written–to communicate about the offender. Left out of the mix is sharing of results from alcohol and drug assessment, criminal history record, drug tests, and the status on supervision. It is up to the offender to: (1) inform the probation agency that he/she has completed treatment, or been unsuccessfully discharged; and, (2) inform the treatment agency of a new charge or detention. The list goes on of how the offender is the transmittal source between the treatment and supervision agencies.

The brokerage system is the predominate form of obtaining services for offenders in need of drug treatment. The probation department acts as a conduit for the 25 to 50 percent of the probation

* The Washington Baltimore High Intensity Drug Trafficking Area (HIDTA) project is funded by the Office of National Drug Control Policy (ONDCP) under grant number 17PWBP528. Special thanks are given to Mr. Joe Kemp and Mr. Tom Carr for their assistance in the development of the HATTS software. Points of view in this document are those of the author and do not necessarily represent the official position of any agency. Any questions can be forwarded to the senior author at 301 489 1705 or ftaxman@bss2.umd.edu.

orders containing a condition of alcohol or drug treatment (Taxman & Byrne, 1994) by providing the offender with the name of a treatment program or assessment agency. The availability of treatment slots as well as the suitability of the offender for particular programs has created a situation where many offenders do not receive needed treatment services (Duffee & Carlson, 1996). The labor intensive manual process of brokering services results in the treatment and supervision system relying on the addict-offender to negotiate through a complicated maze of agencies to fulfill the court order for treatment. The fragmented delivery system results in many needy clients not receiving treatment (Schlesinger & Dorwart, 1992); additionally, the system itself does not provide the precautions to prevent offenders from dropping out of treatment.

Technology offers the potential to change the likely destiny of failed treatment experiences and probation violations. Overcrowded caseloads and counseling sessions impede supervision and treatment staff from sharing information and making joint decisions. With technology, the supervision and treatment system can overcome traditional barriers. Networked personal computers using a shared data base offer a solution to create a seamless system of care among treatment and criminal justice agencies. The seamlessness is based on concepts of boundary spanning to foster development in the organizations to implement a systemic case management approach. In this chapter we will develop the concepts of systemic case management, provide information on an automated approach, and outline some critical issues in implementing automated case management approaches.

The Office of National Drug Control Policy (ONDCP) sponsored the Washington/Baltimore High Intensity Drug Trafficking Area (HIDTA) to reduce drug trafficking and consumption of drugs in thirteen jurisdictions.[1] As part of an effort to reduce recidivism among hard-core addicts in the criminal justice system, the project developed the HIDTA Automated Tracking System (HATTS) to implement the

---

1 The High Intensity Drug Trafficking Area (HIDTA) concept is congressionally mandated geographical approach to reduce harm to society drug trafficking and drug comsumption. HIDTAs assist in coordinating policy and strategic efforts across state, local, and federal agencies. The Washington/Baltimore HIDTA was created in 1994 with a mission to have an interdisciplinary approach of law enforcement, treatment and criminal justice, and prevention. This chapter discusses the treatment and criminal justice component of the project. In this region, the participating agencies are: Montgomery, Prince George's Baltimore, Howard, and Charles counties and Baltimore City in Maryland; Fairfax/Fall Church, Arlington, Prince William, and Loudoun counties and Alexandria City in Virginia; and the District of Columbia

HIDTA programmatic concepts. For the last two years, the project has been involved in automating the treatment and criminal justice system functions as part of strategy to integrate case management into the daily functions of the respective agencies. The software, shared data base, and conceptual framework presents innovative technology to overcome the implementation and manual processes that have impaired service delivery for the last quarter of a century. As we move into the 21st century, HATTS and the systemic case management principles provide a refreshing approach to ensuring quality of care in a public safety environment.

SEAMLESS SYSTEM OF CARE

Since the inception of probation service, the supervision agent is both an "enforcer" and a "social worker." As the social worker, the supervision officer has the ominous duty of brokering services for the client that typically provides the offender with a list of available programs or services. Since the brokerage model is based on the assumption that services are readily available (Moore, 1992), the challenges are usually to connect with the treatment system. As an enforcer, the supervision officer has the responsibility for ensuring that court orders are followed. The brokerage model has lead to the creation of individual case managers to ensure that offenders are provided with needed services. Moore (1992) and Taxman and Lockwood (1996) argue that systemic case management policies are needed to ensure that the individual case manager has the resources, authority, and power to provide needed services.

CASE MANAGEMENT APPROACHES

The brokerage model has led to the creation of individual case management approaches to ensure that offenders are provided with needed services. Individual case management bridges the treatment and criminal justice systems by having personnel devoted to improving access and placement in treatment. Treatment Alternative to Street Crime (TASC) is an example of an agency with the primary focus of linking the criminal justice offender with treatment services (Swartz, 1994). Many case management agencies (e.g., TASC) have expanded their services to include assessment, selection of the treatment program, appointment setting, therapy services, drug testing, and monitoring services. In some jurisdictions the case manager also monitors the progress of the client and provides progress reports to the courts (Anglin, Longshore, Turner, McBride, Inciardi, & Prendergast, 1996).

While case management was created to link treatment and criminal justice systems, it is not surprising that research on the effectiveness of case management has not been as promising as expected (Martin, Inciardi, Scarpitti, & Neilsen, in press; Taxman, Ellis, Spinner & Luongo, 1995; Anglin et al., 1996). Case management is often perceived as a supplement to the treatment and supervision process (Austin, 1993). In the Assertive Case Management study, the case manager assumed responsibility for establishing goals for the offender without input from parole officers and the case managers role often resembled the supervisory functions of the probation and/or parole officer (Martin et al., in press). The individual case manager is not perceived as a system function, but merely one of many actors involved with a client.

Moore (1992) and Taxman and Lockwood (1996) discuss how case management can be defined at the systemic level and applied on individual cases. The systemic approach recognizes that case management is a critical function that is performed within the normal responsibilities of treatment and supervision agencies. At the policy level, the systemic approach identifies the components of care in such a manner that it is easily applied at the individual case level. The importance of the systemic approach is that the treatment and criminal justice agencies agree on standards of care that clarify the role of staff and allocate needed resources. Case management is then built into the normal functions of the treatment and supervision agencies instead. Table 11-1 illustrates the different case management functions, typically ascribed to case managers, that are performed within the treatment and criminal justice. The systemic case management approach integrates these functions.

Table 11-1: Comparison of Case Management Functions with
Supervision and Treatment Function

Case Management Functions	*Supervision Functions*	*Public Health Treatment System*
Identification of Clients	Court Ordered Drug Users	Referrals from other systems
Screening	Intake	Intake
Assessment	Risk Assessment including use of substances	Psycho-Social Tool Addiction Severity Index
Treatment Plan	Supervision Plan	Treatment Plan
Treatment Services	Refer for Service/Provide Space within the agency	Provides Services
Monitor Progress	Responsible for Monitoring	Clinical Activity
Drug Testing	Available but varies by agency	Available but varies by agency
Transition to Another Level of Care	Depends on referral from treatment agency	Varies, depends on treatment agency policy

SYSTEMIC CASE MANAGEMENT COMPONENTS

The concept of systemic case management is premised on bound-aryless organizations bridging services and processes. For the criminal justice client, this involves treatment and criminal justice agencies functioning as a single agency instead of two separate units that try to "coordinate" fragmented services and constantly struggle over who "controls" decision-making about the client. In describing effective boundaryless organizations, Ashkenas, Ulrich, Jick, and Kerr (1995) have identified the following features:

- *Speed*: The ability to respond quickly and change strategies rapidly;
- *Flexibility*: The ability to pursue multiple paths and make rapid shifts in processes to focus on achieving goals;
- *Integration*: The organization pulls together diverse task activities and resources to mobilize the needed efforts to achieve desired outcomes; and,
- *Innovation*: The ability to find new creative and innovative processes to handle standard operating procedures.

The cornerstone of a systems approach is that services should consist of a process of interconnected parts. The emphasis is on a system consisting of several different complementary parts that have integrated decision making in the key areas such as assessment, referral, placement, tracking and monitoring, service planning, transitioning into another level of care, appropriate service mixes, and discharge. The systems approach lends itself to building the infrastructure to support the functions of a service delivery system with clearly defined policies.

Operationally, a seamless system is a service delivery system that links criminal justice and treatment agencies together by umbrella policies and procedures for the specific purpose of improving client outcomes. The agencies integrate decision-making and practice on managing the offender in the community. Instead of each agency defining their own role, the focus is on performing the necessary functions as part of a process. Each function is performed through specific roles and responsibilities that are mutually defined and agreed upon by all of the participating agencies. The service delivery system consists of policies linking all participating agencies to ensure that all of the functions are performed. These policies are designed to affect decision-making at the system level (e.g., resources, staffing, prioritization of target populations, etc.) and operational level (e.g., individual case management, access to services through many different agencies, etc.).

The systemic case management process builds functions that are normal and typical for the treatment of the substance abusing offenders. First, it begins with the recognition that the goal is to reduce recidivism by reducing substance abuse among the offender. With the supervision and treatment agencies ascribing to a public safety goal, the focus of the treatment and supervision is focused on outcomes—particularly reducing criminal behavior. The systemic case management approach integrates the following functions into the daily jobs of the treatment and supervision staff. Screening, Treatment, Analysis, Response, and Systems (STARS) provides the framework for assuring the continuity of care while the treatment or criminal justice system provides services to the client.

Screening and Assessment

An understanding of the needs of the offender is the beginning point of any treatment and/or supervision process. Information gathered usually consists of historical psycho-social, criminal justice, and prior program (e.g., treatment, supervision, etc.) information about the offender. This information provides the basis for making decisions about the type of services that are needed. For the criminal justice client, the screening and assessment is two-pronged–a needs assessment for the therapeutic needs and a risk assessment to understand the offender's risk for engaging in future criminal behavior. Screening and assessment then require the case manager to use the information to make an informed judgment as to the mix of services that are appropriate for managing the offenders behavior in the community. Similarly, the treatment system must conduct an assessment to determine the appropriate service level for the client. Decisions are usually made around the severity of the substance abuse problem that impacts the placement in a residential or outpatient program.

The supervision and treatment systems can benefit from sharing assessment information. The Addiction Severity Index (ASI) is a common tool in the treatment community which collects information on medical, psychiatric, family, social, substance abuse, legal, and employment (McLellan & Altermann, 1991). Many supervision agencies are starting to use the ASI since it gathers comprehensive information on the background of offenders. Yet, often only one agency typically uses the ASI and the information is generally not shared across the systems. Further supervision officers are often interested in the treatment program history of offenders and treatment agencies are often interested in the criminal history of the client; in both situations, the agencies have to rely upon self-report for pertinent information. The failure to share information, even with consent processes, results in both systems operating in a vacuum to make critical decisions about the appropriate placement for the offender.

Treatment Placement

Treatment and/or supervision plans are developed from the assessment process. Although placement typically refers to treatment services, the criminal justice client often requires monitoring and external controls to limit their behavior. Tools of control include electronic monitoring, home detention, house arrest, drug testing, face-to-face contacts, and collateral contacts. From a treatment perspective, the offender may become involved in a number of therapeutic services such as counseling, outpatient services, intensive outpatient, residential- or jail/prison-based treatment. The use of residential or "facility" based services is usually based on the severity of the dysfunctionality of the client. Treatment and supervision staff, using the screening and assessment information, must determine the placement.

Related to the treatment placement function is the ability to gain access to the needed programs and services. This often requires the case manager to determine programs that have available slots and juggle the treatment and supervision system needs. Placement efforts also try to impact the eligibility criteria to ensure that offenders have access to needed services, both in the treatment and criminal justice system (Ridgely & Willenbring, 1992). Treatment providers usually have direct access to treatment slots, although through increased treatment funding for offenders supervision officers also have the same capability.

Analysis and Monitoring

Systemic case management recognizes the dual role of continuous monitoring of the progress of the client and altering treatment and supervision plans. The analysis component is a data gathering process that requires information from the criminal justice and treatment systems about progress in the treatment and supervision plans to make informed decisions. Drug test results, treatment attendance, supervision contacts, employment and school attendance, and other information are critical to determine the progress of the client. The monitoring component includes a series of criteria to determine progress on the components of the treatment and supervision plan. Analysis and monitoring need to be coupled with the ability to make timely decisions about the progress of the client. This is an on-going process that requires the agencies to have timely information about the client.

Although a critical component of the process, analysis is very difficult because of the scattered information about the client. The supervision officer or treatment provider is placed in the position of both gathering and processing information on the offender. Few systems have developed a process for making transitions. For example, many probation departments have a policy of conducting a reassessment every six months. Yet how the information is used has not been clearly established.

Responses

Adjusting the treatment and supervision service mix should occur according to the progress of the client. Plus, the case manager must be in a position to respond to compliance problems. The latter is particularly important given that nearly 50 percent of the offenders drop out of treatment (Simpson, Joe, Broome, Hiller, Knight, & Rowan-Szal, 1997a; Simpson, Joe, & Brown, 1997b) or are in violation of a probation order (Taxman & Byrne, 1994). Managing compliance issues is an important component of the process, and one that is typically avoided (Taxman & Lockwood, 1996).

The case manager must have the power and authority to make treatment and supervision decisions about the client. A new concept, graduated sanctions, allows for swift, certain, and progressive responses to the behavior of the offender. That is, if the offender fails to comply with the treatment program, the probation officer has the authority to increase the level of control over the client by imposing curfews, attendance at supervision meetings, community service, and courtroom detention. Oregon allows the supervision officers to give up to 30 days of incarceration for continuous positive urine tests.

The concept of the responses is that they must occur shortly (e.g., 24 hours after the known event) after the negative behavior. The client also should be aware of the nature of the consequences as part of the treatment plan. For example, if a client has a positive drug test, then the treatment and supervision agency must have agreed on responses to guide action. The process is designed to hold the offender accountable for supervision and treatment requirements. The adjustment uses information to make changes in treatment and supervision services according to the progress of the client. Similarly the concept of responses is to reward positive behavior through a series of incentives. An example of incentives is the reduction of fees for drug testing, provision of bus tokens, or being a peer counselor in a treatment group.

System

Most treatment and supervision systems tend to provide services with regard for their own system. The systemic case management approach provides the client with the most incentives to achieve both treatment and supervision goals (Taxman & Lockwood, 1996). That is, the interagency approach allows the leverage of the criminal justice system to be used to achieve treatment goals. The advantages of the seamless system is that the case management functions are built into the responsibilities of supervision and treatment.

As we have shown, case management functions are ingrained in the daily activities of the treatment and supervision staff assigned responsibility for providing care for the criminal justice client. Under the systemic approach, all of the functions are enhanced by treatment and supervision working together to make joint decisions using similar information. For example, if an offender is low risk, from the criminal justice perspective, then it might be more appropriate to place the offender in a community program than a scarce residential treatment program. Similarly, an offender with a high volume of criminal activities might be best suited for a residential program, instead of being placed in a community program. Such decisions can not be made without sharing information across the systems.

The low-technology version of treatment and supervision (e.g., phone contacts, faxes, etc.) is a very labor intensive process that does not make integrated decision making easy or feasible. Automation provides the opportunity to institutionalize the practices even more so than merely "assigning" staff the responsibilities. The next section will describe how automation facilitates systemic approaches. Even without an automation system, the policies that are required to implement automation are critically important to the foundations of improved service delivery system. These policies provide the mechanism for treatment and supervision agencies to integrate decision making on client level decisions.

SEAMLESS SYSTEM FACILITATED THROUGH AUTOMATION

Automation features systemic case management functions into a system to ensure that the treatment and supervision staff must process and use information from their sister agencies. By providing the medium to share information, staff have information that is easily compiled in a fashion that fosters integrated decision-making. For example, if data is shared among the parties, then treatment and supervision staff can use similar information to make decisions about the client at all phases of the process—referral, placement, participation, change in treatment, change in supervision, and discharge.

Typically, supervision and treatment agencies have separate automation systems with little ability or protocol to share data. Important events, behaviors, and outcomes may be tracked electronically, but they are shared manually by phone, fax, or in a written report. The challenge of incorporating systemic policies into an automation system is to allow the automation to facilitate sharing data across the agencies. The end product is a tool which builds information developed by both systems and minimizes redundancy in data collection.

Another benefit of an automation system is that it maintains historical records on the client from both systems. Currently, client information is available in filing cabinets of individual treatment programs. Treatment staff tend to depend on the client to report prior treatment experiences. Automation allows for the centralization of treatment experiences and allows staff to make decisions based on data instead of the memory of the client or a service provider. For the substance abuse field, the capability of having historical records from many different treatment programs provides the clinical staff with added information about the client's previous treatment history. This is beneficial in making both treatment recommendations and responses to the treatment progress. The integrated automation system provides agency level information that does not rely upon the client to report prior program participation.

As part of a project to implement seamless systems among treatment and criminal justice agencies, the Office of National Drug Control Policy (ONDCP) sponsored the Washington/Baltimore High Intensity Drug Trafficking Area (HIDTA). The HIDTA Automated Tracking System (HATTS) provides an integrated set of automated tools to implement the seamless system (Washington/Baltimore HIDTA, 1997). The design and implementation of the HATTS system in over four jurisdictions illustrates how automation can ease the transition into a systemic case management. The experiences of these jurisdictions also illustrates how policies and current technology can address the presumed confidentiality barriers that have often prevailed in the communication between treatment and criminal justice agencies.

CONFIDENTIALITY ISSUES

A frequently mentioned barrier to treatment and supervision agencies sharing client level information is confidentiality issues. Any viable technological solution must incorporate the different legal and ethical provisions for protecting information while it is being shared by treatment and supervision agencies. According to Vigdal (1995, p. 6):

> Linking alcohol and other drug (AOD) abuse treatment with criminal justice sanctions involves legal and ethical issues that influence both the structure and operation of both systems. Confidentiality is a primary concern, as is protection of the right to privacy.

Access to information created by the treatment system on offenders involved in court-ordered substance abuse treatment programs is highly restricted, with even more controls than the traditional doctor-patient or attorney-client relationships (Holland, 1997; Vigdal, 1995). Public law and regulations have been put into place to protect confidential substance abuse records based on the concept that this protection is critical to the participation and success of the client in treatment program. Information disclosed without consent by the client to agencies or the public has been perceived as having a life-long damaging effect on the client, including the potential discouragement of the substance abusing population from seeking treatment (Lopez, 1994).

Any automation system for treatment and criminal justice data must include the standard criteria required in standard consents forms. The criteria include: (1) a list of the agencies who will receive the information, (2) the purpose of providing the information, (3) the type of information to be shared, and (4) the length of time that the information may be disclosed. Manual and automated systems must terminate access to treatment information whenever a specific date, event, or condition of consent expires (Holland, 1997; Lopez, 1994). Treatment information must also be protected against illegal redisclosure by one agency with granted access rights, to any other agency that does not have consent rights for the specific client and period (Vigdal, 1995).

HARDWARE, SOFTWARE, AND SECURITY ISSUES

HATTS is an example of an integrated automation system that fosters the use of systemic case management functions. As a client/server software application written in Visual Basic, the software is designed to run on a Windows NT server. End users need a personal computer with Windows 95 and a modem or some other method for connecting to the server. The software application has built in the ability for treatment and criminal justice agencies to develop client case files within each agency while simultaneously sharing information controlled by consents based on federal and local confidentiality guidelines.

Data are stored in tables maintained on a central server.[2] Access to the data table is controlled by the HATTS application, and each user is granted rights and privileges through the security screen controlled by a systems administrator. Each user can be granted or denied rights to access specific functions, screens, and reports. Each agency is identified by a unique number, and the agency can create numbers for up to 99 subunits. The security ensures that user access is limited to the functions that have been predefined by the agency and/or consent agreements (see discussion below).

HATTS includes functions of the treatment and criminal justice system. The system offers a flexibility to allow each agency to: (1) operate separately within its own environment or (2) share information across agencies. HATTS creates an environment where information is readily available but only disseminated when an appropriate confidentiality releases and policies are available. HATTS incorporates the confidentiality regulations by providing specific functions to give consent to client level information. As shown in Exhibit 1, each case must indicate the type of information to be shared and the appropriate time frames. With appropriate confidentiality releases stored within HATTS, it is possible for the treatment and criminal justice systems to

---

2 A current modification of HATTS is the ability to operate in a distributed database setting where data is maintained over several different servers feeding into a central server.

share specific information created over a specific period of time as long as the client has signed a release giving consent to provide information to the treatment and/or supervision system. Any information created outside of the specific time period, or not covered by the consent, is not shared. This feature allows each agency to continue to work with the client within their normal business cycle, and only share information where it is agreed to by the client.

Exhibit 1: Sample Consent Form

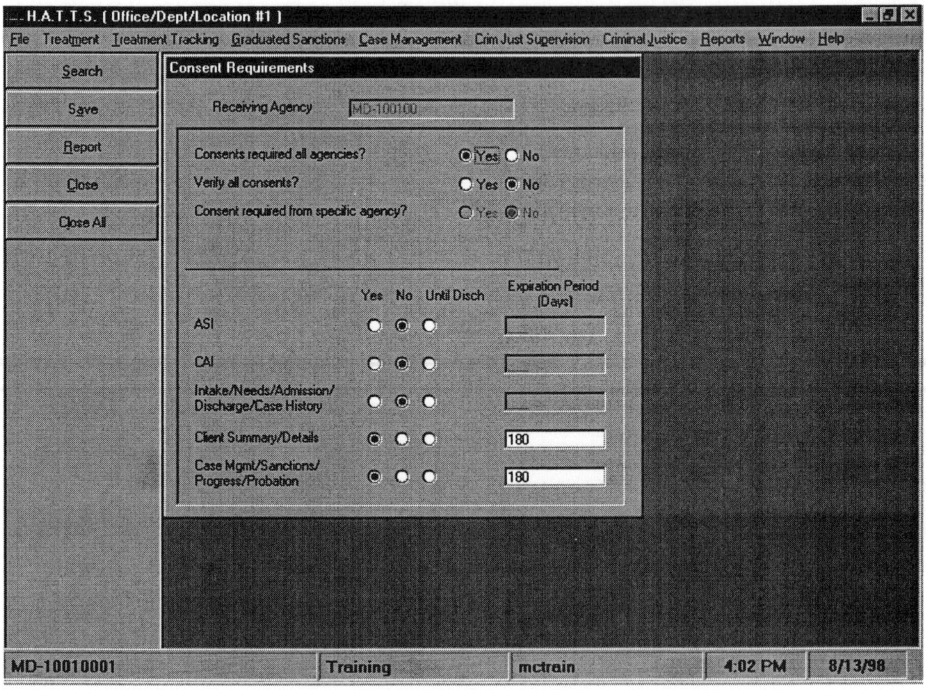

STRUCTURE OF HATTS

Table 11-2 provides a summary of the different components of the systemic case management model, HATTS screens, and functionality. Each of the STARS functions is integrated into the HATTS system to facilitate the analysis, responses, and joint decision making of the systemic case management approach. Not only does HATTS contain the various STARS functions but it also facilitates systemic case management processes. Table 11-2 shows the different screens in relation to the case management function. Throughout the application, both treatment and supervision have a definite role in providing needed information about the client. Instead of highlighting the different screens, the following discussion will be on the products of HATTS.

Table 11-2: Comparison of Seamless System Components
with HATTS Screens and Functionality

Seamless Case Management	HATTS SCREENS	Functionality
Screening	• Consent • Client Information (Demographics and Criminal History) • Addiction Severity Index • Risk Assessment	• Supervising Agent Information • Matches Client to Appropriate Program • Treatment History • Supervision and Case Leveling
Treatment Placement	• Create Appointment with Program • Tracks Treatment Services	• Confidentiality Releases • Determines Placement at Programs • Sets Up Appointment at Program • Establishes a Wait List for a Program
Analysis	• Attendance at Treatment Sessions • Attendance on Supervision • Monitors Supervision Contacts and Conditions • Monitors Drug Test Results	• Summary Screen with Red to Highlight Problem Areas • Highlights Recent Problem Areas
Responses	• Records Graduated Sanctions • Records Changes in Treatment • Records Changes in Supervision	• Summary Screen with Red to Highlight Problem Areas • Highlights Recent Problem Areas
Systems	• Treatment • Criminal Justice • Other Social Service Agencies • Confidentiality Releases	• Highlights Entry and Processing Across Agencies

Below are the different components of HATTS for the treatment and/or criminal justice staff. HATTS has built in an automated consent system which allows information to be shared across and within systems. (Refer to discussion on the confidentiality and release process.) This feature assists in facilitating the ability of the treatment and criminal justice system to coexist in one shared data base while simultaneously maintaining the integrity of the data.

Program Inventory

The system contains both an inventory and descriptive information on the treatment and correctional programs in the region. This program database refers to the type and nature of the services provided by the program; services are captured according to whether they occur on-site or as a referral to another program. The information determines the range of services provided by the program. The descriptive file also contains some information on the personnel structure of the program, the fees, the drug testing practices, and other critical information. The data base contains program capacity information (e.g., number of clients to be served, average daily service levels, etc.) which is used to manage referrals, maintain waiting lists, and coordinate placements in the program. (Refer to the wait list function below.)

Client Intake Process

Basic demographic information obtained by intake workers, supervision agents, or counselors are used to open a case within an agency. Each client is assigned a unique identifier or client ID based on gender, birth date, the social security number, and last name. The unique client ID is used across HATTS to facilitate sharing information where appropriate. Staff can view information from prior cases created within their agency, as well as cases in other agencies (when consent has been granted). Agencies can also store other identifying information with each case (e.g., agency case numbers, aliases, docket numbers, law enforcement identification numbers, etc.); the system uses the different identifiers to search for the client throughout the data.

Referrals and Appointments

HATTS allows agencies to make referrals and appointments to specific programs. At the conclusion of the intake, the staff can make an appointment to a specific program. The staff can monitor the status of the appointment through the system. Admission, treatment progress, and discharge information are all available as real time information on the client's progress.

Confidentiality and Releases

Automated consents are handled in a very unique manner within HATTS. The agency/provider *receiving* an appointment predefines the release policies within HATTS according to the type of information that will be released and length of disclosure. These policies should match the standard parameters and provisions contained within the release of information form signed by the client. The agency/provider *receiving* an appointment can require verification of any outside consent before allowing the system to release any data. They can also define different consent parameters for releasing information to different agencies.

The criminal justice or treatment agency *making* the appointment enters the date the release was signed.[3] All of the predefined policies flow automatically with this specific appointment for this specific client. If the agency *receiving* the appointment established that all consents must be verified with a hard copy of the signed form prior to releasing information, they can perform the verification directly within HATTS on the incoming referral appointment screen.

Assessment

HATTS contains several different tools to assist in examining the client's level of functioning. The publicly available *Addiction Severity Index* (ASI) and Client Assessment Information (CAI) tool compile indepth historical data from critical areas such as substance use, medical

---

3 Either agency can grant staff designated within their agency the authority to override the pre-established consent policies. All overrides must be verified by the *receiving* provider before the system will release any information. An override report is also maintained for management review.

history, family relationships, housing, legal status, mental health history, etc. Typical background characteristics on the clients and extensive narrative text notes are saved, reported, shared, or printed as needed. The ASI is used to compute the composite scores which indicate the severity of the problem. The ASI and CAI are used in the match function to determine which program has the most appropriate services for the offender. (That is, the results of the ASI and CAI are compared to the program inventory to determine the programs that have the most amenable services for the client.)

Service Units

Supervision and treatment staff often track the progress of clients as they proceed across predefined levels and phases within each agency. The intensity and frequency of required contacts may change as an offender achieves different levels. Tasks, duties, and the frequency of participation in different types of treatment services may change as a client graduates from one treatment level to another. HATTS allows agencies to establish the parameters for predefined levels, assign levels to each case, and monitor specific activities associated with each level. The system also produces a tickler report that links the completion of specific events or duties with the projection of events still to be accomplished.

Supervision

HATTS provides documentation of the different conditions of release as well as the client's attendance to these conditions. The supervision screen allows the agent to indicate the number of and types of supervision contacts that have occurred. The supervision agent can maintain case notes in the system, and share this information electronically as desired with treatment agency staff.

Treatment Tracking

Treatment staff can record daily treatment events, kinds of services provided, and progress notes. Feedback on participation in treatment can be shared immediately with the supervising agent, if the consent is entered into HATTS.

Graduated Sanctions

Staff can document the treatment and supervision mishaps and the responses by the different system(s). The screen provides the date and various types of responses, and allows each system to have current information on changes in behaviors to effectively coordinate responses to noncompliance.

Drug Testing

The screen documents the results from drug testing including the date of the test, the type of drug(s) tested, and the results, whether positive or negative. All positive tests are highlighted. This screen allows users to enter the results manually, and also displays results gathered from an automated drug testing system that can be linked to HATTS. HATTS also includes provisions for scheduling drug tests, checking in clients, maintaining a chain of custody, and sharing automated test results controlled by consents from the client.

Matching Client and Program

Built into the system are important tools for the screening and treatment placement functions. The system maintains a registry of treatment and supervision programs (i.e., outpatient, residential, day reporting, etc.) including information on the services offered in the program, the linkages with other programs, and the program capacity. The registry allows the system to create a reservation system of available slots and a waiting list of clients for that program. The registry also "matches" the service needs of the client with the services offered by a particular program. The matching is based on the information provided in the client assessment information compared to the services provided by the program. The system rank orders the treatment programs that are most suitable for the needs of the client. The rank order can be used to determine which program is likely to offer the most benefit to the client. Along with the matching functions, the system maintains the treatment and supervision history of the offender that can also facilitate placement decisions. Prior treatment and correctional program experience (e.g., type of program, discharge status, and progress) can be instrumental in determining the next appropriate program for the client.

Summary Screen

A summary screen highlights the status of the client in six critical areas: treatment, supervision, drug testing, graduated sanctions, case management, and arrests. The summary screen provides linkages to the contributing information which means that the supporting information is readily available to interested parties. To make the analysis functions easier, the summary screen provides the status of the client in the critical areas. The status of the client in treatment, supervision, and drug testing is available in order to consider the next steps for the client. The summary screen provides the treatment and supervision staff with critical pieces of information to foster decisions about appropriate responses for the client given his/her performance in treatment and supervision. This enhances the analysis and response capabilities of a systemic case management process.

IMPLEMENTING HATTS

The systemic case management approach is based on the developing policies and practices that facilitate shared decision making among the agencies. Software tools like HATTS provides the mechanisms to implement the policies and practices in an environment grounded in sound principles. The usual agency standard operating procedures are extended to develop system operating procedures. That is, policies define the appropriate services (e.g., assessment, treatment, supervision, testing, and responses) which guide the daily practices of staff. To encourage staff operating in different organizational systems with different goals and objectives, the software reduces the barriers that impact timely sharing of information. Automation reduces the reliance on formal reports and paper documentation and provides an electronic means to share historical data, assessments, events, and progress information.

Identifying the Policies and Procedures

Manual and automated systems are not "turn-key" systems with ready-made processes. Part of the systemic case management approach is to develop the needed umbrella policies that pertain to the STARS functions. Stated simply, it is critical that the treatment and criminal justice system agree on the different components of care–assessment, placement criteria, treatment dosages, drug testing dosages, and supervision dosages–and develop the appropriate policies and resources to deliver the services. By making an inventory of key practices in the treatment and criminal justice system along the STARS functions, the agencies can identify areas where interagency policies are lacking.

In each arena, the policy makers must determine the appropriate units of care. For example, many treatment and supervision agencies have different practices regarding drug testing offenders in treatment. Some treatment agencies test offenders while they are in treatment while others rely on the criminal justice system to test offenders; in some jurisdictions little or no testing occurs by either system. In the systemic case management approach, the jurisdictions must determine: (1) how frequently the offender should be drug tested while in treatment, who is responsible for testing, and how the information will be shared among the participating agencies; (2) how frequently the offender should be drug testing after treatment, who is responsible, and how any relapses or positive drug tests results will be handled by the treatment and supervision systems; and (3) what are the appropriate responses to positive drug tests. Similar policy decisions must be made on treatment and supervision issues.

Developing Staff Skills to Analyze and Assess Based on Data

Automation, the systemic case management processes, and integrated decision-making all represent significant changes in the landscape of treatment and corrections. Each changes the daily operations of the correctional and treatment staff by providing the staff with information that is infrequently available. Even more importantly, the automation presents challenges to ensure that information is used to guide decisions as well as provide a mechanism to monitor staff responses. Automation, although a frequently sought after feature, presents challenges to existing organizations by providing staff with new skills to handle computers. Staff must be trained on using computers and using information.

One of the biggest challenges is developing skills to use historical and current information to guide decision making. In a manual system, the tendency is to make decisions based on readily available information such as the most recent incident, recalled events, and client appearance, or attitude. Automation extends the information that can be used in decisions by providing historical events in an orderly fashion. Staff have available a chronological order of events to use in making decisions. This is critically important because it has the potential to change decision making from reactive to informed. Decisions are based on historical facts which allows the staff to examine the intensity of the behavior and the responses. For example, if an offender has a history of testing positive, an examination of the history reveals periods of negative tests and some changes in the living arrangements of the client. Together this information assists the treatment and supervision staff in making decisions about the next appropriate steps for the clients.

Breaking Cross-Cultural Barriers

The availability of information from treatment and criminal justice agencies presents new opportunities to reduce the barriers that often evolve from "philosophical differences." At the staff level, information drives the ability to see the client as a person instead of two parts—the treatment or criminal justice version of the person. The competition between treatment and criminal justice responses often arises from treatment and criminal justice staff having different information about the client and then using that information to make the best "informed decisions." These differences are generally capsized as philosophical differences between health and safety needs. However, through the automation system relying on shared information that is used by both systems, the philosophical differences disappear. Staff share information as a means to make the best possible decision for the addict-offender, instead of a criminal justice or treatment decisions. The cultural barriers between the systems tend to be resolved through the ability to have similar information that can be discussed and analyzed by both treatment and supervision staff.

Working Within Confidentiality Requirements

Staff daily practices often differ from organizational policies. While formal policies may restrain staff from disclosing certain types of client information without consents, informal practices may exist that contradict these policies. Staff may have developed working relationships between criminal justice and treatment agencies where sharing verbal and written information on clients commonly occurs without a signed consent. Case management and referral staff may focus more attention on making the link between agencies, while waiting for another client contact to get a signed consent. Supervision agents may not be aware of consent requirements because the agencies have not historically developed internal confidentiality checks and balances, or monitored consent procedures.

HATTS, or similar software tools, reinforces agency policies by requiring staff to operate within confidentiality regulations. The software mandates that staff fulfill consent requirements before any information sharing occurs. The process itself requires the agencies to review and define policies regarding the sharing of information with other agencies. Technology promotes good business practices while also benefiting staff with a timely sharing of information.

Standardizing Policies for Sharing Automated Information

Agencies use memorandums of understanding, qualified service organization agreements, and consent forms to allow sharing of client data. Differences exist in how the federal confidentiality regulations are interpreted and implemented by state and local government agencies. The length of time for sharing data, as defined within a preprinted consent form, can vary between agencies and jurisdictions. Criminal justice agencies often request different types of treatment data based on the types of programs they operate, the caliber of staff, and the nature of past relationships with treatment agencies.

MOVING INTO THE 21st CENTURY WITH
TECHNOLOGY AND SERVICES

Improved technology has contributed to the development and implementation of personal computer-based management information systems that can be used by multiple agencies. This discussion features how case management is critical to the everyday functions performed by treatment and supervision agencies. Case management is integral to the outcomes of clients involved in treatment services. For the offender in treatment, case management provides the linkage between the criminal justice and treatment system. The challenge has been that it has been difficult for supervision and treatment staff to perform the functions, particularly the analysis and responses, without adequate information. Technological improvements make once difficult functions easy while also contributing to the use of up-to-date information to ensure that treatment and supervision goals are pursued. An automated system that allows treatment and criminal justice staff to share a data base enhances the ability to understand the full range of information about the status of the offender. In the end, it reduces the difficulty of sharing information across the agencies.

Information is a "strategic organizational resource" which few correctional and treatment agencies have at their fingertips (Cochran, 1992). As an organizational resource, the availability of information to make decisions at all levels of the organization—front-line staff to administrators—will improve the practice in the field and public perception of the value of these services. HATTS provides the forum for moving the field into the next century by giving public agency software tools that are user-friendly, affordable, and grounded in theoretical principles of care. HATTS provides the forefront by giving correctional and treatment agencies a tool for coordination and collaboration which have been described as barriers to effective service delivery. By removing the barriers, technology allows the agencies to achieve their goals while empowering the staff to continue to do quality work. In the end, technology will provide the vehicle to allow treatment and correctional agencies to hold both agency staff and offenders accountable. By doing so, corrections and treatment will garnish support with the public by the improve professionalism, competency, and effectiveness (Cochran, 1992).

REFERENCES

Anglin, M. D., Longshore, D., Turner, S., McBride, D., Inciardi, J., & Prendergast, M. (1996). *Studies of the functioning and effectiveness of treatment alternatives to street crime (TASC) programs: Final report.* Los Angeles, CA: UCLA Drug Abuse Research Center.

Ashkenas, R., Ulrich, D, Jick, T., & Kerr, S. (1995). *The Boundaryless Organization: Breaking the Chains of Organizational Structure.* San Francisco: Jossey-Bass.

Austin, C.D. (1993). Case management: A system perspective. *Journal of Contemporary Human Service,* 451-458.

Cochran, D. (1992). The long road from policy development to real change in sanctioning practice. In J.M. Byrne, A.J. Lurigio, & J. Petersilia (Eds). *Smart sentencing: The emergence of intermediate sanctions.* (pp. 307-319). Beverly Hills, CA: Sage.

Duffee, D.E., & Carlson, B.E. (1996). Competing value premises for the provision of drug treatment to probationers. *Crime and Delinquency, 42*(4), 574-592.

Holland, S.R. (1997). Confidentiality of substance abuse treatment client records in the criminal justice system: Overview of the federal law and regulations. Unpublished paper presented at the Center for Substance Abuse Treatment Criminal Justice Networks Technical Assistance Workshop, Denver, Colorado.

Lopez, F. (1994). *Confidentiality of patient records for alcohol and other drug treatment.* U.S. Center for Substance Abuse Treatment: Technical Assistance Publication Series, 13.

Martin, S.S., Inciardi, J.A., Scarpitti, F.R., & Nielsen, A.L. (in press). Case management for drug involved parolees: A hard ACT to follow. In Inciardi, J.A., Tims, F.M., & Fletcher, B.W. *The Effectiveness of Innovative Approaches to Drug Abuse Treatment,* Westport, CT: Greenwood Press.

McLellan, A.T. & Altermann, A.I. (1991). Patient treatment matching: A conceptual and methodological review with suggestions for future research. In Pickens, R.W., Leukefeld, C.G., & Schuster, C.R. *Improving Drug Abuse Treatment* (pp. 114-135). Rockville, MD: National Institute on Drug Abuse Research Monograph Series, No. 106.

Moore, S.T. (1992). Case management and the integration of services: How service delivery systems shape case management. *Social Work, 37,* 418-423.

Ridgely, S.M., & Willenbring, M.L. (1992). Application of case management to drug abuse treatment: Overview of models and research issues. In Ashery, R. (Ed.), *Progress and Issues in Case Management.* U.S. Department of Health and Human Services: NIDA Research Monograph 127.

Schlesinger, M., & Dorwart, R.A. (1992). Falling between the cracks: Failing national strategies for the treatment of substance abuse. *Daedalus, 121* (3), 195-237.

Simpson, D.D., Joe, G.W., Broome, K.M., Hiller, M.L., Knight, K., & Rowan-Szal, G.A. (1997a). Program diversity and treatment retention rates in the drug abuse treatment outcome study (DATOS). *Psychology of Addictive Behaviors, 11*(4), 279-293.

Simpson, D.D., Joe, G.W., & Brown, B.S. (1997b). Treatment retention and follow-up outcomes in the drug abuse treatment outcome study (DATOS). *Psychology of Addictive Behaviors, 11*(4), 294-307.

Swartz, J. (1994). TASC–The next 20 years: Extending, refining, and assessing the model. In Inciardi, J.A. (Ed.), *Drug Treatment and Criminal Justice*. Beverly Hills, CA: Sage.

Taxman, F.S., & Lockwood, D. (1996). Systemic case management practices: The HIDTA seamless system approach. Report to the Office of National Drug Control Policy.

Taxman, F.S., & Byrne, J.M. (1994). Locating absconders: Results from a randomized field experiment. *Federal Probation, LVIII*(1), 13-23.

Taxman, F. S., Ellis, L., Spinner, D.L., & Luongo, P.F. (1995). Changing behavior of hard core offenders: Results from a modified TC in a jail setting with a continuum of care. Unpublished paper.

Vigdal, G.L. (1995). *Planning for alcohol and other drug abuse treatment for adults in the criminal justice system*. U.S. Center for Substance Abuse Treatment: Treatment Improvement Protocol Series 17.

Washington Baltimore HIDTA, 1997. *HATTS: Training manual*. University of Maryland, College Park.

PART IV
CRIMINALITY AND TECHNOLOGY

INTRODUCTION

Part IV, Criminality and Technology, contains three chapters focusing on innovative criminality utilizing the computer. In Chapter 12, Peter Mercier provides an overview of computer crime, and examines the current attitudes of faculty, staff, and students at a midsize, mid-Atlantic university. His findings indicate the majority of the sample believe that accessing another person's computer account should be illegal and find this activity to be reprehensible, while most feel that there is nothing wrong with copying commercially sold software. Mercier suggests that levels of computer crime occurrences are worthy of continued research because unauthorized computer access and computer software "piracy" cost organizations millions of dollars annually. Such investigating and prosecuting poses new technological challenges for the criminal justice system.

The next two chapters focus on specific types of computer crimes from different perspectives. David Carter and Andra Katz, first in Chapter 13, explain computer crime victimization. They conducted a national study of corporate security directors to examine their experiences with computer crime.

Next, in Chapter 14, the same authors document how computers are used as tools by International Organized Crime. Based primarily upon interviews with officials from over thirty law enforcement and intelligence agencies around the world, the authors were able to document nine categories of circumstances where computers were used as a tool by continuing criminal enterprises. These included: record keeping, counterfeit currency and documents, counterfeit products, sexually-related commerce, gambling, theft and fraud, telecommunications fraud, illegal immigration, and the black market. This chapter provides a current definition and perspective of international organized crime as entrepreneurial crime and then discusses each of the categories of computer applications.

Chapter 12

ON-LINE CRIME: IN PURSUIT OF CYBER THIEVES, SOFTWARE PIRATES, AND OTHER COMPUTER CRIMINALS

PETER J. MERCIER

Over the last several decades, the amount of financial, military, and intelligence information, proprietary business data, and personal communications stored on and transmitted by computers has increased significantly. It is clear today that neither governments, the military, nor the world's economy could operate without computer automation (Parker, 1976; Chang & Chang, 1985). Everyday, more than one-hundred million electronic messages are transmitted throughout the world's networks, and banking networks transfer trillions of dollars (BloomBecker, 1988). Increasingly, computers transacting large volumes of business are linked to each other via various military or financial networks or the Internet. According to Schwartau (1994), four out of every five computer crimes investigated by the Federal Bureau of Investigation (FBI) in 1993 involved unauthorized access to computers via the Internet.

Information stored and transmitted by computer is vulnerable to attack. No one knows the true scope of computer crime, but informal estimates suggest that billions of dollars are stolen or lost annually, and nearly every organization using computers has been affected in some way by computer intrusions. Additionally, the problem goes beyond the borders of the United States. The British National Computer Center reported that more than 80 percent of British organizations suffered a security breach in the last several years (Cohen, 1995). The increasing use of interconnected networks makes these crimes easier than ever.

197

Although exact estimates are not available, limited research suggests that computer-related crime appears to be on the increase in both incidence and severity. Media reports indicate that this increase may be attributable, in part, to a generation of "hackers" who become initially involved in computer deviance as children while in school (Hollinger, 1988, 1993). Thus, in addition to providing an overview of computer crime, this study seeks to determine whether students' attitudes about illegal computer use vary from those of faculty and staff at a midsized mid-Atlantic university.

UNAUTHORIZED ACCESS TO COMPUTER SYSTEMS

Because we live in an age of automation and computer connectivity, almost no organization is exempt from computer intrusions. Yet, there are several common targets frequently attacked: military and intelligence computers may be targeted by espionage agents, financial institutions (e.g., banks) by professional criminals, businesses by their competitors. Any company may be the target of its employees or exemployees, universities the target of students or former students, and any organization the target of "hackers" who either access computer systems for the intellectual challenge or operate as paid professionals (Bequai, 1982; Sterling, 1992).

Unauthorized Access to Military and Intelligence Computers

National security is increasingly in the hands of computers which store information ranging from the positioning of satellites to plans for troop deployments throughout the world. Just as common criminals have learned that computers are where the money is found, espionage agents have learned that computers are where intelligence information is located. More and more, espionage is becoming a game of computer breakins (Schwartau, 1994).

Intrusion into U.S. government computers is common, despite efforts to enhance computer security. In his book *The Cuckoo's Egg*, Cliff Stoll (1990) describes, in fascinating detail, how a 75 cent accounting imbalance at Berkeley Laboratories in California led him to the discovery of a West German hacker who was extracting information from defense computers in more than 10 countries, including the United States. Some of this information was sold to the Soviet KGB.

In June, 1988, computer hacker Kevin Mitnick remotely accessed a Defense Department network. Though he allegedly stole a prerelease version of Digital Equipment Corporation's VMS V5.0 Operating System software and temporarily stored it on a Navy computer at the Patuxent Naval Air Station in Maryland, officials claim that he obtained no classified information. Mitnick, who was subsequently arrested by the FBI after an intensive cross country manhunt, fine-tuned his "hacking" skills as a student in suburban Los Angeles during the late 1970s. He spent much of his adolescence breaking into computer systems, starting with those that ran the Los Angeles Unified School District's attendance, grade reporting, and scheduling applications (Shimomura & Markoff, 1996).

In January, 1990, three Silicon Valley workers were arrested for breaking into government and telephone-company computers. They reportedly accessed systems that provided them with information on military exercises, flight orders, FBI investigations into the late Philippine President Ferdinand Marcos, and instructions on how to eavesdrop on private telephone conversations. Some of the military information that was compromised due to these intrusions was classified as "SECRET" (Schwartau, 1994).

Unauthorized Access to Business Computer Systems

Just as the Cold War ended, a new era of worldwide economic competition began, and rivalries among national economies make industrial espionage a growing threat. Even "friendly" nations have become our economic enemies. In one case, Boeing Aircraft accused the French company Airbus of bugging Boeing employees' hotel rooms and airline seats and tapping their phone lines in an effort to obtain secret corporate information (Schwartau, 1994).

Although most intrusions into business computer systems are committed by employees (Schwartau, 1994), businesses are increasingly the target of both competitors and the curious (Forester & Morrison, 1990). Even computer companies such as Apple found viruses in their electronic mail systems. One virus succeeded in shutting down the system and erasing all of Apple's voice mail. Apple also reported that computer criminals may have reverseengineered the secret code that underlies its Macintosh computers. This copyrighted and seemingly highly protected code could be used to build a clone of the Macintosh computer (Schwartau, 1994).

Attacks Against Financial Computer Systems

These days, our money may seem to be nothing more than bytes in a computer. Our paychecks are deposited electronically. Our bills are paid electronically. Therefore, it is not surprising that there has been a natural progression in electronic theft (Forester & Morrison, 1990).

Banks are always targets for computer criminals (Forester & Morrison, 1990). In 1988, seven individuals conspired to steal money from the First National Bank of Chicago. The group used a wire transfer scheme to move $25.37 million belonging to Merrill Lynch and Company, $25 million belonging to United Airlines, and $19.75 million belonging to the BrownForman Corporation to a New York bank and then to two separate banks in Vienna, Austria. The transfers were authorized over the telephone, and followup calls made by the bank to verify the requests were routed to the residence of one of the suspects. Investigators were able to use these telephone records to trace the crime to the suspects. Had these criminals been a little more clever, they might have gotten away with $70 million (Schwartau, 1994).

Often, financial attacks are perpetrated by insiders who know the technical "ropes." In 1994, a MCI switch technician was arrested for allegedly selling thousands of telephone credit card numbers. The total cost to the company was estimated at $50 million (Power, 1995).

Even juveniles have turned to computers to obtain merchandise illegally. In 1996, three 16-year-olds were arrested in Hampton, Virginia, for using an online service to illegally obtain more than $14,000 worth of computers and software. After obtaining credit card information by downloading some programs from the Internet, the three juveniles were able to place orders to various computer mailorder companies using the stolen credit card numbers. The mail order companies, located in New Jersey, shipped the computers to an address in Hampton, Virginia. The victims whose credit card numbers had been stolen lived in Philadelphia and other parts of the Northeast and New England (Chernicky, 1996).

Grudge and Fun Attacks Against Computer Systems

Not all computer criminals are seeking information or material gain. Some simply want to wreak damage and destruction. One of the betterknown cases in this category is that of a Texas insurance company employee, a systems security analyst, who worked for the company for more than two years before being fired. After he left the firm, its IBM system crashed, and the company suffered a major loss of commission records used to prepare the monthly payroll. The program responsible for the problem was traced to the former employee's computer terminal and account. Investigators were able to show that he had planted a "logic bomb" in the program while still employed with the company. In this case, he essentially programmed the system to crash if his name were ever to be removed from the company's payroll (Cohen, 1995).

Similarly, many computer criminals are not interested in money. Except for the fact that they are breaking the law—the federal government and 48 states have criminal statutes prohibiting computer trespass—they do not fit the criminal stereotype—those who access computer systems to commit fraud or espionage. However, these individuals do break into computer systems affiliated with the military, universities, banks, and businesses. Many of them are juveniles, sometimes as young as 13, who think of their computers as advanced video games. In June, 1989, a 14 year old Kansas boy used a small Apple computer to crack the code of an Air Force satellite positioning system. The teenager, who reportedly began his career as a hacker at the age of 8, specialized in breaking into Hewlett-Packard's HP3000 minicomputers, used by businesses and a number of government agencies (Cohen, 1995).

SOFTWARE PIRACY

The theft of copyright-protected software is currently one of the emerging crimes associated with computers. Some people justify making and using unauthorized copies of software and may not understand the implications of their actions or the restrictions of the U. S. copyright law (Swinyard, Rinne, & Kau, 1997).

Any computer user may steal copyrighted software. The problem of software piracy has arisen partially because our intellectual property laws have not kept pace with the evolution of technology (Michalowski & Pfuhl, 1991; Fagin, 1997). Additionally, it is very difficult to "police" and control violations pertaining to software-copyright laws because of the way personal computers function (Fagin 1997); there is no technological mechanism to stop the installation of copyrighted software from one computer to another. Although software developers use a number of different approaches to prevent individuals from duplicating their products, software piracy remains a multi-billion dollar, international crime problem (Parker, 1989).

COMPUTER-RELATED CRIME RESEARCH

As we approach the 21st century, the use of personal computers will continue to grow. Each year, more Americans become computer literate, with levels of computer competency especially high among a younger generation whose expertise comes not only through their educational experiences but also through their recreational use of video games (Hollinger, 1993).

Current literature (Nycum, 1986; Hollinger, 1988, 1993; Michalowski & Pfuhl, 1991; Collier & Spaul, 1992; Coldwell, 1997; Fagin, 1997; Johnson, 1997; Swinyard et al., 1997) reveals that scarce research has been conducted regarding computer-related crime; however, several relevant victimization studies suggest the magnitude of theses occurrences. The first national survey of computer crime, conducted by the American Bar Association (1984), finds significant victimization of businesses by computer. The majority (77%) of this criminal activity was perpetrated by the companies' own employees (Zajac, 1986). More than 25 percent of the responding businesses experienced financial harm from computer crime-related incidents during the year prior to the study, estimating their annual losses from $2 million to $10 million (American Bar Association, 1984).

In 1986, a survey of Forbes 500 corporations disclosed that 56 percent of the respondents experienced losses attributable to computer crime during the previous year–the average loss for the corporations was $118,932. Similar to the American Bar Association's study, the

Forbes' study revealed that most of the perpetrators (63%) were employees of the victimized firms. Interestingly, more than one-half of the organizations experiencing victimization did not report any of the incidents to law enforcement authorities (O'Donoghue, 1986). Like the two nationwide surveys of businesses, a 1989 statewide survey conducted by the Florida Department of Law Enforcement found that one out of every four businesses experienced some type of computer-related crime during the previous year. As in the two nationwide surveys, the Florida study shows that the majority (85%) of these crimes were committed by employees of the victimized firms (Herig, 1989).

In his landmark book, *Crime by Computer*, Donn Parker (1976) expresses concern that the computer education process is criminogenic. While in the process of experimenting with this new technology, Parker (1976) argues, students are often encouraged to demonstrate their knowledge by committing some type of deviant or criminal act involving computers. However, in a survey of 200 Midwestern computer science students, Hollinger (1984) reports that most disapproved of incidents in which a computer was used as the instrument of crime. Yet, nearly one-quarter of the respondents in this study indicate that they would, more than likely, modify confidential information stored in a computer account if they had the opportunity. Only 3 percent disclose that they definitely would not.

In structured interviews comparing a small sample of computer science students (n=8) and young, known computer criminals (n=3), Hollinger (1988) theorizes a linear progression regarding computer deviance—involvement among the more deviant computer users starts with software piracy, leads to unauthorized browsing of another's computer files or email, and is followed by more malicious "cracking" into someone else's account. Additionally, Hollinger (1988) notes little difference in admitted levels of illegal computer activity between students who had been arrested for computer-related crimes and peers who had yet to be detected for similar activities.

Another study (Hollinger, 1993) using self-report questionnaires administered to a large sample of college students at a major Southeastern university reveals that software piracy and unauthorized computer-account access are still relatively infrequent occurrences on campus; however, a significant minority of students do admit to participating in computer-related deviant acts. Of the 1,766 respondents, 10 percent acknowledged participation in some type of software piracy during a 15-week semester in 1989; only 3.3 percent admitted some involvement in unauthorized computer access.

Review of the literature has surfaced only two studies measuring students' attitudes toward computer-related crime. The first, a study conducted by Coldwell (1997) measuring attitudes between students in different academic disciplines, disclosed that students in the engineering and technology disciplines do not consider "hacking" into others' computer systems to be unethical as compared to students in the other disciplines (Coldwell, 1997). Coldwell (1997) theorizes that students in engineering and technology are socialized into their disciplines by their faculty, and in many cases, feel more comfortable with machines than with people. Additionally, Coldwell (1997) posits that many of these students are taught to be clinically objective and appear to be less concerned about social consequences for their actions.

In the second attitudinal study, a cross-cultural analysis examining differences in morality and behavior toward software piracy between students in the U.S. and Singapore, Swinyard et al. (1997) note that the Singaporean students are significantly more inclined than the U.S. students to overtly make pirated copies of software. According to Swinyard et al. (1997), American students are influenced by legal restrictions on copying software as versus the loss of revenue suffered by computer software companies. Therefore, they are more likely than the Singaporean students to discreetly copy computer software programs because of the stricter copyright laws in the U.S. Additionally, the study reveals that the Singaporean students find it significantly more acceptable to copy computer software and keep it for personal use as compared to the U.S. students. Swinyard et al. (1997) explain this contrast as a result of cultural differences. Whereas Asian cultures believe that individual developers of technology are obliged to share their developments with society, Western cultures emphasize individual freedom and benefits over societal interests.

Because the literature suggests that most computer-related crime is conducted by employees (American Bar Association, 1984; O'Donoghue, 1986; Zajac, 1986; Herig, 1989) and students (Parker, 1976; Hollinger, 1988, 1994; Coldwell, 1997), a college campus seems an ideal setting for an attitudinal study. Generally, college faculty and staff not only use computers on a regular basis to conduct their day-to-day activities, but are also given broad access to university computers. This access may allow faculty and staff to review student records, grant proposals, research projects, and other similar information. Likewise, today's students are a generation of young people who grew up with computer video games and are encouraged to learn and experiment with computer technology.

Therefore, this research addresses the following questions: Do students and faculty/staff differ in their attitudes about unauthorized access of computer systems and software piracy? Do students from varying academic disciplines differ in their attitudes about unauthorized access of computer systems and software piracy? This research focuses on attitudes and seeks to advance knowledge about computer-related crimes and the potential for perpetration. Attitudes may not only influence latent criminal behavior but also future policies and laws related to computer activity.

METHODOLOGY

Since limited research suggests that computer software piracy and unauthorized computer access have a potential relationship to school-aged computer users and academic instruction (Hollinger, 1988, 1993; Coldwell, 1997), an attitudinal survey was administered to a sample of faculty, staff, and students at a midsize, midAtlantic university during the spring and fall semesters of 1997.

Instrument

The instrument for this study is a 16-item, Likert-type survey measuring attitudes about various computer-crime issues. For the purposes here, seven items measure attitudes about unauthorized access to computer systems and six items measure attitudes about computer software piracy. Unauthorized access is defined as "acquiring another user's password," "unauthorized use of someone else's computer account," "unauthorized browsing [in] another user's computer files," "unauthorized copying of another user's computer files," "unauthorized file modification," and "deliberate sabotage of another user's computer programs" (Hollinger, 1988, p. 199). Software piracy is defined as making a "copy of proprietary computer software" for one's personal use or for another user and/or receiving a "copy of propri-

etary computer software from another user" (Hollinger, 1988, p. 199).
Though response choices were "strongly agree," "agree," "disagree,"
and "strongly disagree," these response choices are collapsed to reflect
"agree" and "disagree" for statistical analysis purposes.

Sample

Of the 180 faculty and staff randomly selected, 60 returned surveys
for a total response rate of 33 percent. In addition, 325 students were
conveniently sampled in 15 randomly selected undergraduate and
graduate classrooms. Among the student sample, 39 majors and 6 discipline areas are represented.

The student sample is young while the faculty and staff sample is
middle-aged. Furthermore, the majority of the sample is female,
Caucasian, and considers themselves to be somewhat computer literate. Table 12-1 amplifies the sample's characteristics.

Table 12-1 Sample Characteristics

Variable	*Students*	*Faculty/Staff*
Age:		
Mean	21.7	41.7
Range	17-56	58.3
	Measured by Percent	
Sex:		
Male	40.2	41.7
Female	59.8	58.3
Race/Ethnicity:		
Caucasian	73.2	69.5
African-American	15.1	20.3
Hispanic	3.4	1.7
Asian/Pacific Islander	3.1	1.7
Other	5.2	6.8
Marital Status:		
Single	82.6	11.9
Married	11.2	71.2
Other2	6.2	16.9
Class Standing		
Freshman	32.6	NA
Sophomore	18.8	NA

Table 12-1 Sample Characteristics - continued

Variable	Students	Faculty/Staff
Junior	19.7	NA
Senior	21.0	NA
Graduate	7.9	NA
Computer Literacy:		
None	9.0	6.7
Somewhat	71.2	56.7
Very	19.8	36.6
Hours per week working on a computer		
None	6.5	1.7
1-5	46.3	16.7
6-10	24.1	18.3
11-15	9.6	8.3
16-20	4.6	16.7
More than 20	8.9	38.3

[1] Includes Native American, Alien, and Other categories.
[2] Includes Divorced, Widowed, and Cohabiting categories.

RESULTS

Table 12-2 shows that students, staff, and faculty overwhelmingly disapprove of people gaining access to others' computer accounts, reading their electronic mail, and destroying their computer files without authorization. Furthermore, they strongly support the illegality of this behavior. Additionally, the majority find these activities to be reprehensible and offensive, and they believe that those who engage in computer deviance should be punished and prosecuted in accordance with the law.

Table 12-2. Percentage Distribution of Attitudes Toward Unauthorized Computer Access

Unauthorized Access	Students		Faculty/Staff	
	Agree	Disagree	Agree	Disagree
Accessing another person's computer account for the purpose of browsing their e-mail should be illegal.	92.6	7.4	91.7	8.3
Accessing a company's computer system without authorization should be illegal.	92.0*	8.0	96.7*	3.3
I feel that accessing another person's computer account and destroying their files is reprehensible.	91.2**	8.8	96.7**	3.3
I feel that it is okay to access a university's computer system for the purpose of changing grades.	16.1	83.9***	3.5	96.5***
I find it offensive for a person to access another person's e-mail account without authorization.	92.6*	7.4	100.0*	0.0
I disapprove of people accessing (hacking) computer systems without authorization.	87.0***	13.0	98.3***	1.7
People (hackers) who access computer systems without authorization should be punished and/or prosecuted in accordance with the law.	87.3**	12.7	96.7**	3.3

*p < .01   **p < .005   ***p < .001

According to Table 12-3, the majority of students feel that there is nothing wrong with copying and sharing computer software among friends, while the majority of faculty and staff disapprove of this behavior. However, students, faculty, and staff overwhelmingly disapprove of people copying computer software and then selling it to others. Of those responding, nearly 59 percent of the students agree that there is nothing wrong with copying commercially sold software compared to 25 percent of the faculty/staff; 81 percent of the students compared to 30 percent of the faculty/staff feel that there is nothing wrong with sharing commercially sold software among friends; 46 percent of the students find this activity to be reprehensible, compared to 59 percent of the faculty/staff; 43 percent of the students disapprove of others copying commercially sold software compared to nearly 70 percent of the faculty/staff; and only 42 percent of the students believe that people who copy commercially sold software should be punished or prosecuted for copyright infringement violations compared to nearly 66 percent of the faculty and staff.

Table 12-3. Percentage Distribution of Attitudes Toward Software Piracy

Software Piracy	Students		Faculty/Staff	
	Agree	Disagree	Agree	Disagree
I feel that there is nothing wrong with copying commercially-sold computer software.	58.5**	41.5	25.0	75.0**
I feel that there is nothing wrong with sharing commercially-sold software among friends.	81.2**	18.8	30.0	70.0**
I feel that copying commercially-sold software and selling it to another person is okay.	16.7	83.3**	3.3	96.7**
I feel that copying commercially-sold computer software is reprehensible.	46.3	53.7*	59.3*	40.7
I disapprove of people copying commercially-sold computer software.	43.1	56.9**	69.5**	30.5
People who copy commerically-sold software should bepunished and/or prosecuted for copyright infringement violations.	42.2	57.8**	65.5**	34.5

*p < .01   **p < .005   ***p < .001

Finally, Tables 12-4 and 12-5 examine, by discipline area, the percentage of students who disapprove of unauthorized computer access and software piracy. As Table 12-4 reflects, the majority of students in all of the discipline areas overwhelming disapprove of others' accessing computer accounts and files without authorization, although students in the engineering and technology disciplines appear to have less aversion to this activity. This result tends to support Coldwell's

(1997) attitudinal study of college students, which found that students in the engineering and technology disciplines do not consider unauthorized access to another person's computer system to be unethical. Furthermore, Coldwell (1997) argues that students in engineering and technology are socialized into their disciplines and appear to be more comfortable with machines than with people. Students who are attracted to the engineering and technology disciplines may "have something missing, socially" (Coldwell, 1997, p. 415); however, this would be difficult to validate without additional research.

Table 12-4. Percentage of Students by Discipline Disapproving of
Unauthorized Computer Access

Unauthorized Access	Business	Humanities	Education	Natural Science	Social Science	Engineering and Technology
Accessing another person's computer account for the purpose of browsing their e-mail should be illegal.	93.1	87.1	94.1	95.2	95.6	81.6
Accessing a company's computer system without authorization should be illegal.*	82.2	90.6	100.0	97.6	92.6	84.2
I feel that accessing another person's computer account and destroying their files is reprehensible.	85.2	90.6	91.2	95.0	94.8	81.6
I feel it is okay to access a university's computer system for the purpose of changing grades.*	75.0	71.9	88.5	78.6	91.2	73.7
I find it offensive for a person to access another person's e-mail account without authorization.	85.7	87.5	91.2	100.0	95.6	84.2

Table 12-4. Percentage of Students by Discipline Disapproving of
Unauthorized Computer Access - continued

Unauthorized Access	Business	Humanities	Education	Natural Science	Social Science	Engineering and Technology
I disapprove of people (hackers) accessing computer systems without authorization.	82.1	84.4	88.2	92.9	89.0	79.0
People (hackers) who access computer systems without authorization should be punished and/or prosecuted in accordance with the law.	85.7	93.8	85.3	92.9	88.8	76.3

*p < .05

In contrast, Table 12-5 reveals that most students approve of copying commercially sold software, especially if it is to be shared among friends. However, the majority of students in all discipline areas disapprove of people copying commercially sold software and selling it to others. Interestingly, students in the natural sciences and the engineering and technology disciplines appear more likely to approve the use of pirated software as compared to those students in the other disciplines. Presumably, students and professionals in the natural sciences and in engineering and technology utilize computers and various types of software more frequently than those in other disciplines. These attitudinal results coincide to what Hollinger (1993) found in his computer crime study on college campuses; engineering and science majors reported the highest levels of software piracy.

Table 12-5. Percentage of Students by Discipline Disapproving of Software Pirach

Unauthorized Access	Business	Humanities	Education	Natural Science	Social Science	Engineering and Technology
I feel that there is nothing wrong with copying commercially-sold computer software.	46.4	53.1	47.1	29.3	45.6	23.7
I feel that there is nothing wrong with sharing commercially-sold software among friends.	21.4	28.1	20.6	7.1	18.4	21.1
I feel that copying commercially-sold computer software and then selling it to another person is okay.	96.4	78.1	82.4	83.3	83.0	79.0
I feel that copying commercially-sold computer software is reprehensible.*	44.0	63.3	35.3	45.0	47.7	35.1
I disapprove of people copying commercially-sold computer software.**	50.0	64.5	35.3	42.9	43.6	26.3
People who copy commercially-sold software should be punished and/or prosecuted for copyright infringement violations.*	63.0	61.3	38.2	35.7	40.7	27.0

*p < .01   **p < .001

DISCUSSION AND CONCLUSION

As we move into the 21st century, computer-related crime appears to be one of the greatest challenges facing the law enforcement community. Several factors make computer crime a difficult problem to address. First, individuals who violate the law have integrated highly technical methods with traditional crimes and developed creative new crimes as well. Second, they use computers to cross state and international boundaries electronically, thus complicating investigations. Finally, the evidence of these crimes is not always tangible and may only exist as some type of programmable code or electronic impulse (Carter & Katz, 1996). Unfortunately, the police, and even "cyber cops," have fallen behind in the computer age and must overcome a steep technological learning curve.

Computer crime poses an increasingly real threat to our society. Money and intellectual property have been stolen, corporate operations impeded, and sensitive or classified information compromised as a result of computer crime (Forester & Morrison, 1990; Stoll, 1990; Schwartau, 1994; Shimomura & Markoff, 1996). As previously mentioned, the economic impact of computer crime is staggering.

Most of the empirical research to date focuses on prevalence and incidence rates of computer-related crime on college campuses and in the corporate world. In a study measuring computer-crime attitudes, Coldwell (1997) finds that students in the engineering and technology disciplines do not consider "hacking" into other people's computer systems to be unethical. Additionally, Coldwell (1997) posits that these students do not seem to be aware of the social consequences of computer crime as compared to those in other disciplines. Similar to Coldwell (1997), this study reveals that students in the engineering and technology disciplines appear to have less aversion to people accessing computer accounts without authorization as compared to those in the other disciplines. As Coldwell (1997) suggests, there may be some type of underlying socialization going on with those who study engineering or major in one of the technological specialties; however, additional research investigating this purported socialization connection is necessary in an effort to either confirm or refute this claim.

Generally, most of the respondents in this study disapprove of people accessing computer systems without authorization, and they support the illegality of this behavior. In other words, there are no significant differences between students and faculty/staff regarding unauthorized access to computer systems. On the other hand, there are some significant differences between students and faculty/staff regarding software piracy. The majority of the students feel that there is nothing wrong with copying and sharing computer software among friends, while the majority of faculty and staff disapprove of this behavior. This result may give rise to an increased interest in Hollinger's (1988) theory, which supposes that computer deviance follows a linear progression with software piracy as its first stage. His theory is supported by others who propose the notion that *career criminality* is on a continuum. Clinard and Quinney (1973) argue that criminality progresses from minor offenses to more severe crimes for career criminals. This relationship may be similar for those who have "careers" in computer deviance.

Like most research utilizing survey data, this study has its limitations. The present study can not be generalized to the population because a random sampling of students was not obtained. Although the instrument used here is reliable and has internal consistency, the possibility exists that respondents may not have accurately or honestly answered some of the items.

Even though relevant literature (Parker, 1976; Bequai, 1982; American Bar Association, 1984; O'Donoghue, 1986; Zajac, 1986; BloomBecker, 1988; Stoll, 1990; Sterling, 1992; Hollinger, 1993; Shimomura & Markoff, 1996) suggests that computer-related crime is a significant problem facing our society, the true nature and extent of it is not known. Continued research measuring both attitudes and prevalence rates should be considered.

Researchers should continue to explore computer crime in greater detail with an emphasis on learning the origins, methods, and motivations of a growing technologically informed criminal group. And as the literature (Parker, 1976; Coldwell, 1997) suggests, students may be socialized to learn "hacker" ethics at an early age through the educational process. Decision makers in law enforcement, government, and business may use this emerging body of knowledge to develop policies, methods, and regulations in an effort to detect computer crime incidents, investigate and prosecute the perpetrators, and prevent future crimes.

Just as law enforcement agencies have developed specialized units to investigate white collar crime, domestic violence, and drug use, they must initiate similar programs for computer crime (Carter & Katz, 1996). Because computer crime investigations are very specialized, law enforcement personnel must receive the appropriate technological training to keep pace with those committing these offenses.

The computer age has allowed our society to flourish in many ways. Unfortunately, the computer age has ushered in new types of crime for law enforcement personnel to address. The challenge of the criminal justice system is to seek ways to keep the drawbacks affiliated with computer technology from overshadowing the great promise of the computer age.

REFERENCES

American Bar Association. (1984). *Report on computer crime.* Washington, DC: Task Force on Computer Crime, Section of Criminal Justice.

Bequai, A. (1982). *Computer crime.* Lexington, MA: D. C. Heath and Company.

BloomBecker, J.J. (1988). *Introduction to computer crime.* Santa Cruz, CA: National Center for Computer Crime Data.

Carter, D.L., & Katz, A.J. (1996, December). Computer crime: An emerging challenge for law enforcement. *FBI Law Enforcement Bulletin,* 1-8.

Chang, P.T., & Chang, R.H. (1985). Social issues and computerbased management information systems. *Free Inquiry in Creative Sociology, 13,* 7579.

Chernicky, D. (1996, April 20). Hampton teens arrested for online fraud. *The Daily Press,* C12.

Clinard, M.B., & Quinney, R. (1973). *Criminal Behavior Systems: A Typology* (2nd ed.). New York: Holt, Rinehart and Winston.

Cohen, F.B. (1995). *Protection and Security on the Information Superhighway.* New York: John Wiley and Sons.

Coldwell, R.A. (1997). University students' attitudes towards computer crime: A research note. In R.C. Hollinger (Ed.), *Crime, Deviance and the Computer* (pp. 413-416). Brookfield, VT: Dartmouth.

Collier, P.A., & Spaul, B.J. (1992). Problems in policing computer crime. *Policing and Society, 2,* 307320.

Fagin, J.A. (1997). Computer crime: A technology gap. In R. C. Hollinger (Ed.), *Crime, Deviance and the Computer* (pp. 197-209). Brookfield, VT: Dartmouth.

Forester, T., & Morrison, P. (1990). Computer crime: New problem for the information society. *Prometheus, 8,* 257271.

Herig, J. A. (1989). *Computer crime in Florida: 1989.* Tallahassee, FL: Florida Department of Law Enforcement.

Hollinger, R. C. (1984, November 7). Computer deviance: Receptivity to electronic rulebreaking. Paper presented at the annual meeting of the American Society of Criminology, Cincinnati, OH.

Hollinger, R. C. (1988). Computer hackers follow a Guttmanlike progression. *Sociology and Social Research, 72,* 199200.

Hollinger, R. C. (1993). Crime by computer: Correlates of software piracy and unauthorized account access. *Security Journal, 4*, 212.

Johnson, D. G. (1997). Crime, abuse, and hacker ethics. In R. C. Hollinger (Ed.), *Crime, Deviance and the Computer* (pp. 447-467). Brookfield, VT: Dartmouth.

Michalowski, R. J., & Pfuhl, E. H. (1991). Technology, property, and law: The case of computer crime. *Crime, Law and Social Change, 15*, 255275.

Nycum, S. H. (1986). Computer crime legislation in the United States. *Israel Law Review, 21*, 6489.

O'Donoghue, J. (1986). *The 1986 Mercy College report on computer crime in the Forbes 500 corporations: The Strategies of Containment.* Dobbs Ferry, NY: Mercy College.

Parker, D. B. (1976). *Crime by computer.* New York: Charles Scribner and Sons.

Parker, D. B. (1989). *Computer crime: Criminal justice resource manual.* Washington, DC: National Institute of Justice.

Power, R. (1995). *Current and future danger: A CSI primer on computer crime and information warfare.* San Francisco: Computer Security Institute.

Schwartau, W. (1994). *Information warfare: Chaos on the electronic superhighway.* New York: Thunder Mouth Press.

Shimomura, T., & Markoff, J. (1996). *Takedown.* New York: Hyperion.

Sterling, B. (1992). *The Hacker Crackdown: Law and Disorder on the Electronic Frontier.* New York: Bantam.

Stoll, C. (1990). *The Cuckoo's Egg: Tracking a Spy Through the Maze of Computer Espionage.* New York: Pocket Books.

Swinyard, W.R., Rinne, H., & Kau, A. K. (1997). The morality of software piracy: A crosscultural analysis. In R. C. Hollinger (Ed.), *Crime, Deviance and the Computer* (pp. 391-400). Brookfield, VT: Dartmouth.

Zajac, B. J. (1986). Computer fraud in college: A case study. *Journal of Security Administration, 9*, 1321.

Chapter 13

AN ASSESSMENT OF COMPUTER CRIME VICTIMIZATION IN THE UNITED STATES

ANDRA J. KATZ AND DAVID L. CARTER

With the growth of technology and the evolution of computerization, we have not only seen new types of crime emerge, but the character of these crimes has changed rapidly as a result of developing technological capacities. Certainly there has been some empirical exploration of these offenses, most of which has been done by private security organizations largely along the lines of a risk assessment for specific industries. While these inquiries have provided new insights, they have generally been narrowly focused and unpublished. While there have been increasing numbers of books and publications on computer-related crime, they tend to address specific issues or cases. In essence, a comprehensive, contemporary, and empirical review of (1) the character of computer-related crime and (2) the consequences of computer-related crime appears not to exist. Given the dramatic economic impact these offenses can have, greater information is needed for policy makers, law makers, and investigators.

Several factors suggest why computer-related crime has not been comprehensively investigated:

• Given the emotional concerns of the public and criminal justice officials associated with violent crime in America today, the seemingly "distant" or impersonal nature of computer-related crime is more easily ignored (except for its victims).

• In the authors' preliminary research, it has been found that many law enforcement officials do not envision computer-related crime as a problem that effects them, thus little attention has been given to it.

219

• Many of the crimes–such as theft of intellectual property, unlawful transfers of money, telecommunications fraud, and data tampering–are sufficiently distinct from the types of crimes that criminal justice officials are accustomed to dealing with that they do not understand their character and impact.

• The technical nature of computer-related crime is somewhat intimidating, or at least confusing, to those with limited computer-related experience, thus the potential crime issues of these technologies are avoided.

• In the authors' experiences and preliminary research, it has been found that many view computer-related crime somewhat "unidimensionally"–i.e., such as theft from a computer–not envisioning the wide array (and ever-broadening) nature of computer-related offenses. As such, the impact and breadth of the problem is diminished from their perspective.

• Technology and technological capability coupled with the innovation of computer criminals (who tend to be very bright), changes so rapidly, it is difficult to keep abreast of changes and developments.

A SYNOPSIS OF THE LITERATURE

According to Parker, the lack of attention historically paid to computer crime is no accident. "In 1970, a number of researchers concluded that the problem was merely a small part of the effort of technology on society and not worthy of specific explicit research" (1989, p. 5). However, "the increase in substantial losses associated with intentional acts involving computers proved the fallacy of this view" (Parker, 1989, p. 5).

Another setback for computer crime research came in the mid-1970's. "Researchers believed that the involvement of computers should be subordinate to the study of each specific type of crime, both manual and automated" (Parker, 1989, p. 5). To reinforce this, researchers pointed out the fact that "the uniqueness of characteristics of computer crime across all the different types of crime was not considered sufficient to warrant explicit research" (Parker, 1989, p. 5). Consequently, research focused on "real" crimes (i.e., violence) while treating computer criminality with secondary, or even tertiary importance (Katz, 1995). Essentially, the potential impact of computer crime was not envisioned. Just as there has been little research in this venue, law enforcement officials have given it limited attention because of its seemingly "distant and complex" nature. Preliminary research has shown that "many public law enforcement officials do not envision computer-related crime as a problem that affects them" (Carter, 1995a, p. 2). Yet, a wide array of anecdotes show this not to be the case. Recognition is slowly changing with the creation of computer crime units in the Secret Service, Air Force OSI, and FBI; growth of such organizations as the Florida Association of Computer Crime Investigators and the High Tech Crime Investigators Association; and computer crime specialists in local police departments as well as new units in such diverse organizations as the Royal Canadian Mounted Police, Royal Thai Police, and London Metropolitan Police. Still, as one respondent to this study observed,

> I feel the weakest link is the lack of education in [public] law enforcement relating to computer-technology crimes. The law enforcement community has devoted [itself] to the high priority violent crimes lumping computer crimes into a low priority status, yet the losses to computer crime could fund a small country.

Despite common assumptions, computers are not used solely as a tool in white-collar crime, but have also served as instrumentalities for crime against persons. Pedophile bulletin board systems (BBS) and the "set-ups" of young people for sexual assault based on contacts and discussions through commercial on-line systems and the Internet are examples. Linking computers to violent crime may be one method to generate increased resources for research and planning in this arena.

Coupled with their "impersonal" nature, computer crimes are inherently technical (Katz, 1995). These crimes "are sufficiently distinct from the types of crimes that criminal justice officials are accustomed to dealing with that they do not understand their character and impact" (Carter, 1995a, p.2). Additionally, "the technical nature of computer-related crime is intimidating to those with limited computer-related experience, thus the potential criminality related to those technologies is something which simply cannot be understood" (Carter, 1995a, p.2).

Cyberspace in its current, largely unregulated, state has created a breeding ground for a variety of criminal enterprises. Crimes and incidents of malfeasance, ranging from theft, stolen services, smuggling, terrorism, pornography, sexual harassment, stalking, and the spread of hate messages by extremists, have and continue to be occurring at substantial levels (Katz, 1995).

Ingenuity on the part of criminals, coupled with easy access, has led to a new generation of perpetrators. The ability to commit computer-related crimes is both increasingly easy and probable. Not only does cyberspace provide a seemingly unlimited supply of information, but also an unlimited supply of victims. The frequently high stakes pay-off from a computer crime, the speed at which crimes can occur (with some incursions lasting as little as three milliseconds), the ability to include a programming code instructing the software to "erase itself" after the incursion is executed, and the fact that the criminal can be in another country when executing the criminal commands are all among the reasons to believe that computer crimes will increase at a substantial pace (Carter, 1995b).

Who Commits Computer Crime: "Insiders" or "Outsiders"?

While there is some debate about who poses the greatest risk as a "technocriminal," the fact remains that anyone who has the capabilities or skills may pose a threat to computer security (Katz, 1995). Determining whether a crime is the job of an employee or an "outsider" is often difficult to do. However, certain "red flags" may emerge. One example is that of companies which rely on a closed local area network (LAN). The fact that there is only limited or, in some cases, no external network access from the company virtually eliminates the probability for "outsiders" to penetrate the system. Although a closed LAN is a safeguard, doing business in today's society oftentimes does not make it economically feasible for businesses to electronically cut themselves off from the outside world (Katz, 1995). Businesses that are "well-connected" are able to significantly surpass the commerce of those who remain electronically isolated. The pursuit of growing business options is often initiated by corporate leaders with limited thought of the security threats. A balance must be struck. One security official told the researchers, "Security is viewed as an 'add on;' 'an obstacle;' 'a necessary evil.' CEOs should view us as an investment. With effective security, profits will rise and losses will fall."

While "outsiders" may pose a serious threat, at this point in time computer crimes tend to be "inside" jobs. According to Van Duyn (1985, p. 4), "insiders pose a far greater threat to the organization's computer security than outside 'electronic invaders' possibly could." The reason being that "insiders are familiar with their employers' data processing operations and the type of data each system and application is storing and processing" and therefore know exactly where to look for information. The emergence of networking and user-friendly protocols are beginning to change this balance.

As Van Duyn (1985) notes, vulnerability from within an organization is the most dangerous and poses the most serious threat. A number of studies support this conclusion. In fact, "one study estimated that 90 percent of economic computer crimes were committed by employees of the victimized companies" (U.N. Commission on Crime and Criminal Justice, 1995). A more recent study conducted in North America and Europe found that 73 percent of the risk to computer security was from internal sources, while only 23 percent was attributable to external sources (U.N. Commission on Crime and Criminal Justice, 1995). Unlike "outsiders" attempting to break into a system, "insiders" are oftentimes able to more easily circumvent safeguards therefore reducing their chances of being detected. Moreover, if the employee has authorized access to the information, but chooses to steal or destroy it, then detection is even more difficult.

"Insiders" also have a distinct advantage, for not only do they often know immediately where to look for the data, but, if in doubt, "they can reference the systems documentation which usually includes programming specifications, file and record layouts, a data element dictionary, and so on" (Van Duyn, 1985, p. 4). Most significantly, "insiders" have a better idea on how to locate and gain access to crucial information such as financial, marketing, manufacturing, technological, or research data.

Consistent with evidence that "insiders" pose the greatest threat to computer security, Parker (1989) cites several factors which alone or in conjunction with others help to create an atmosphere conducive to computer crime within organizations. The first factor identified by

Parker (1989) is that perpetrators are often young. He notes that it is not youth, in and of itself, which translates into a generation of computer criminals. However, "younger people in data processing occupations tend to have received their education in universities and colleges where attacking computer systems has become common and is sometimes condoned as an educational activity" (Parker, 1989, p. 39).

Differential association may also help explain vulnerabilities which expose organizations to computer crime (Katz, 1995). Modifying the theory to a workplace environment, Parker (1989, p. 39) states that it "is the white-collar criminals' tendency to deviate in only small ways from the accepted practices of their associates." The vulnerability erupts from "groups of people working together and mutually encouraging and stimulating one another to engage in unauthorized acts that escalate into serious crimes" (Parker, 1989, p. 39). The potential for one-upmanship becomes magnified as the acts escalate in risk and sophistication.

METHODS

One of the difficulties in conducting exploratory research is to properly define and frame the variables to be assessed. Intuitively, one knows the issues at hand and the broad goal to be accomplished; however, operationalizing those variables can become problematic. In the current study, the research parameters were more strongly directed by current anecdotal information about computer-related abuses than previous research.

Based upon a content analysis of anecdotes obtained from interviews with practitioners working on computer crime cases, information downloaded from various sources on the Internet and key word searches of news services, the authors framed a number of variables for analysis. This was followed by further interviews with corporate security directors and investigators in order to clearly define critical information which was needed. During this process it became evident that obtaining interval and ratio information from businesses (such as explicit details on victimization, losses, active investigations, and personnel actions associated with computer abuse) would be virtually impossible. One reason was the lack of comprehensive and accessible records. More importantly, however, was the reluctance of businesses to admit their computer-based vulnerabilities.

After four iterations of the survey draft, an instrument was developed using nominal and ordinal variables which would seek much of the desired information, albeit less robust than originally planned. The survey was pretested among a small group of academicians and practitioners who reviewed it for clarity, terminology, substance, and structure. Modifications were made based on the feedback and balanced with the research project's goals.

Given the nature of the study, it was determined that the best source of information would be corporate security professionals. A purposive sampling frame was first selected from the American Society of Industrial Security (ASIS) membership. As defined by Kerlinger (1973, p. 129), purposive sampling is a nonprobability sample which is "characterized by the use of judgment and a deliberate effort to obtain representative samples by including presumably typical areas or groups in the sample." Such was the case in this study based upon the sampling needs.

Since ASIS has a worldwide membership of people who hold a wide range of positions it was necessary to segregate the membership based upon the member's position (i.e., corporate security directors) and businesses likely to have computers which would be the target of crime or abuse. In order to control, to the extent possible, the subjectivity of this stratification, the researchers were careful to include a broad range of business in the sampling frame. Airlines, telecommunications companies, banks, utilities, retailers, manufacturers, energy companies, the defense industry, and government agencies are examples of this range. The sampling frame was also limited to United States residents both for reduced mailing costs and because of the time and complications associated with surveying overseas members.

The actual sample of 600 people was randomly selected from the purposive sampling frame. The sample size was based on the recognition that, given the subject, the response rate would likely be low. Consequently, the researchers used a larger sample size as a means to increase the probability of representativeness of the population and ensure a sufficient number of responses to meet the assumptions needed for statistical testing.

Given that the data are at nominal and ordinal levels, the primary test for bivariate analysis was the Chi-Squared (X2) test of independence to determine significant relationships between the variables. When a relationship was identified, Phi was used to determine the strength of correlation (covariance). Finally, Cramer's V was examined as a gauge of the overall strength of the association. A weakness of Cramer's V in the current study is that many of the variable scales are narrow and, as a consequence, the ability to discriminate the variance is reduced (thus, Cramer's V would consistently be low). Despite this limitation, when all three statistics are viewed collectively, they provide reliable indicators from which conclusions may be drawn.

The sample members were sent a letter of introduction containing a statement of confidentiality, a survey, and a return envelope. Recipients were urged to complete the survey as soon as possible and promised a copy of the results if they sent a business card or called a toll-free number (88 people requested the survey findings.) Two weeks after the survey was mailed, a postcard reminder was sent with the closing date two weeks after that.

A total 183 surveys were returned (30.5%); however, not all could be used because they were improperly completed, not legible, or the respondent refused to complete the survey because of corporate policy. As one respondent noted, "(u)nderstandably, companies that have experienced some of the [computer crimes] are reluctant to disclose their experiences." There were 151 usable responses for a usable return rate of 25.2 percent. While the overall response rate is lower than desired, the number of usable responses is sufficiently high to provide insightful descriptive trends in addition to exceeding the assumptions and cell sizes needed for statistical testing.

VICTIMIZATION

The extent and nature of computer crime appears to be on a rapidly ascending curve. A study conducted by the American Bar Association in 1987 found that of the 300 corporations and government agencies surveyed, 72 (24%) claimed to have been the victim of a computer-related crime in the 12 months prior to the survey (U.N. Commission on Crime and Criminal Justice, 1995). The estimated losses from these crimes ranged from $145 million to $730 million over the one-year period. This broad range is illustrative of the problem in estimating losses. Not only is it difficult to identify and document these crimes, it is even more difficult to place a monetary value on the loss of intellectual property wherein the actual value may not be known for months or years.

Two years later, the Florida Department of Law Enforcement (FDLE) surveyed 898 public and private sector organizations which conducted business by computer. Of the 403 (44.9%) respondents, 25 percent reported they had been victimized by computer criminals (FDLE, 1989). The Florida study found embezzlement of funds by employees to be a major source of the crimes; however, no attempt to estimate losses was made because, according to one of the researchers interviewed, "losses would have been nothing more than a guess."

In perhaps one of the most comprehensive studies, conducted in 1991, a survey was done of 3,000 Virtual Address Extension (VAX) sites in Canada, Europe, and the United States to assess computer security threats and crimes. The results show that 72 percent of the respondents reported a security incident had occurred within the previous 12 months with 43 percent reporting the incident was criminal in nature (U.N. Commission on Crime and Criminal Justice, 1995). By far, the greatest security threats came from employees or people who had access to the computers; however, a number of external security breeches from hackers telephoning into the systems or accessing via networks was reported. The ABA and FDLE studies scarcely even mentioned this "external threat" and gave little attention to it as a growing problem. This is not surprising, however, since, as noted previously, networking in the late 1980s was predominantly used by the military, academics, and researchers. Access was comparatively limited and networking technology was more expensive. However, the 1991 United Nations study suggested that external threats via remote access was a problem which would grow in the years to come. Despite this concern, past research suggests that threats of computer crime generally come from employees, just like much of the theft in retail businesses.

The data in this study show a trend of victimization which increased significantly over previous studies, with 98.5 percent of the respondents reporting they had been victimized—43.3 percent reported being victimized more than twenty-five times. While these numbers seem dramatic, security professionals with whom these results were discussed stated they were surprised at the frequency of admitted victimization, not actual victimization. One respondent stated, "Do we know the national or even local scope of the computer crime threat? Probably not, but it has to be higher than anyone wants to admit."

This level of victimization leads one to ask who are the perpetrators? Consistent with previous research, the most common perpetrators reported in this research were employees. The primary threat comes from full-time employees, followed by part-time and "outsource" employees, with computer hackers a close third, a finding which was expected since there appears to be a correlation between theft and access to computers (Hefernan, 1995). However, the important dynamic to recognize is that "access" is changing dramatically with networking.

THEFT

Not surprisingly, the fastest growing computer-related crime was theft. However, an interesting facet of this crime supports the forecast of Toffler—the most common "commodity" stolen was information. Respondents reported that intellectual property was the most common target of thieves including such things as new product plans, new product descriptions, research, marketing plans, prospective customer lists, and similar information. One respondent observed the conflict between security and business by stating, "Outside individuals hacking into our computer is a problem and a potential threat. Its hard to stop without jeopardizing business communications and networking."

To illustrate one method of information theft, a security experiment was described to the researchers during an interview. A major corporate research laboratory uses the Internet to search for information on new product plans. In a test of the system, an information specialist "hacked" into the Internet communications of two researchers and recorded their search inquiries and the Uniform Resource Locator (URL) addresses (including both Web sites and Gophers) the researchers "visited." The key word search inquiries and access sites were given to an independent researcher in the same field who immediately hypothesized the type of product the company was working on and the "new dimension" of the product. When confronted with the results of this experiment, the researchers confirmed the hypotheses were correct. While this was a security experiment, the survey respondents had more concrete experiences of direct theft. One respondent, commenting on information theft, framed the problem this way, "company plans, research, products, etc. have been lost this way creating financial losses and job losses."

The research findings show there was a significant relationship between personal use of company computers and increases of intellectual property theft ($X^2 = 15.64869$, df = 6, p <.01). Personal use of computers ranged from simple word processing to use of spread sheets for personal finances to accessing the Internet. In many cases, these uses were either permitted or, more typically, overlooked. Perhaps one of the problems is that when an employee has a workstation where personal activities are performed, the employee begins to view this portal as being proprietary. As a consequence, the impact of thefts, particularly that of intellectual property which does not have a "tangible" value, is not as readily perceived as being wrong, thereby making the theft psychologically "easier."

Generally speaking, thefts were discovered by an audit trail showing access to information where the user had no legitimate need, by an informant who told the business of the theft, or the theft was surmised based on external information, such as the actions or products of a competitor. There is a wide body of research which shows the value of stolen trade secrets and intellectual property (Hefernan, 1995; Tripp, 1995; U.S. Congress, 1995). Traditionally this information was stolen by compromising employees, photocopying documents, burglary, or surveillance of company personnel and practices. Increasingly, however, theft from computers is the desired methodology because it is more comprehensive, more reliable, easier, more "consumable" and contains less risk for detection and capture.

Intellectual property was not the only target of thieves; there was also a significant relationship between personal use of company computers and employees stealing or attempting to steal money ($X^2 = 13.8424$, df = 6, p <.05). In most cases, employees who attempted to steal money were identified before an actual loss was sustained. The reason for this was that it was easier to account for monetary losses, which required some type of electronic transaction, as opposed to intellectual property theft which simply requires the copying of files. Moreover, monetary files had more security controls and were monitored more closely than information files. Finally, there are fewer monetary files than information files. As a consequence, cash accounting is easier to monitor.

Despite this, monetary thefts have nonetheless occurred. In Detroit, a "small time" computer hacker cracked a bank's computer system, opened a new account, and methodically transferred small amounts of money into it from existing accounts. One survey respondent summarized the issue succinctly, "Losses are sometimes very large. We just lost $1 million."

The analysis of these variables proved insightful. When part-time employees and computer hackers were tested against the same dependent variables, no significant relationship was found. This reinforces the fact that full-time employees pose the greatest threat to theft by computer. Moreover, both the vulnerability of intellectual property and the extrinsic value it holds makes such information a tempting target.

UNAUTHORIZED ACCESS TO FILES: "SNOOPING"

The practice of "snooping" refers to a person's unauthorized opening of files in order to "see what's in there." A snooper's motive may be curiosity, the challenge of entering an unauthorized area, or evaluation of the information to determine if it has value and can be taken. Somewhat akin to a criminal trespass, it is sometimes difficult to ascertain if a law was broken, a company policy was violated, an ethical standard was breached, or the behavior was simply poor judgment. Snooping tends to vary along this continuum, depending largely on security controls, custom within the organization, and corporate policy on accessing information. One security professional told the researchers that most cases of snooping in his company were simply curiosity or "cyber-voyeurism" where there was no malicious intent. Even in cases of hackers, he felt that most were interested in the challenge rather than to commit a theft.

Despite these experiences of one professional, the data indicated otherwise. There were significant relationships between snooping by full-time employees and stealing or attempting to steal intellectual property ($X^2 = 15.48614$, df = 6, p <.05) and stealing or attempting to steal money ($X^2 = 23.72249$, df = , p <.001). In the case of stealing intellectual property, it appears snooping was done to identify the nature of available information, its potential value, and the ability to steal the information. In the case of money, snooping was most likely done to better understand the file structure, determine transaction protocols, locate accounts most susceptible to theft with a lower probability of discovery, and test security for access control and authentication roadblocks (something akin to a burglar "casing" a target). Clearly in both cases, snooping was a significant precursor to criminality.

Significant results were also found among part-time employees' snooping and stealing or attempting to steal intellectual property ($X^2 = 19.17477$, $df = 6$, $p < .005$) and part-time employees stealing or attempting to steal money ($X^2 = 25.66591$, $df = 6$, $p < .001$). Importantly, the findings of both full-time and part-time employees are strongly supported and based on similar reasoning. While not as strong overall, there was a significant relationship between snooping by hackers ($X^2 = 17.68774$, $df = 6$, $p < .01$) and stealing or attempting to steal intellectual property while there was no significant relationship between snooping by hackers and monetary theft. With the growth of networking, a similar analysis in the next few years or so may find different results.

Conventional wisdom seems to suggest that snoopers are more of a nuisance than a threat. However, the data suggest that snooping is an exploratory activity which leads to a theft or attempted theft in a significant number of instances. Organizational policy, employee supervision, and security measures should be reviewed to ensure that snooping activities are detected and resolved.

VIRUS INTRODUCTION

Viruses are created for a wide array of reasons and can have many different effects depending on the creator's intent. For those malcontent computer users who are looking for "ready made" viruses, there is a BBS in France, accessible via the Internet, which has a large collection of diverse viruses which can be downloaded and then introduced into the targeted computer. Certainly the capacity to infect a computer is available and is occurring on an increasing, although not epidemic, basis.

According to the data, 66.3 percent of the responding businesses reported viruses had been introduced into business computers over the past five years. When tested, the data show significant relationships of virus introduction by hackers attempting or stealing intellectual property ($X^2 = 34.62849$, df = 9, p <.001) and by hackers attempting or stealing money ($X^2 = 36.52177$, df = 9, p <.001). This is supported by anecdotal evidence that hackers would try to destroy any evidence of their presence, destroy evidence of their crime, and increase the difficulty of detecting and investigating a theft (or intrusion) by introduction of a virus. Essentially, the virus was meant to be a smoke screen for the incursion. This does not mean that hackers only used viruses to cover up a theft–indeed there is evidence that viruses are also introduced as a means to "protest" a company policy or simply as a game. What the strong findings suggest are that in a notable number of cases where computer thefts occur, a virus is introduced. The caveat to investigators is to be certain to also look for evidence of thefts whenever a virus is introduced via network or modem access.

Beyond hackers, there was also a significant relationship between a part-time employee's theft or attempted theft and a virus introduction ($X^2 = 36.18864$, df = 9, p <.001). The rationale is the same for part-time employees as it is for hackers. Interestingly, there was no significant relationship between virus introduction and any behavior by full-time employees. Anecdotal evidence suggests that employees have placed viruses in computer systems for a number of reasons. According to the National Computer Security Association, an important reason for the increase in computer viruses is the massive terminations and layoffs afflicting the corporate landscape. Some employees may feel that they are being coldly dismissed after years of loyalty and a growing number see inserting a virus into the corporate computer system as a way of striking back.

Interestingly, 82.6 percent of the respondents reported that antivirus software had been loaded on company computers. Given the relative inexpense and ease of such software in comparison to the damage which could be caused by the virus, it would seem that virus protection would be prudent insurance for the security professional to take. Thus it was surprising that not all companies had antiviral software. While not directly comparable, it appears that the portion of respondents who do not have antiviral software is about the same as those who are not connected to the Internet nor have external modem access. One might assume that if these are the same companies, security personnel are concluding that a virus threat does not exist since the computer has no "external connectivity." If this is the case, the researchers suggest that full-time employees also pose computer security risks. They obviously could–and have–introduced viruses as noted above.

This leads to the reasons viruses are introduced. While not empirically measured, interviews and anecdotes shed light on these motivations. Harassment of other employees, particularly with respect to "company politics" serves as one reason for viruses. If a fellow employee can cause problems to others, particularly in a company where one's success is measured in a competitive atmosphere against other employees, then a virus can be a good tool to gain an advantage. Harassment could also be the intent of a person who externally introduces the virus. For example, there is evidence that activists in both the environmental and animal rights movements have infected computers of companies which the activists view as having corporate policies which are harmful to their respective causes.

Retribution is a second reason. Employees who feel they have been treated unfairly, terminated without just reason, or are not appreciated, are likely to direct some type of revenge toward the company. A computer virus seems to be one method which fulfills that need because it can cause significant damage to the company, yet there is little chance one will get caught. A third reason for infecting a computer may simply be called "gamesmanship." In these cases the virus is typically introduced by a hacker to "play with" the system but with no intent to cause permanent damage. Despite this lack of malice, the business will still suffer some financial loss because of lower productivity while the virus is present and the cost related to eradicating the problem. Moreover, there could be accidental damage caused by the virus itself or attempts to repair the problem.

Another reason for infecting a computer is to impede the commerce of a business. Whether it is a hacker working at the behest of a competitor or an employee who has "sold out," a virus intended to impede commerce will typically cause major damage such as erasing files, mixing information so that it makes no sense, or locking up hardware so that the system software has to be reloaded. Whatever the effects of the virus, there are significant losses from actual costs of the virus eradication and system repair, there are losses from commerce during operational slowdowns–and in some cases stoppages–while the problem is being resolved, and undetermined losses of market share which may occur as a result of the problem. A final reason for infecting computers is to hide evidence of thefts. If a virus erases information, disrupts audit trails, or jumbles information, losses, even if detected, may be attributed to the virus, not a theft.

Since computer viruses are readily available with new ones being written all the time and the fact they are introduced by employees and hackers alike, the problem is truly real. The need to anticipate their insertion into a computer system is a logical security precaution which policy makers should address. As computer systems are increasingly networked, the problem will only increase.

HARASSMENT

Crime and misconduct are, of course, not products of technology but the products of human behavior. The technology is simply a way to facilitate criminality. While there is no general agreement among criminologists about what causes crime, the evidence suggests that causal or precipitating factors are on a continuum which includes, as a fundamental variable, opportunity. Technology provides the opportunity to commit crimes in several ways: the opportunity to have access to a valuable commodity, the opportunity to seize that commodity with relative ease, and the opportunity to take the property with a low probability of being apprehended. With the growth of networking and new hardware configurations and software, opportunities for crime have opened into a much broader arena.

As one illustration of this phenomenon, the data show that harassment of employees significantly increased as Local Area Networks (LAN) ($X^2 = 7.40053$, df = 3, p <.05) and file servers were increasingly used ($X^2 = 8.12483$, df = 3, p <.05). There are a number of reasons why employees would harass others including sexual harassment, various types of jealousy of others, the "teasing" of others which gets out of control, exercising power over others, company politics, retribution for being "wronged," and competitiveness that impedes the success of another. With the ease and anonymity which can be provided over networks, harassment has been a form of misconduct which appears to have flourished.

There was a significant relationship between full-time employee computer abuse and harassment of employees ($X^2 = 21.44211$, df $= 9$, p $<.05$). This statistical finding along with anecdotal evidence demonstrate a consistent theme which suggests that full-time employees who abuse their computer access privileges will do so for a number of reasons, including harassment. Perhaps one approach to minimize harassment is to have good access controls for E-mail while ensuring that the system does not permit E-mail to be delivered anonymously; instead messages should always be easily and readily identifiable. While some have argued that such controls stifle the creativity of employees who want to share innovative ideas for feedback, the process also stifles harassment. Thus, decisions have to be made on a case-by-case basis of whether harassment is a problem and a balance must be stricken between competing interests and system control.

DESTRUCTION OF "VIRTUAL PROPERTY"

In this study, "virtual property" specifically refers to both computer systems operating programs and data kept in computerized files. The data indicate that when people attempt to steal intellectual property there is a significant likelihood that there will be some destruction of the computer system or file server's operating programs. This is true whether the person is a full-time employee ($X^2 = 39.02557$, df $= 9$, p $<.001$), part-time employee ($X^2 = 39.12260$, df $= 9$, p $<.001$), or hacker ($X^2 = 60.49559$, df $= 9$, p $<.001$).

While there are very strong relationships for all three groups, the strongest was with the hackers. Perhaps this should be expected since hackers must access computers more "forcefully" thereby the probability for operating program damage would increase. Moreover, hackers do not have the same proprietary interest in virtual property that employees do nor do they have the same level of concern about identification and punishment as would an employee. Interestingly, while hackers are significantly less likely to steal information in comparison to employees, when they do attempt to steal, they are the most likely to damage operating programs.

Similar significant results were found when destruction of data files were tested against theft or attempted theft by full-time employees (X^2 = 33.40446, df = 9, p <.001), part-time employees (X^2 = 36.70534, df = 9, p <.001), and hackers (X^2 = 42.2734, df = 9, p <.001). Once again, the significant relationships are all strong with the hackers being particularly noteworthy. These findings reinforce those related to destruction of operating programs and add to the significance of the results. One point which becomes imminently clear from the results is that businesses are not only the victims of intellectual property theft, but they are consistently victims of virtual property destruction.

While not explicit in the data, one may speculate why operating programs and data files were destroyed during the course of thefts or attempts. There is a probability that the damage was accidental as a result of a trespassers probing restricted areas and attempts to take protected information. In some ways, this is similar to using an electronic sledge hammer to commit a cyber-burglary—there is bound to be collateral damage as a result.

Of course, the damage could also be intentional. The thief may simply need to damage the operating program as a means to access and steal the desired information. Another reason for the destruction may be an attempt to hide evidence of the intruder's presence; essentially, covering one's tracks. A third reason is to impede both discovery and investigation of the theft. It may be inevitable that the theft will be discovered, but if an investigation can be impeded, the thief's chance of evading detection or prosecution will be increased. A final reason may be to prevent a "competitive theft." That is, if information has potentially significant pay-off and competition is high, there is a likelihood that others may attempt to steal the information. As a means to prevent other thieves—i.e., competitors—from stealing the intellectual property, an intruder may destroy the operating programs.

When destruction of either operating programs or data files occurs, there is not only an intrinsic loss associated with that property, but also a loss of productivity, system repair costs, potential loss of market share, and costs associated with "catching up" after repairs are made and/or information is recovered. Costs grow geometrically, thus the losses can be substantial.

As a final point in this area, the data show significant relationships between the destruction of data files and the use of local area networks (X^2 = 13.10538, df = 3, p <.005) and the use of file servers (X^2 =

8.62766, df = 3, p <.05). There were no significant relationships between data file destruction and those companies using mainframe or mini-computers. Even when adjusting for the fact that there were fewer companies using these machines, thus lower chi-squared cell expectations, no relationships were found. Perhaps because the file servers and LANs are inherently more "network friendly" explains their relationships with property destruction.

There are some important policy implications from these findings. First, when damage to any virtual property has occurred, it should be assumed that a computer incursion has occurred until shown otherwise. The investigation should include an examination of "holes" in both authentication software and access control to determine if previously undetected security risks exist. Second, when an audit trail shows access to "unusual areas" of the system by a user, particularly systems operations, this may be a warning sign of a potential security breach. Somewhat surprisingly, some security officials have noted that audit trails are either inadequately used or used to ensure that an employee or intruder is not improperly using a legitimate user's access. One must recognize the painfully obvious fact that since many thieves are employees, an audit trail's notation of improper or unusual access could be an internal incursion. Third, security counter measures should be applied to operating programs as well as data files. A number of security professionals have stated that their primary foci have been on "perimeter" and file controls, but comparatively limited security to operating programs, per se. Finally, connectivity appears to have a strong relationship with property destruction. While intuitively apparent, suffice it to note that the data support this assumption and counter measures should take "networkability" into consideration.

As a final note, there were no significant relationships found between theft or attempted theft of money (by any group of individuals) and any of the destruction variables. While cross-tabulated data indicated the probability existed, that probability is only intuitive, not statistical. Since there were notably fewer attempts to steal money and the data's scales have limited sensitivity, discrimination between the relationships could not be detected thus no conclusions can be clearly drawn on this point.

TELECOMMUNICATIONS FRAUD

Telecommunications fraud takes many forms ranging from thefts of long distance billing numbers, unauthorized access to telephone accounts, the "black market" of cellular telephone billing numbers, unauthorized access to satellite communications links, and nearly every derivative or permutation of these frauds which can be creatively developed. Regardless of how it was accomplished, telecommunications fraud was widespread.

This particular category of crime was difficult to expressly isolate as being penetrated exclusively by computer. While the researchers attempted to isolate noncomputer perpetrated telecommunications fraud (such as unauthorized use of a company's long distance access) from that which was clearly computer-related, our successes were limited. One reason for this limitation was that the respondents could not always distinguish how the fraud occurred. A second reason was that most respondents had been so overwhelmed with this problem, they "forced" answers to variables which were actually not directly responsive, yet clearly indicative of a problem.

The greatest problem respondents indicated in this area was the extent of "unexplained" telecommunications fraud. Obviously, fraudulent long-distance and cellular billings were identified, but security investigators had difficulty locating the source of the fraud. That is, while telephone or billing numbers could be identified, the abuser typically could not be isolated; even if the number was assigned to a specific employee. In many cases, the billing times could not be correlated with employee use/abuse or the magnitude of billing costs would eliminate the employee as a suspect. Both of these factors indicate unauthorized access.

There is strong anecdotal evidence that hackers enter computer systems and take advantage of the electronic avenues open to them. This includes invasion—or in the worst case scenario, seizure—of internal telecommunications switches, use of corporate long-distance and satellite channels (frequently for modem connections), or stealing long-distance account numbers. In the latter case, the stolen account numbers would be either for personal use, distribution to others (usually friends) for their use, or selling the numbers on the black market. An analysis of these variables shows a significant relationship between telecommunications fraud and hacker intrusions ($X^2 = 13.44125$, df $= 6$, p $<.05$), suggesting this to be a major problem.

There is a significant relationship between full-time employees who steal intellectual property via computer and increases in telecommunications fraud ($X^2 = 18.07281$, df $= 6$, p $<.005$). On further examination of these variables via anecdotal evidence, it appears that employees who steal information are also likely to improperly use telecommunications access—whether land-line or cellular. It is not clear what the employees are using the long distance for (e.g., conversations, modem access, fax, or—most likely—a combination of the three). The point to note is that the employee who is an intellectual property thief will also fraudulently use telecommunications access (they will also probably make personal copies on the company's photocopier and steal pens from the supply room).

Overall, the respondents reported that they had a major problem with telecommunications fraud. As telephone systems are increasingly managed by computer systems, particularly as interactive technology merges all telecommunications, data transmissions, networking, cable television, teleconferencing, and other facets of information transfer, the likelihood that telecommunications fraud will increase is high and its losses will grow even more.

The cellular phone industry has been particularly victimized by systems which receive billing code transmissions. Thieves, using a scanner of sorts, set up in areas where there is likely to be a heavy cellular presence and then simply snare the billing code from the air. The codes can then be down-loaded from the scanner into a computer using programs available on the Internet, and entered into stolen cellular telephones which are, in turn, sold on the black market. The monetary losses are staggering. While efforts are being made to encrypt the codes as well as using other techniques such as "call profiling" and Personal Identification Numbers, technology criminals have demonstrated their creativity to meet challenges and will undoubtedly find methods to defeat these security measures. The need to constantly monitor criminal capabilities and address them via counter measures is possibly the only way to minimize the losses. In essence, it is an on-going process.

SECURITY COUNTER MEASURES

In light of these technological threats to proprietary information, the researchers sought to determine practices and experiences with different security counter measures. Specifically, data encryption, operations security, surveillance of computer users, training of personnel, and use of Internet firewalls were examined. These factors were selected because preliminary research found them to be common practice in the computer security environment.

The analysis shows there was a significant relationship between file or data encryption and reduced theft of intellectual property ($X^2 = 9.97955$, df = 3, p <.01). Consequently, encryption should be considered as an important security tool for confidential information. A *caveat* is provided, however. Anecdotally, it was learned that encryption must be reviewed, and perhaps changed on a regular basis—the breaking of such systems has not only occurred, it has become somewhat of a game. As an illustration, RSA-129 is a 129-digit number created in 1977 by the creators of an encryption system said to be "probably secure." At the time it was created, it was estimated to take 40 quadrillion years to factor it with methods of the time. The code's creators recognized that technology was rapidly evolving, consequently analytic capacities would also increase dramatically. In light of these changes, the encryption team projected that the code would remain secure well into the 21st century. In 1994, the code was "cracked" by a group of 600 Internet volunteers (Rosener, 1994). The point to note is that technology is challenging traditional assumptions, including the assumption of long-term security via encryption.

Another important relationship found that as operations security of companies' computer systems and file servers increased, thefts of intellectual property significantly decreased ($X^2 = 8.24674$, df = 3, p <.05). Operations security included such things as monitoring users, creating audit trails of system users, and physical surveillance of users and systems. With regard to this last point, there was a significant relationship specifically found in the use of surveillance and decreased theft of intellectual property ($X^2 = 8.90941$, df = 3, p <.05). As a test of reliability for these findings, an additional analysis of increased operations security was run against specific intellectual property thefts with significant results ($X^2 = 7.51429$, df = 3, p <.05). An operational problem appears to emerge, however.

Anecdotal evidence suggests employee morale goes down, job satisfaction is reduced, employee productivity decreases, and individual creativity is less apparent when there is an increase in security surveillance of computer users. Balancing the need to use surveillance to reduce intellectual property thefts as opposed to the potential negative effects of this countermeasure may be a difficult one to achieve. In all likelihood, the decision will have to be made on a case-by-case basis after an evaluation of the organizational culture and the risk-benefits involved.

The protection of money, according to the respondents, poses different problems. While the value of intellectual property is difficult to assess, it can more easily be protected through encryption. However, there are unique limitations to encryption and different operations security requirements for computerized "cash accounts." Because of the inherent value of money as well as the ease of use and transfer of currencies–particularly in a "readily usable state"–virtually anywhere in the world, there was significant relationship between the need to use alternate security counter measures and the reduction of theft of money ($X^2 = 8.89489$, df $= 3$, p $<.05$).

Throughout the research one constant thread which had a significant relationship between minimizing theft, thus increasing security, was increased employee training ($X^2 = 8.00518$, df $== 3$, p $<.05$). Consistently, respondents reported that crimes and computer abuse (such as harassment via E-mail and use of business computer systems for personal use) were reduced after employee training.

The final countermeasure tested was the use of firewalls. While there are different methodologies, as a rule firewalls are software controls which permit system access only to users who are specifically registered with a computer. As users attempt to gain access to the system they are challenged to ensure they have an authenticated password. Typically, the user will be challenged several times–i.e., "layering"–for added protection. While firewalls are widely used, there were no significant relationships found between this countermeasure and protection of information. Indeed, several respondents comments suggested that hackers had penetrated their firewalls. A number of security professionals have reported discovery of "Password Sniffer" and "Password Breaker" programs, downloaded from the Internet, which were used to breach security. What is not known was the sophistication or level of security provided by these firewalls, thus the finding of no significance could be a function of security practice rather than the countermeasure, per se. That is, the finding should not be misinterpreted to say that firewalls do not work, rather there was no consensus on their success. This lack of consensus is likely based on inadequate security levels, irregular upgrade or maintenance, or an operational limitation associated with the firewall's use. The need for an organization to comprehensively review its authentication software is essential because of the comparative ease in breaking these systems as they currently exist (Bishop & Klein, 1995).

These observations are supported by Collinson who stated that "...firewalls are often set up incorrectly and may actually increase the risks a company faces by fostering a false sense of security" (1995, p. 217). Typically, a firewall is developed to defend against known incursion methods. However, computer criminals are creative and have clearly shown their ability to penetrate many firewall systems. Moreover, when new barriers are developed, they are approached like a puzzle, rather than an obstacle. The firewall is essentially a sophisticated electronic damn. Unfortunately, once an intruder finds a passage around this barrier, access to critical information becomes much easier for the hacker. Some evidence suggests that less investment is placed in internal security controls when a firewall is in place. As discussed, there are a number of vulnerabilities to this approach. Effective information system security requires a more holistic, proactive vision with an underlying assumption than any countermeasure can be compromised. Clearly, this is an area which needs closer examination, particularly given the level of reliance on this security measure.

CONCLUSIONS AND RECOMMENDATIONS

As evidenced by the research, the threat of computer crime is real. Those who maintain it is not a serious problem simply have not been awakened by the massive losses and setbacks experienced by companies worldwide. Money and intellectual property have been stolen, corporate operations have been impeded, and jobs have been lost as a result of computer crime. Similarly, information systems in government and business alike have been compromised and it has been with some luck that more damage has not been done.

There are issues of privacy, confidentiality, and ethics involved not to mention the economic impact which is staggering. In an interview with the British Banking Association (BBA), the authors were told that the BBA estimated the global loss to computer fraud alone to be about $8 billion a year. To add other losses as discussed previously brings the total economic effects of computer crime to a level beyond comprehension. Building on this scenario is the fact that as a result of new technologies, emerging technologies, and a growing generation of people who are not only computer literate but also network literate, the problem will grow.

Researchers must explore the problems in greater detail to learn the etiology of this growing criminal group, their methodologies, and motivations. Decision makers must react to this emerging body of knowledge by developing policies, methodologies, and regulations to detect incursions, investigate and prosecute the perpetrators, and vigilantly prevent future crimes. Our institutions have already fallen behind the criminals; at this point the question is not can we catch up, but whether we can keep the gap from widening.

The results of this study empirically support many elements of the anecdotal evidence. First, computer security incidents have significantly increased over recent years. Second, a primary target of computer thieves is the intellectual property of a business. Third, the people most likely to steal information are employees who have access to computer files. Fourth, the number of computer incursions (and attempts) by hackers outside of the business is increasing. In only a few years, the hacker threat will most likely equal if not exceed the threats posed by employees. Fifth, security professionals need to provide training to computer users about "cyber abuse," crime, the ramifications of information losses, and security precautions which must be taken (as well as the rationale for those precautions). Sixth, there must be a recognition that the threat of a virus infecting systems is real. Moreover, this threat will grow with more creative, hence destructive, viruses being created and a wider spread of the viruses as a result of the growth in networking. Seventh, the "snooping" of files is a problem which can lead to theft and damage of important information. Eighth, harassment via computer is a real problem which organizations must address, not dismiss. Ninth, destruction of virtual property is a correlate to thefts and attempted thefts. This destruction has both direct costs for reparations and indirect costs for losses of productivity. Tenth, telecommunications fraud exists on a massive scale costing millions of dollars every year. Finally, a number of established security procedures appear to work effectively; however, they can be foiled if not regularly reviewed and revised to meet changing conditions and technologies.

REFERENCES

Baum, M.S. (1995, November 20). As cited in: Why many businesses can't keep their secrets. *Wall Street Journal*, B1.

Bishop M., & Klein, D.V. (1995). Improving system security via proactive password checking. *Computers and Security, 14*, 233-249.

Carter, D.L. (1995a). A typology of computer-related crime. A paper presented at the International Conference on Organized Crime, The Police Staff College, Bramshill House, England.

Carter, D.L. (1995b). Computer-related crime. *FBI Law Enforcement Bulletin.* (August).

Collinson, H. (1995). Recent literature. *Computers and Security, 14*, 215-220.

Florida Department of Law Enforcement. (1989). *Computer Crime in Florida.* An unpublished report prepared by the Florida Department of Law Enforcement, Tallahassee, Florida.

Herfernan, R. (1995). Securing Proprietary Information (SPI) Committee of the American Society of Industrial Security. Committee presentation at the ASIS Annual Meeting, New Orleans, LA, September 12, 1995.

Katz, A.J. (1995). Computers: *The Changing Face of Criminality.* A doctoral dissertation submitted to the School of Criminal Justice, Michigan State University, East Lansing, Michigan.

Kerlinger, F. (1977). *Foundations of behavioral research.* New York: Holt, Rinehart and Winston.

Manzi, M. (1995). Personal interview with Special Agent Merle Manzi, Florida Department of Law Enforcement and Vice-President of the Florida Association of Computer Crime Investigators (FACCI). Interview on November 11, 1995.

Monkerud, D.D. (1995). Computer security and computer crime. *Uniforum Magazine.* (Electronic E-mail copy). (December).

Parker, D. B. (1978). *Crime by computer.* New York: Charles Scribner's Sons.

Parker, D. B. (1989). *Fighting computer crime.* New York: Charles Scribner's Sons.

Rosener, J. (1994). *CyberLaw.* April, (America Online).

Rosener, J. (1995). *CyberLaw.* October, (America Online).

Toffler, A. (1990). *Powershift.* New York: Bantam Books.

Tripp, B. (1995). *Survey of the Counterintelligence Needs of Private Industry.* Washington, DC: National Counterintelligence Center and the U.S. Department of State Overseas Security Advisory Council.

U.N. Commission on Crime and Criminal Justice. (1995). *United Nations Manual on the Prevention and Control of Computer-related Crime.* New York: United Nations.

U.S. Congress. (1995). *Annual Report to Congress on Foreign Economic Collection and Industrial Espionage.* Washington, DC: Government Printing Office.

Van Duyn, J. (1985). *The human factor in computer crime.* Princeton, NJ: Petrocelli Books, Inc.

Chapter 14

COMPUTER APPLICATIONS BY INTERNATIONAL ORGANIZED CRIME GROUPS

DAVID L. CARTER AND ANDRA J. KATZ

As the global environment has changed, so has the character of international organized crime. The growth of common markets in Europe, Asia, Africa and the Western Hemisphere; global communications networks including satellites and the Internet; the availability of easy and comparatively inexpensive travel; and evolving social and political systems–the most notable of which is the change in Eastern Europe–have all influenced an evolution in criminal enterprises. Just like any other social or economic group, organized crime continuously evolves along with the global community. It should be no surprise, therefore, to see criminal enterprises increasingly rely on computerization.

How extensive is that reliance? How are computers used by organized crime groups? Has the way that criminal enterprises "do business" changed as a result of computers? These are among the questions explored by the authors.

THE STUDY OF INTERNATIONAL ORGANIZED CRIME

This study relied on qualitative research methods including interviews with law enforcement officials, intelligence analysts, government officials, investigators, and corporate security directors all of whom work with international organized crime and have some knowledge or evidence associated with computer applications by these

247

groups. The interviews, in most cases, followed a consistent protocol which documented the interviewees' experience and observations on current trends. The exceptions were interviews which were done under incidental situations. Even in these cases, the researchers were able to ask and record primary questions from the protocol.

Of the forty-seven people interviewed, most were from Europe and Asia, although some interviewees were from North America and five were from Africa. (Corporations from which security directors were interviewed are not included in this list for confidentiality reasons.) Persons were selected for the interviews based on their knowledge and experience in light of the positions they hold with their organizations. Corporate security directors were included in the research because of the increasing involvement of organized crime in cargo theft, theft of intellectual property, manufacture and distribution of counterfeit commodities, and industrial espionage.

In addition, the researchers were given access to a wide range of investigative reports and documents. A content analysis was completed with these materials to the extent possible. In a few cases, the authors were permitted to read and take notes from the documents, but not copy them.

An analysis matrix was designed to document the interviewees' responses to key questions. In addition, on selected variables, the interviewees were asked to give their perceptions on a five-point scale. Based on these responses and the collective observations documented in the interviews, the information was integrated for analysis in this paper.

With respect to reporting results, because of the critical nature of information involved in this study–frequently of a "classified" or "confidential" nature-interviewees were guaranteed confidentiality in their specific responses to control questions. While the researchers were given access to some "classified" information, that information was used as background and to give direction for further study, but not included in this chapter.

Typically in research, one reviews previous research to integrate the findings as well as to identify consistencies and inconsistencies. In the current study, there is a virtual void in the literature. Empirical research on computer crime, per se, is very limited–particularly recent research during the era of explosive technological growth and an exponential expansion of networking. As a result, limited literature is cited.

DEFINING ORGANIZED CRIME

Historically, organized crime has been viewed in terms of the "traditional" or "familial" crime syndicates broadly known as La Cosa Nostra or the Mafia. In the past fifteen years, the perspective of organized crime has been broadened, largely as a result of drug trafficking, to include the South American drug trafficking groups (e.g., Medellin and Cali Cartels; Mexican Drug Cartels), Asian crime groups (e.g., Triads, Tongs and Yakuza) and the many emerging groups from Central and Eastern Europe. As we look toward the future, it is increasingly evident that organized crime must be viewed from an even broader context–a new paradigm.

Law enforcement organizations are beginning to respond to this change. For example, Interpol defines organized crime as "any enterprise or group of persons engaged in a continuing illegal activity which has as its primary purpose the generation of profits and continuance of the enterprise regardless of national boundaries." From another perspective, the German Bundeskriminalamt (BKA) operationalizes organized crime as "the planned commission of criminal offenses, determined by the pursuit of profit and power, involving more than two persons over a prolonged or indefinite period of time, using a commercial or business license scheme, violence, and/or intimidation."

While some variance exists in these definitions, clearly the trend among international law enforcement organizations is away from the "familial" view and toward a more "entrepreneurial" perspective. The movement toward viewing organized crime as "enterprise crime" is because of its market-driven nature–any commodity where a profit can be earned is open to organized crime.

Entrepreneurial groups appear to develop through an evolutionary process. Experiences of investigators indicate that individuals–and perhaps small groups–who have common criminal interests tend to loosely amalgamate for certain criminal purposes. Just as in the case of many new business initiatives, if the crime amalgamation seems to work–i.e., generate profits–then the enterprise takes on more structured characteristics. Some groups may be short-term alliances with minimal structure–essentially adhocracies–others become quite sophisticated organizations. Clearly, however, levels of structure and sophistication vary widely on a continuum with a notable degree of ebb and flow between crime groups. This fluid nature makes it difficult to develop a clear picture of these enterprises as well as to give an accurate assessment of their activities. The adoption of computer technology to criminal enterprises follows a similar developmental path.

COMPUTERS AS INSTRUMENTALITIES OF ORGANIZED CRIME

Why are computers increasingly becoming an important tool to criminal groups? The reasons are quite simple: In many venues computers permit faster, more productive work at lower cost with fewer personnel. Based on this project's interviews as well as a content analyses of other sources of information, several applications have been identified wherein criminal enterprises have used computers.

Maintaining Records of the Enterprise

Evidence by law enforcement and intelligence, organizations have found crime groups keeping computerized records in a manner similar to businesses. Records which have been discovered include:
- Contraband shipment schedules
- Income and expenses of contraband or commodities
- Data bases of conspirators and "customers"
- Locations, account numbers, and status of monetary transactions (typically money being laundered)
- Records of monetary transfers and payments
- Data bases and "status" of bribed or vulnerable officials
- Dossiers of officials, conspirators, and others with whom the crime group has an interest

In most cases of record keeping, there was some type of file protection, although typically the protection was rudimentary. For example, password controls built into a word processing program or a commercial encryption program were the most common forms of protection. While these controls would keep the casual user from accessing the files, the protections could be circumvented comparatively easily by persons with the appropriate expertise. In some cases, criminals attempted to erase hard drives and physically destroy floppy disks. In most of these instances, computer forensics experts were able to recover much of the data. Some evidence indicates that criminals using computers for record keeping are becoming more technologically literate with respect to file protections and data erasure. As a result, evidence gathering could become more difficult.

An emerging issue is "remote record keeping" via networks. Rather than a criminal enterprise keeping records on a hard drive, records were kept on a remote computer in a different country which could be accessed as needed. In one case, a criminal enterprise conspirator, operating out of England, kept remote records on a computer in the Czech Republic. The criminal's apparent intent was that, if arrested, there would be no records of the enterprise at his home or office. While no arrests were made nor could these allegations be proven, the informant providing the information was deemed reliable. With the growth of Internet Service Providers around the world and increased ease of networking, this scenario is certainly feasible.

Using Technology to Counterfeit Currency and Documents

Computer technology has provided a revolution in the counterfeit currency and document business. Past counterfeiting activities required skilled engravers and printers as well as expensive photographic and printing equipment. Using these traditional methods successful counterfeiting was a labor-intensive task which required expert workmanship and equipment which was bulky and somewhat uncommon, making investigations easier. In addition, because of the required skill levels and equipment, there were relatively few successful counterfeit operations.

However, with color scanners, color printers, sophisticated word processing and graphics software suites, and computer-driven color balancing photocopiers, successful counterfeiting has not only significantly broadened, but has also become much more difficult to detect. As one example, the U.S. $100 bill was the most frequently counterfeited currency in the world. With computerized counterfeiting, the global market was becoming flooded with counterfeit $100 bills (particularly in Central and Eastern Europe). As a result, the U.S. Treasury changed the bill's design and incorporated a watermark (like most of the rest of the world's currency) and other security factors. It was announced by the Treasury Department that the new $100 bill was virtually impossible to counterfeit. It was reported by interviewees that within a month of the new bill's introduction into circulation, good counterfeit copies surfaced in Eastern Europe. High resolution color scanning of an original can even pick up the watermark and colors of fibers in the paper which are, in turn, reproduced by high quality printers.

The same scanning process and graphics software are used for counterfeit passports. Counterfeiters maintain scanned "masters" of various passports–Dutch and German documents appear to be particularly popular–in computer files. They are then able to readily enter appropriate names, photographs, and identity information in the files to prepare a high quality counterfeit.

Another particularly unique application of the technology has been found to make new certificates of origin and ownership papers of stolen vehicles using the actual Vehicle Identification Number (VIN) of the stolen auto. Like the passports, master files of documents–such as certificates of origin and titles–are scanned into the computer. They are then printed using the stolen vehicle's description and VIN along with the new "owner's" identification. Sophisticated auto theft rings operating from Poland to Morocco have used this method.

While this approach to counterfeiting can obviously occur anywhere, it has been most evident in Northwest Africa. However, growing use has been found in Southeast Asia.

Supporting the Distribution of Counterfeit Products

The marketing of counterfeit products–ranging from Rolex watches to Microsoft software to Levi's jeans–is well documented. The extent to which "traditional" organized crime is involved is debated; however, there is strong evidence that such groups are strongly involved in the "marketing" and distribution of these products in what is referred to by Her Majesty's Customs and Excise Service (of the U.K.) as the "fakes trade."

While skilled craft workers have been quite successful in designing and manufacturing counterfeit products, customs and corporate security investigators frequently relied on product logos and subtle design and coloration characteristics to distinguish licensed products from counterfeit ones. This too is changing because of computer technology.

As in the case of counterfeit currency and documents, criminal enterprises have been using color scanners and computer-driven color printers to scan legitimate logos, product tags, and such things as "jackets" and labels of videotapes, audio tapes, and software. Using the scanned images as masters, skilled printers are able to prepare these materials to complement the "knock off" products. One corporate security director told the authors that this process was an additional "wrinkle" for investigators to overcome because the process made the product look more legitimate to the consumer. (In some cases, counterfeit products not only looked a great deal like the original, the quality was also good.) With authentic appearing packaging, the enterprise could sell more of their counterfeit products at higher prices and still undercut the legitimate manufacturer's sales.

The counterfeit trade is also growing in the area of fake computer components. Particularly popular appear to be counterfeit modems and hard drives, which, apparently can be duplicated and manufactured with comparative ease. As with any counterfeit product, they are marketed under a popular brand name at a significant savings. Interestingly, these counterfeits appear to work quite well and be reliable. When consumers receive a good product at a low price there are few complaints.

By far, the vast majority of counterfeiting described in this section is occurring in southeast Asia. The exception appears to be the counterfeit movies on video cassette which are increasingly originating from Eastern Europe. Interestingly, even "hard-core" pornographic videotapes have been counterfeited and distributed.

Techno-Exploitation of Sexually-Related Commerce

Most people have heard news accounts about various forms of individual sexually-related misconduct occurring via the Internet of which organized crime has virtually no involvement. Keeping in mind that the sole purpose of a criminal enterprise is to make a profit, the focus of organized crime in cyberspace is to promote sexually-related commerce.

According to investigators from Europe, North Africa, North America, and Asia, new criminal enterprises have emerged, largely consisting of intelligent, young entrepreneurs who are familiar with the capabilities and potential of computers as a tool for sexual commerce. These emerging groups do not neatly fit into traditional definitions of organized crime, yet they nonetheless are on-going enterprises which are frequently violating the criminal law in order to gain a profit. A problem exists, however, because many of these groups' activities fall into the "gray area" of law. That is, some of their activities are lawful (or at least it may be debated that they are lawful). Other activities may be lawful in their country or state/province of origin but are unlawful in other areas where clientele may be served. Because of these legal ambiguities and the fact that sexual commerce is viewed as being less serious than other forms of crime, comparatively little attention is given to these groups with the exception of child pornography.

Predominantly originating from North America, Scandinavia, and Asia, among the activities of these groups are:
- International transmission of pornographic photographs.
- International transmission of obscene written materials.
- International transmission of child pornography.
- International sales of sexual aids, particularly those related to sexual fetishes.
- Advertising, negotiation, and appointments for both male and female prostitution (so-called "cyber-brothels").
- Subscription/fee E-mail services for sexual fantasies.
- Live video sex-shows via the Internet where customers can type instructions for the way they want live "models" to perform.

Some unusual complications emerge from these enterprises. In one alleged case, Algerian and Jordanian officials were seeking to close access from a Web site in Denmark which was marketing pornographic photographs of Middle Eastern women. The unique element of this case was that aspects of the photographs apparently desecrated Islam, thus the violations were deemed serious. In another unusual case, it was alleged by a French firm that sexual aids being sold through a web site were actually counterfeit products violating international copyright treaties.

Officials admit it is difficult to determine which activities in this arena are unlawful. It frequently depends on the jurisdiction of the consumer, yet legal precedence has typically not advanced as quickly as the technology. One U.S. Customs investigator stated that there have been times a case was started on intuition, only to learn later that there was not a specific U.S. law violation. The investigator went on to note, however, that many people who are involved in computer-based sexual commerce are also frequently associated with some other form of criminal enterprise.

While unlawful sexual commerce does not pose the same threat as many other forms of organized crime, it does help fuel the underground economy and provide income to criminal enterprises which, in turn, may support other forms of criminality.

Unlawful Gaming

Gambling has always been a favorite–and profitable–activity for organized crime groups. Casino skimming operations in Las Vegas, "panchinko" rigging in Japan, and unlawful sports betting around the world have turned huge profits for criminal enterprises. It was only natural that entrepreneurial criminals would turn to computerization– particularly the Internet–in order to expand their reach, hence their profits.

At this point, it appears most unlawful computerized gaming operations–notably in North America and Asia–are not networked but are accessible via modem. However, accessibility to such operations is increasingly available through the Internet. The operations generally work the same whether it is a Bulletin Board Service (BBS) or web site. Typically, the user must "join a club" to be given access to the site for gambling. Part of the membership ruse is to pay "dues" which are used as bets. Most typically, gamblers supply a credit card number wherein they can purchase "units" to wager–a unit is essentially an electronic poker chip. (Most typically, all wagers and transactions are converted to U.S. dollars regardless of the country of origin.)

In some cases, when a member joins and is given his/her personal identification number, he/she can then make a deposit–usually either by wire or money order–to a front company which serves as the "bank" for the gambling operation. All bets and communications are then conducted via the computer link. When the gambler wins he/she is typically given credits which can be used for further wagers or he/she can request payment, typically through the front company which serves as a bank. Credit card "credits" are typically not used for two reasons: (1) the gamblers want their winnings quickly in a readily convertible form and (2) it is feared that the issuance of too many credits to a given card number would raise questions leading to investigations.

Interestingly, one British investigator said that the financial transaction accounting procedures for these unlawful gaming operations were quite accurate and reliable. The reason: Operators make money from the "repeat business" of gamblers—if they cannot trust the enterprise, they will not bet their money.

Among the types of networked and BBS gambling operations which have been discovered are sports Books (e.g., soccer, football, horse racing, Olympics, boxing, etc.), elections, "numbers" rackets or unlawful lotteries, and video poker simulators.

Computer-Assisted Theft and Fraud

As computers are increasingly used to account for and make financial transactions, criminals are increasingly accessing them to unlawfully transfer funds, defraud, or steal information. The most common target of computer-assisted thefts by criminal enterprises is intellectual property. As information becomes an increasingly valuable commodity, organized criminals have learned how to market stolen information for high profits and substantially less risk than more traditional illicit commodity trafficking. Theft of such information as trade secrets, new product information, product pricing plans, and customer lists has proven to be highly profitable. The cost to a business competitor to pay for this stolen information is far less than original research, development, and marketing. Increasingly active in this arena are criminal enterprises in Japan, the United States, France, and Germany. While these transactions typically do not have the violence and emotional daring associated with more traditional organized crime activities, the economic toll can be far higher.

The second area of computer-assisted theft by organized crime is fraud. The Florida Division of Insurance Fraud has discovered fraud through altered computer programs which underreport insurance agency incomes. Medical and pharmaceutical overpayments through Medicare/Medicaid have also been fraudulently made in many ways through the altering of computer records and, more commonly, the use of shell companies billing the government for medical services, equipment, and pharmaceuticals. While these forms of theft net significant amounts of money, they typically are not products of broad-based organized crime, although they frequently meet the technical definition of a criminal enterprise.

Criminal enterprises have been found to be involved in frauds related to thefts of credit card numbers for which purchases are made via fax, telephone, and, in some cases, over the Internet. One criminal enterprise emerging from West Africa (notably Nigeria, Liberia, Ivory Coast, and Sierra Leone) involved the purchasing of computer equipment, memory, and peripherals via telephone orders using stolen credit cards from North America and the United Kingdom where "clearance" of the credit card's validity could take weeks. The new equipment would then be sold in its original packages to individuals or commercial outlets where manufacturer's orders were small or slow to arrive. Other forms of credit card fraud using similar methods have occurred in Malaysia and South Africa. Evidence suggests that these thieves are somewhat like "outsource employees" of organized crime groups. That is, the thieves are simply paid for the "live" numbers they steal and members of the criminal enterprise "core group" perform the remaining criminal acts.

Telecommunications Fraud

Telecommunications fraud is a particularly profitable area of computer-related crime that has many approaches. Previously, individual criminal entrepreneurs were committing these crimes, but they are increasingly being pushed out by organized crime groups because the profits are so high and the risk is so low.

There are three types of telecommunications fraud by computer in which criminal enterprises appear to be most involved. One is the theft of telephone credit card numbers which can be gained by accessing computer records, some computerized voice mail boxes, and telephone billing files. Prime targets are large multinational corporations because discovery of the fraudulent billings takes longer. The billing numbers are either sold "on the street" or, as is increasingly the case, sold to other crime groups for their use. In one case, stolen corporate telephone billing numbers from a United States-based multinational company were being sold to various drug trafficking groups which in turn used the stolen numbers to make arrangements for drug transactions and shipments. Payment for the stolen numbers was cheaper than paying for numerous international calls and it was more difficult for investigators to link the calls to their principle investigative targets.

The second type of telecommunications fraud, which has actually decreased, involves hacking into telecommunications "switches" (which are computers) for the purpose of routing calls and changing billing numbers. While individual hackers still break into the switches, organized efforts to do this have largely stopped as a result of more aggressive security precautions by telecommunications carriers.

The third area of telecommunications fraud is the largest and fastest growing: cellular phone theft and fraud. This too was started by individuals and small groups but is increasingly involving criminal enterprises. The process originally involved the capture of cellular telephone billing numbers being emitted from users' telephones. Using a device which detects and records the number, it could then be sold and programmed into a person's wireless phone. The number is typically usable for about one month before it is detected as being stolen. The fraudulent user would then need to purchase a new number.

Because of the large number of cellular telephones in use and the ease in which a large number of billing codes could be captured (a telephone does not have to be in use, but simply turned on in order to emit the billing code), the process became one of "assembly line theft." Essentially, a "client" pays a flat fee and receives a new billing number each month or whenever the number they are using is canceled. (It is recommended that a stolen number not be used over one month in case it is being traced by investigators.) The "service provider" typically has the computer equipment to readily reprogram the client's cell phone. Averaging about $30 a month ($60 if a "new" telephone is also obtained) with several hundred clients in a "territory" and several territories within a given geographic area, the profits can add up quickly and, again, with minimal risk.

As computer-driven telecommunications systems become more prevalent around the world, as reliance on computerized switching increases, with broader use of international telecommunications for data transmission, and as video-conferencing increases, the amounts of money which can be made through telecommunications fraud becomes staggering.

Support of Illegal Immigration Enterprises

Outside of refugees fleeing into countries such as Zambia and Thailand from neighboring countries embroiled in civil war, the European Union countries have experienced some of the largest influx of illegal immigrants (notably from Central and Eastern Europe). Seeking both peace and economic opportunity, the new immigrants have made many sacrifices–including financial ones–to achieve their goals. As in other cases when governments are slow in responding to a crisis–if they respond at all–criminal enterprises will fill the void.

In these cases, evidence has indicated that organized crime groups previously involved mostly in black market smuggling have created new processes to smuggle immigrants into Western countries with "appropriate" documentation, typically for a substantial fee. While computers play a comparatively smaller role in these enterprises, they nonetheless help expedite the scheme through the use of such processes as logistics and arrangements via E-mail, computer-forged immigration documents, and general record keeping related to this enterprise.

Since there has been substantially increased investigations in these human smuggling enterprises in the European Union, the criminal enterprises have explored new immigration options. For example, a Korean immigration investigative supervisor recently told the authors that his office has seen an increase in the number of immigrants from Europe, many with counterfeit passports which are of high caliber (presumably computer generated) and difficult to distinguish from legitimate documents.

While illegal immigration from Mexico and Central America into the United States remains a problem, it is actually one of a smaller scale than the European Union has experienced since the fall of the Iron Curtain. Moreover, while there are some organized groups–known as "coyotes"–smuggling the immigrants into the United States, they have not shown the same level of technological sophistication as the European enterprises.

EXPANDING THE REACH OF THE BLACK MARKET

In virtually every country in the world there is a Black Market available to provide people with products they need or desire but simply cannot obtain through the open market processes. The Black Market trades in any commodity which will turn a profit, particularly if the commodity is contraband (ranging from prohibited pharmaceuticals to Cuban cigars), counterfeit (Rolex watches have remained a long-standing popular Black Market item), or stolen property (anything which is popular but either too expensive to purchase "off the shelf" or difficult to locate.) In nearly every Black Market, organized crime is omnipresent.

Outside of its illegal commodities and avoidance of licensing and taxes, the Black Market operates much like any business. It is market-driven; requires suppliers, transportation, and distribution networks; it has a payroll; it must remain competitive; and is obliged to keep its customers satisfied in order to maintain repeat clientele. Because of the similarities with legitimate businesses, Black Market criminal enterprises have increasingly resembled legitimate business operations.

Just as in any business, the Black Market needs to make its inventory descriptions known to both the "sales staff" and potential clients. Photographs, product descriptions, costs, inquiry processes, and related information for a wide variety of "commodities" have been found in computer files; in a few cases the files are accessible through a restricted BBS. Additionally, some Black Market merchandise is increasingly available for order through the Internet (under the guise of a legitimate business), vastly expanding the enterprises's market, hence profits. In addition, computerization via networking or a BBS provides increased anonymity to specific individuals in the criminal group.

Black market items found to be using computerization–beyond traditional items such as clothing, watches, or electronics–include such diverse "commodities" as high demand/popular items which have been stolen or counterfeited (e.g., electronics, designer clothing, watches, etc.); arts and antiquities; endangered species skins and by-products; armaments; body parts; and children available for adoption.

Particularly with the global expansion of the Internet, in all likelihood, its application to the Black Market will increase. The reason: It's good business.

CONCLUSION

Given the growth and widespread accessibility of computers, it is reasonable to assume that applications of the technology by organized crime groups will increase. The conclusion which one would thus draw is that the criminal justice system must examine its policies and preparedness to deal with this criminal phenomenon. In light of this, there are several important policy implications from this research.

First, it reinforces the need for law enforcement and prosecutors to revisit their definition of organized crime. The view of criminal enterprises in the traditional "familial" structure remains the predominant perspective in law enforcement. Ironically, this is a particularly American police characteristic–law enforcement organizations in many other countries are more likely to accept the entrepreneurial model of organized crime (whether or not computerization is involved).

Second, with the acceptance of a new benchmark of organized crime–i.e., enterprise crime–criminal justice officials must take one more step to recognize the role of technology in this genre of criminality. Computers must be as readily accepted as a criminal instrument as is a gun. These two factors alone require a substantial paradigm shift for investigators and prosecutors in organized crime cases.

Criminal justice personnel need training on the entrepreneurial model of crime, computers as a criminal instrument, investigation and evidence collection techniques, as well as an overview of the various laws and factors related to these forms of investigations. In essence, criminal justice personnel must be resocialized with respect to organized crime. This is a process which requires time, patience, and aggressive learning goals.

Given that many criminal enterprises are chameleon-like, masquerading as legitimate business, and law enforcement is comparatively slow at embracing technology as a criminal tool, the role of playing "catch up" has already been caste. Future research will provide insight on the ability of law enforcement to deal with these groups.

It took American law enforcement nearly seventy years to identify, accept, investigate, and prosecute the heart of Italian/Sicilian organized crime. While La Cosa Nostra remains, its power and influence is only a skeleton of what it once was. In many ways the Mafia has been neutralized.

Given the speed of computers, the diverse character of information and communications systems, the ease of international travel, and the growing innovation of criminals, we do not have seventy years to control these emerging entrepreneurial groups. By that time, such groups will have metastasized, becoming institutional elements in our economic and political systems.

REFERENCES

Baum, M.S. (1995, November 20). As cited in: Why many businesses can't keep their secrets. *Wall Street Journal*, B1.

Bishop M., & Klein, D.V. (1995). Improving system security via proactive password checking. *Computers and Security, 14*, 233-249.

Carter, D.L. (1995a). A typology of computer-related crime. A paper presented at the International Conference on Organized Crime, The Police Staff College, Bramshill House, England.

Carter, D.L. (1995b). Computer-related crime. *FBI Law Enforcement Bulletin.* (August).

Collinson, H. (1995). Recent literature. *Computers and Security, 14*, 215-220.

Florida Department of Law Enforcement. (1989). *Computer Crime in Florida.* An unpublished report prepared by the Florida Department of Law Enforcement, Tallahassee, Florida.

Herfernan, R. (1995). Securing Proprietary Information (SPI) Committee of the American Society of Industrial Security. Committee presentation at the ASIS Annual Meeting, New Orleans, LA, September 12, 1995.

Katz, A.J. (1995). Computers: *The Changing Face of Criminality.* A doctoral dissertation submitted to the School of Criminal Justice, Michigan State University, East Lansing, Michigan.

Kerlinger, F. (1977). *Foundations of behavioral research.* New York: Holt, Rinehart and Winston.

Manzi, M. (1995). Personal interview with Special Agent Merle Manzi, Florida Department of Law Enforcement and Vice-President of the Florida Association of Computer Crime Investigators (FACCI). Interview on November 11, 1995.

Monkerud, D.D. (1995). Computer security and computer crime. *Uniforum Magazine.* (Electronic E-mail copy). (December).

Parker, D. B. (1978). *Crime by computer.* New York: Charles Scribner's Sons.

Parker, D. B. (1989). *Fighting computer crime.* New York: Charles Scribner's Sons.

Rosener, J. (1994). *CyberLaw.* April, (America Online).

Rosener, J. (1995). *CyberLaw.* October, (America Online).

Toffler, A. (1990). *Powershift.* New York: Bantam Books.

Tripp, B. (1995). *Survey of the Counterintelligence Needs of Private Industry.* Washington, DC: National Counterintelligence Center and the U.S. Department of State Overseas Security Advisory Council.

U.N. Commission on Crime and Criminal Justice. (1995). *United Nations Manual on the Prevention and Control of Computer-related Crime.* New York: United Nations.

U.S. Congress. (1995). *Annual Report to Congress on Foreign Economic Collection and Industrial Espionage.* Washington, DC: Government Printing Office.

Van Duyn, J. (1985). *The human factor in computer crime.* Princeton, NJ: Petrocelli Books, Inc.

NAME INDEX

SUBJECT INDEX